D0762221

The secret life of

GLENN
GOULD

The secret life of

GLENN GOULD

A GENIUS IN LOVE

Michael Clarkson

ECW PRESS

Published by ECW Press
2120 Queen Street East, Suite 200, Toronto, Ontario, Canada M4E 1E2
416.694.3348 / info@ecwpress.com

LIBRARY AND ARCHIVES CANADA CATALOGUING IN PUBLICATION

Clarkson, Michael, 1948–
The secret life of Glenn Gould : a genius in love / Michael Clarkson.

ISBN 978-1-55022-919-6

1. Gould, Glenn, 1932-1982. 2. Pianists — Canada — Biography. I. Title.

ML417.G69C62 2009   786.2092   C2009-905965-7

Editor: Jennifer Hale
Cover Design: David Gee
Cover photo © City of Toronto Archives, Fonds 1257, Series 1057, Item 3068
Text Design: Tania Craan
Typesetting: Mary Bowness
Printing: Friesens   1   2   3   4   5

Mixed Sources
Cert no. SW-COC-001271
© 1996 FSC
FSC

The publication of *The Secret Life of Glenn Gould* has been generously supported by the
Canada Council for the Arts which last year invested $20.1 million in writing and
publishing throughout Canada, by the Ontario Arts Council, by the
Government of Ontario through Ontario Book Publishing Tax Credit,
by the OMDC Book Fund, an initiative of the Ontario Media
Development Corporation, and by the Government of Canada through
the Book Publishing Industry Development Program (BPIDP).

Canada Council for the Arts   Conseil des Arts du Canada   Canada   ONTARIO ARTS COUNCIL   CONSEIL DES ARTS DE L'ONTAR

PRINTED AND BOUND IN CANADA

ECW PRESS
ecwpress.com

To Jennifer (Vanderklei) Clarkson,
the virtuoso in my life

CONTENTS

Introduction   ix

Chapter ONE
FLORA   1

Chapter TWO
FRANNY *and* GOULDIE   11

Chapter THREE
SLEEPING *with the* PIED PIPER   27

Chapter FOUR
A PROPOSAL   45

Chapter FIVE
GLADYS *and* CYNTHIA   59

Chapter SIX
Overlapping VOICES   67

Chapter SEVEN
The EMPTY SEAT *in the* AUDIENCE   77

Chapter EIGHT
That SPRING *in* BERKELEY SQUARE   89

Chapter NINE
Lots of FEMALE FRIENDS   105

Chapter TEN
The BEGINNING *of a* TRIANGLE   115

Chapter ELEVEN
The MUSIC INTENSIFIES   135

Chapter TWELVE
Crushed by CAROL   141

Chapter THIRTEEN
To TORONTO   147

Chapter FOURTEEN
The BREAKUP   163

Chapter FIFTEEN
The VOICE *on the* RADIO   169

Chapter SIXTEEN
CATHARSIS *through* MUSIC   177

Chapter SEVENTEEN
TRANSITION   189

Chapter EIGHTEEN
RHAPSODY *in* MOO   203

Chapter NINETEEN
The LIST   217

Chapter TWENTY
MONICA – *The* LINK *between*
two SECRET KINGDOMS?   229

Chapter TWENTY-ONE
The LAUGH HEARD *around the* WORLD   241

Chapter TWENTY-TWO
SUSAN K.   249

Chapter TWENTY-THREE
DEATH   259

Chapter TWENTY-FOUR
Whatever HAPPENED TO . . .   269

Acknowledgments   283
Sources   285

We both fell in love talking about tranquility of spirit and we re-enforced each other's determination to find that quality and bring it into our lives.
— Glenn Gould, writing about a woman two years before he died

The slow, impending death of a great entertainer. It's rare that we could actually see such a thing, but there it is, in Glenn Gould's legendary 1981 performance of Bach's *Goldberg Variations*. Fans have watched the video for decades as if it were his epitaph.

And, in a way, an epitaph is what it turned out to be.

As the camera slowly zooms in on the solitary pianist, at first we see Gould with his head all but buried in his Steinway, hunched over and getting as close to the keyboard as possible, an old man shriveling before our eyes. It is difficult to distinguish what is more compelling — the stark visual of the man or his melancholic music, slow and contemplative, surely a reflection, an outpouring of his troubled soul, a lonely artist losing control of his environment. He looks ill, as though he has taken a pounding, physically and emotionally, as though life should not have required five decades to bring him to his knees. Wearing heavy-rimmed glasses, he could be blind. And yet there is poetry to this scene — a bittersweet self-consciousness as Gould chatters and sings quietly to himself. Tender and loving is the voice from his piano. The video ends with Gould dramatically dropping his hands and, finally, his weary head. Arguably the greatest piano virtuoso of his time was expiring. And, in ways, these *Goldberg Variations* — a beautifully complex score written by Johann Sebastian Bach — reportedly as a charming sleeping pill in 1740 to please an insomniac Russian count — helped put Glenn Gould, age fifty, to sleep. Within seventeen months of this recording, he was dead and the album was released posthumously to rave reviews, winning a Grammy award.

History tells us that Gould died from a stroke and a blood clot, possibly because his immune system had been weakened through prescription drug abuse and an unhealthy lifestyle, and more than forty books and twenty documentaries by or about Gould would seem to back this conclusion. But now, nearly three decades later, we discover through this book perhaps another important cause of his demise — heartsickness.

In his last seven years, Gould suffered an unprecedented string of heartbreaks with women, beginning with the death of his mother, Flora, in 1975, and reportedly ending with a marriage rejection from Birgit Johansson, a piano teacher in Stockholm, several days before his stroke. "Oh why couldn't I have given him the time? Was it because of me he died?" the charismatic Johansson told relatives. "Why didn't I do more for him?"

Sandwiched between the loss of Gould's two beloved "piano teachers" were the collapse of his ten-year affair with Cornelia Foss, the wife of famous composer Lukas Foss, and two shadowy relationships which ended mysteriously — with soprano Roxolana Roslak and pianist Monica Gaylord. "Don't tell anybody about me and Glenn," Gaylord told Gould's assistant at his funeral.

Many of these relationships were painful enough for the sensitive Gould, but perhaps even more so because he kept them secret. He confided in no one when they fell apart, often due to his own emotional shortcomings and personal demands.

Gould, who told friends he would not live past fifty, may have known what was coming. Some evidence of this is seen in the two recordings of his signature *Goldberg Variations*. In the twenty-six years between those records, released in 1956 and 1982, something happened to Gould, and even he saw it. In the early 1980s, while reviewing his initial recording, Gould remarked, "I could not recognize, or identify with, the spirit of the person who made that recording. It really seemed like some other person, some other spirit had been involved." In this statement, Gould seemed to be admitting what many people thought impossible — that Gould had matured, had been swayed by his life experiences and by the outside world to the point his spirit had changed. There is additional video evidence to support the changes in the two "Gould-berg" signatures. A 1964 film shows a spritely Gould as a hip artist on a more passionate, hopeful mission — a man in a hurry to get somewhere. Perhaps what helped to change Gould through the years was the ebb and flow of his personal life, the bumps and the bruises of his romances with Foss, Roslak and Johansson, and with piano instructor Franny Batchen in the 1950s. The turmoil in those relationships was something that perhaps affected his music as well. And yet, Gould's clandestine, somewhat eccentric romances were not all sad songs. They seemed to enrich his life and his art in positive ways, giving to both deeper meaning, spiced with emotions he reluctantly was forced to acknowledge.

Meanwhile, long after his death, Gould still lures new listeners to his piano, connecting with them on a haunting, personal level. "He feels and you feel," says New York writer Nicole Audrey. "I can feel his pain and joy — it touches me. He speaks directly to me." But during his career, just who was Gould playing for? His audience? Himself? His demanding mother? All are likely true, but he was also richly inspired by — and bared his soul at the keyboard to — a secret society of women, the girlfriends who stirred his hard-to-fetch feelings, compelled him to propose marriage and acted as sounding boards and motivators for his unforgettable interpretations of the classics and his own compositions. They were the voices, the silent chorus behind the solitary genius.

Fast-forward to a snowy, "warm-as-toast-in-your-parka" kind of December day in 2006, the sort of day that Glenn Gould would have adored, when the first seed for this book was planted. My granddaughter, Skye, and I tossed crumbs on the frozen ground to pigeons in a small park in midtown Toronto. She looked up innocently at a sign that read: GLENN GOULD PARK.

"Who was he, Papa?" she asked.

"He was a famous pianist from years ago."

"Who was he, Papa?" Skye repeated.

Beyond his famous music, I knew that some of Gould's appeal was his eccentricity and the mystery surrounding his private life, that he supposedly gave up his earthly pleasures for his art as a monk might do, but I suspected there was more to his story. An inquisitive writer/researcher for four decades, I was not satisfied with the answer I had given my granddaughter and I decided to find out more. My timing was good — when I discovered that 2007 was the twenty-fifth anniversary of Gould's death and seventy-fifth anniversary of his birth — I decided to write a freelance feature story about Gould for the *Toronto Star*. My initial research revealed a wide-held cliché: a man who bared his soul at the piano stool, touching everyone who heard him play, but the rest of the time protected himself in a cocoon of hats and overcoats. Gould was uncomfortable with people touching his skin, perhaps affected by Asperger's Syndrome, a variant of autism, which can make a person shy — a control freak who could not live without a structured, solitary life. Of the books and documentaries about Gould, each has added its piece to the puzzle, mostly regarding the musical enigma and his phobias, but I do not think they tell us enough about the man, the spiritual, emotional and romantic soul, who was one of the greatest Canadians of all time. We still do not really know what made him tick or why he appeals to us, his millions of listeners. His music moves people and they want to know more about what made him so sensitive, about his heart, and if in ways he was like them.

More than a quarter century after his death, Gould's sexuality remains largely a mystery to his fans who still wonder about him on Internet blogs. Never during his lifetime was Gould publicly linked to a woman. He never married and usually cut people off if they talked about his private life. This led people to assume he had something to hide and was gay or bisexual. It is interesting to note that, while previous biographers have been timid about touching upon Gould's romantic life, they forged ahead with other embarrassing details about his health, habits and psyche.

Gould was mum about the influence of his personal life on his music; of the *Glenn Gould Reader*, a collection of the pianist's thoughts and writings published after his death, Canadian composer and music educator R. Murray Schafer said, "[Its index] contains hundreds of names from the world of music, entertainment and letters, but no names of relatives, teachers or student friends."

In general terms, Gould was private. "I guess it's all part of my fantasy to develop to the fullest extent a kind of Howard Hughesian secrecy," he said. "I'm a very private person, I think."

Added Gould's friend, violinist and conductor Yehudi Menuhin, "No supreme pianist has ever given of his heart and mind so overwhelmingly while showing himself so sparingly."

After finding Cornelia Foss in New York in 2007 following a six-month search involving Gould's old friends and colleagues, I started to doubt the long-held belief that Gould was asexual. She told me that Gould was a good lover during their long affair in the 1960s and 1970s. After my feature story about Gould and Foss appeared in the *Toronto Star* on August 25, 2007, a rival newspaper, the *Globe and Mail*, chastised biographers for not broaching his interpersonal relationships and for ignoring the contribution of the women who helped to shape his life and perhaps his music. "There are many women who are just left out of history because they've been left in the shadows," Kathy Chamberlain, chair of the steering committee for the *Writing Women's Lives* project at the City University of New York, was quoted in the *Globe and Mail* article. "Often . . . the woman is also creative and perhaps has played the role of muse."

Indeed, Gould's women seem to show a reflection of him in their images. Until now, biographers have focused more on trying to explain what came out of his music box, not about the engine that drove it. The vault to his private life has largely remained locked since his untimely death in 1982 for a number of reasons: his obsession with privacy and controlling his image, the loyalty of his carefully chosen friends and lovers as well as the choice that biographers made to predominantly focus safely on his music and eccentricities. It is hardly surprising that a full-blown biography of Gould, including details of his romances, has never been published until now (Kevin Bazzana's *Wondrous Strange* came closest). After all, the first true biography of the first prime minister of Canada wasn't published until 2007 (*John A: The Man Who Made Us*, by Richard Gwyn, *Random House Canada*).

Now, through the memories of Gould's girlfriends and soul-mates, we will see a fresh portrait of the brilliant pianist, revealing tenderness, compassion and even some romance. He was a man who not only *tried to survive* his uncomfortable body on earth, but who actually enjoyed much of it. His music was twelve-tonal and his documentaries contrapuntal —

meaning that both were filled with overlapping voices — and so was his private life. When some romances ended, his obsession and jealousy, even coldness, revealed itself. But in his relationships with people like Franny Batchen there is a kindness, a remembrance of her that lasted decades. Through these women, the reader will view Gould's famous fears and phobias through a different lens — his fear of people, of flying, of eating, of confrontation, of commitment and the potential to have children. A person with serious phobias can function professionally, but if one does not get help it can catch up with you, as it often does with the thirteen percent of the population that suffers from a phobia.

This is not a book about sex (though there is sex in it). Rather, I think it reveals Gould as a much more complete person than we previously thought — emotionally, spiritually, socially and sexually. He was not so much a self-contained fortress who could live without people, sustained only by his otherworldly music, not always a soloist. My findings, based on interviews with more than one hundred people, are that he was at the same time both very different and very everyday — he loved and lost and, yes, touched and was touched. He kissed and cried, and he also won many victories, including personal triumphs, and showed warmth as a surrogate father and would-be husband. And he was an unofficial teacher to many young musicians, helping them get their careers on track. You will see a lot of "buts" and "yets" in this book because Gould was a study in paradoxes and contrasts. "Almost anything you could say about Glenn Gould, you could say the opposite and have it be somewhat true," said his writer friend Tim Page.

The story of Gould's various romances was not an easy one to get; indeed, Gould seemed to have relationships with women who were loyal to his wish for privacy. Except for Gladys (Shenner) Riskind, none of them came forward readily to help me with this project; I approached all of the others and in some cases it took much debate to convince them to talk about their relationships. Until I contacted her in London in 2007, Batchen had never given an interview about her romance with Gould more than fifty years previous. In her 1995 book about performance anxiety, *The Confidence Quotient,* Batchen mentioned Gould only in quoting one of his musical techniques; she never wrote about the intense personal connection she had had with him. Verna (Sandercock) Post was so private about her romance with Gould, she did not even inform her boss Walter Homburger (Gould's agent) about it. In the following chapters it will become clear just how tight-lipped pianist Monica Gaylord still remains about her "friendship" with Gould.

I have many people to thank in the acknowledgments at the end of this book, starting with Batchen (the late Frances Barrault), Riskind, Post, Foss, Roslak and many others who talked openly with me. I would have loved to have had follow-up, in-person interviews with Foss and Roslak, but they declined.

Along with this book, I have contributed initial research and consulting for a documentary on Gould's inner life by White Pine Pictures, based in Toronto, and producers Peter Raymont and Michele Hozer, *Genius Within: The Inner Life of Glenn Gould.* In 2008, Cornelia Foss painted several portraits of Glenn Gould, one of which she displayed on a website (www.cbfosspaintings.com). It shows a slightly different take on the eccentric all wintered up in his signature driving cap, gloves and scarf: his expression seems less foreboding, softer, cheekier and more human than the pianist history has come to know. This, I think, is one of the views we get of him in *The Secret Life of Glenn Gould.*

He demanded love and affection from both his
parents and happily received it at his mother's knee,
where after long hours of [piano] practice, he would lay
his head and demand pats as one would give a dog.
                                    — Gould's cousin Jessie Greig

FLORA

Chapter ONE

The first woman in Glenn Gould's life was Florence Emma Greig. They called her Flora or Florrie and she was born on Halloween, in 1891, in Mount Forest, Ontario. She boasted deep Scottish roots, supposedly descended from a Scottish tribe, the MacGregors, a warlike clan of the eighteenth century. Flora was a distant cousin of Norwegian composer Edvard Grieg, and of William Lyon Mackenzie, the first mayor of Toronto and leader of the Upper Canada Rebellion in 1837.

Flora's family eventually moved to Uxbridge, Ontario, where she would meet her husband Russell Herbert "Bert" Gold, who had mostly English ancestors and some Scottish. Bert was nine years younger than Flora when they married on her birthday in 1925 in the new United Church of Canada. The Greigs were Presbyterian and the Golds Methodist before the United Church absorbed Canadians of both denominations. The couple moved to a middle-class house at 32 Southwood Drive in Toronto's Beach district, where her only child, Glenn Herbert Gold, was born on September 25, 1932, during the Great Depression, when she was nearly forty-one. The baby came after several miscarriages and, according to his father, was "the answer to a prayer." Flora hoped little Glenn would one day become a concert pianist, as her own dreams to become a concert pianist did not materialize; in fact, she had a theory that an unborn child's brain could be influenced by his mother's environment. Before Glenn was born, she filled her days and nights with music, playing piano and organ, singing and listening to the phonograph and the radio. These days, some scientists believe this technique actually works.

The family changed its name to Gould in 1939 when Glenn was seven, reportedly because they did not want to be mistaken as Jewish in the contentious wartime climate. Flora and Bert were hardworking, upright and decent people of high morals, but they did not show their emotions and at times could even be prudish and cold. They looked older than their ages and could have passed for Glenn's grandparents. In the eyes of those who knew them, the Goulds gave Glenn a world-class education in music and a less-than-primary education in life. They exposed him to the premier musicians and teachers, but did not instruct him in the fundamentals of personal feelings and social skills, neglecting to acclimatize him to the things that would become fearful monsters later in his life — germs, crowds, confrontations, other people's opinions and romance. As devout Christians, Flora and Bert made Glenn's second home the church, where he made his public debut playing hymns on the organ. As an adult, he recalled services "with evening light filtered through stained glass windows, ending with ministers who conducted their benedictions with the phrase, 'Lord, give us the peace that the earth cannot give.'" His debut was apt, for early in parenthood, the Goulds had begun to worship a secondary deity — Master Glenn. When his mother realized he had perfect pitch and could command a piano while his friends were out whacking each other with hockey sticks, she began to believe he was a special gift to the world, perhaps even the reincarnation of a composer — and she told him so. In doing so, some people believe, she may have laid the groundwork for his subsequent self-worship.

From the beginning, Glenn was much closer to his mother than his father. Into adolescence he called her Mama. Physically, Flora was frail and unattractive, sometimes anxious and perhaps a hypochondriac, whereas Glenn was generally healthy, but a little fragile with poor posture. Robert Fulford, who lived next door to the Gould family, was one of Glenn's best friends in their youth. He recalls Gould being healthy, but that his mother was too doting — "perhaps planting the seeds of hypochondria that colored his adult life." When other children wore T-shirts, she bundled him up in sweaters; when they drank Kool-Aid, Glenn was given cod liver oil on a silver spoon; when others went gleefully to the midway at the Canadian National Exhibition, Flora kept her son home and away from all those free-floating germs. She even frowned upon things like sports and sleigh rides. The skinny Gould was not macho and avoided hockey and baseball; this may have been one reason why he had a cool relationship with his father, who was more sporting, an outdoorsman who built the family's summer cottage on Lake Simcoe. Not only did Glenn not know one end of a hammer from the other, he was a pacifist and did not like his father's fur business; his strong will eventually convinced his father to stop fishing.

Gould found school "a most unhappy experience." He said, "I got along miserably with most of my teachers and all of my fellow students. I suppose the fact that after school I didn't go out to play hockey and could only play the piano gave me a feeling that music was a thing apart . . . representing a sort of means to isolation." It is possible that young Glenn never became accustomed to other children and social structure because he was allowed to take so much time off school. In second grade at Williamson Road School, he was absent forty-two days with supposed illnesses, which some biographers have traced to his mother's over-protectiveness and to the boy's anxiety when separated from her. This situation would continue into adolescence when, according to Gould's cousin Jessie Greig, "he demanded love and affection from both his parents and happily received it at his mother's knee, where after long hours of [piano] practice, he would lay his head and demand pats as one would give a dog." Greig, who was six years older than Gould and watched him grow up, added that "these pats were a reward for a day well spent and a fulfillment of his great need for love and acceptance."

As an only child, Glenn did not have to share things and was spoiled, even by his own account. His mother was *always* there for him, even when he didn't need her, and this may have caused some friction, competition and jealousy between his parents. At about age twelve, Gould told Fulford that at the family cottage, he would sleep with his mother one night and his father would sleep with her the next — "this arrangement having been worked out some years before," Fulford said. Both Flora and Bert were amateur musicians and singers who enjoyed performing at church, Bert playing violin, and Flora the piano and the organ. From the time Glenn was four years old until eleven, he had his mother as his music and piano teacher. She was described as a nurturing teacher, but she was strict and did not allow Glenn to play wrong notes or to add his personal touch to passages. As young as three, Gould showed remarkable skill: while sitting on his mother's lap he had perfect pitch. By five, he could play songs she had taught him and could even create some of his own. He boldly announced, "I'm going to become a concert pianist." Later, he would become known for his precision at the keyboard. He likely had his mother to thank for that, and yet, as Flora spent four to six hours a day with her son at the piano, his work strangely was never good enough for her. The Goulds could afford to spend money on Glenn's training because Bert's furrier business was lucrative, and so they enrolled Glenn at age eleven with revered teacher Alberto Guerrero, a former concert pianist. At thirteen,

Gould made his debut on the organ during a concert in Toronto and received sparkling reviews.

Through his adolescence, Glenn deeply loved his mother, and they would exchange innocent Valentine's Day cards until he was at least twelve, but they were both strong personalities and sometimes came to loggerheads. During an argument with her, Glenn got angry and worried that he might cause her bodily harm, but he held back and became ashamed of the emotions he had felt. "The experience caused him to retreat into serious introspection and, when he emerged, he swore to himself that he would never let that inner rage reveal itself again," said Andrew Kazdin, Gould's record producer in New York in the 1960s and 1970s. "He was determined that he would live his life practicing self-control." Indeed, even as a child, Gould rarely cried — if he fell in the schoolyard, he would hum to himself to block the pain. Like other boys, he was gangly and awkward in his early teens, but eventually grew into his big ears; he took longer, however, growing in other ways.

A loner with few friends, at age thirteen Gould had a number of pets — a budgie named Mozart, four goldfish, Chopin, Haydn, Bach and Beethoven, and an English setter, Nicky — and he also brought home stray pets. "By the time I was six," he later said, "I'd already made an important discovery: that I get along much better with animals than with humans."

On a secondary level, young Gould had a number of grandparents, aunts, uncles and nannies in and out of his life. "He said he grew up amongst very elderly people, uncles and aunts and grandparents, as well as his parents, and that it affected him," said Father Owen Carroll, a Catholic priest and teacher, who was Gould's friend for many years after they met in 1955. "They were Protestant and Presbyterian. He said that, because of that, he didn't really know young people." And yet, black-and-white pictures from the cottage, which have been widely circulated through books and magazines, could have been fashioned by

Norman Rockwell, showing young Glenn full of summer smiles, sometimes in suit and tie, with floppy-eared dogs and unidentified boys at his side. Perhaps it was what his parents wanted others to see, or what he wanted others to see — the beginning of image making. What the photos do not show are the introvert, the artsy geek roughed up by bullies.

As a teenager at Malvern Collegiate Institute, Gould was often absent, spending much time studying music at the Royal Conservatory of Music and being tutored at home by a teacher. Gould said he disliked high school, partly because he did not want to be forced into being social. Dr. Helen Mesaros — a psychiatrist who published a book in 2008, *Bravo Fortissimo Glenn Gould: The Mind of a Canadian Virtuoso* — believes Gould skipped his youth and became repressed socially and sexually while putting most of his time and energy into his classical music. He spurned jazz and popular music, possibly partly because they represented the public airing of emotions and the lyrics often talked of everyday life. Into his teens, he did not date girls or attend sock-hop dances. "The loss of the opportunity to dance, play and sing popular music, to engage in youthful fashion and other teenage behavior left him with unfinished business from this stage of development," she said. Mesaros added that Gould may have been threatened by the emergence of his instinctual drives for romance and instead "resorted to an ascetic lifestyle with a heavy emphasis on his intellectual and creative pursuits." She believes that he never had a serious romantic relationship during his life, except with the piano. (Of course, in her research, Mesaros was not privy to the findings of this book — that Gould began courting women fairly seriously, albeit secretly, when he was about twenty.)

In adulthood, Gould would refer to his childhood as happy. In the two-storey, middle-class home on Southwood Drive, among the maple trees swaying with breezes from Lake Ontario, the young Gould lived in relative solitude and could be free to create without the stifling opinions of peer pressure. At the cottage near Uptergrove, Ontario, a ninety-minute drive north of Toronto, Gould loved walking the countryside with dogs and playing piano until all hours of the night. He admitted he grew up a little puritan in his thinking. In the 1930s and 1940s, Toronto was much smaller and less cosmopolitan than it is today and, with a strong British flavor and peaceful, private people, it became known as Toronto the Good. Gould despised loud colors, especially red, which he deemed aggressive, and loved black-and-white movies. It's possible that Gould got an idealistic view of life, women, animals, nature and music from his mother. It seems to be a myth, however, and one not discouraged by Glenn himself, that he did not have other influences on his life and music apart from his mother and German composers. For instance, Guerrero, who taught Gould for nine years, obviously had a big sway on his style; Gould became known for sitting in a low chair, hunchbacked, and playing with "flatter" fingers than most other pianists — traits that Guerrero taught to all his students. Guerrero encouraged such a low stance at the keyboard that Gould's father fashioned a special, low-slung chair he would take with him all his life wherever he performed or recorded.

In another Guerrero student, Malcolm Troup, Gould perhaps saw a reflection of what he would become. Ever since they studied together at Malvern Collegiate Institute and the conservatory, Gould had admired Troup, who was two-and-a-half years his senior. Born in Toronto of English parents, Troup began composing at age nine. Gould often talked incessantly about Troup, according to another student in their Guerrero class, Ray Dudley. "Troup was a kind of character . . . and I think he had a tremendous influence on [Gould]," Dudley said. "[Troup] was radical in everything he did — in the way he dressed, the way he spoke, even the way he wrote. He'd write long, involved essays on some esoteric subject and then read them to the class. Well, I think Glenn would just sit there, fascinated. And Troup usually came into class with holes in his socks or wearing clothes that were rather dirty looking. He was always trying to create a sensation with his appearance." At one time, Dudley and Gould were close and would play pianos together at Gould's cottage.

As a virtuoso pianist, Troup also resembled Gould before Gould resembled Gould. At age seventeen, Troup made his concert debut with the CBC Toronto Orchestra playing Rubinstein's Concerto in D. Troup was at times flamboyant and theatrical, as well as talented. Sometimes dressed to the hilt, he always performed with his own style, with a tendency to lean forward at the keyboard, caressing it as he played Franz Liszt music. And he was controversial — on a live CBC-TV show in the 1950s, Troup had the audacity to use the word "masturbatory" on the air. "He said something like, 'Society is too concerned with masturbatory toys in place of the real thing,'" according to filmmaker Warren Collins, a friend of Gould and Troup. "Malcolm liked to shock and to startle." Gould's admiration for Troup apparently lasted through the years; in 1973, Gould wrote a letter to the University of Manitoba, recommending that Troup be appointed the school's music director.

If music was king in Gould's upbringing and through his teenage years, sex and romantic intimacy were paupers. As in many other British-style homes of the era, matters of the bedroom were rarely discussed by the Goulds and it was likely up to young Glenn to find out about relationships with women all by himself. "He is a confirmed bachelor at thirteen," Fulford wrote in the Malvern newsletter on April 3, 1946. Later, Fulford added, "He never to my knowledge told dirty jokes or speculated about the sexuality of girls." Indeed, during Gould's first concert tour in Western Canada in 1951, the newspaper *The Albertan* asked if nineteen-year-old Gould was interested in girls, to which his mother Flora smiled and replied, "No, he hasn't time for them yet. And I'm glad he hasn't right now." Even though he lived at home with his parents until he was twenty-seven, that would all change.

*She was a great hostess and great at
drawing people out of themselves.*
— Filmmaker Warren Collins of Frances Batchen

FRANNY *and* GOULDIE

Glenn Gould was seventeen, still wearing the suit and tie his parents bought for him, when he met Frances Batchen at the Royal Conservatory of Music in Toronto. He was sitting on a sofa with an acquaintance of Batchen's. "I was on an errand at the conservatory and I went up to them and started talking about a two-piano recital which I was about to do with someone else," she recalled decades later, as Frances Barrault. "I was telling them about the pieces we were going to do when the man who was with my friend began describing the music to me in detail, so intelligently, that I said to him, 'Oh, you *must* be Glenn Gould,' which he was."

He *must* be the young man who had won all those Kiwanis Festivals against older competition; he *must* be the young buck who had strong opinions about Mozart in the cafeteria; he *must* be the one who turned professional three years earlier, with Beethoven's "Tempest Sonata" at the Eaton Auditorium; he *must* be the uncanny pianist who delivers the phrasing, the delicate tone, the poetry of a polished European; he *must* be the young man who was scheduled to appear soon on CBC Radio nationwide. It was practically love at first sight, she recalled. "What gets a woman attracted to a man? He was handsome, intelligent, sexy and talented with enormous control over himself. He was just very interesting." But in the beginning, she

11

remembers vividly, it was the music that brought them together. "Oh, it was the music!" They both adored Bach. "His music, his Bach, just seemed perfect," she said.

Actually, Batchen already knew of the handsome stranger because young Gould had been receiving rave reviews in the newspapers for his performances. Everybody at the conservatory talked about him, and how unusual he was, and how he was a magician transporting listeners to another place. In the early 1950s, millions of Canadians were turned on by classical music (nearly half of the music on CBC was classical). Many kept pianos in their homes, becoming intimate with Beethoven, Mozart and Bach. Gould — whose interpretations of the classical masters were off-center and at times downright rebellious — allowed listeners to shake off their stiff British roots and ascend to another dimension as his piano music got you up and off your feet, floating into a world of sea and sky until you could become intoxicated. As an orphan who had suffered a rough early life, Batchen was in a lot of emotional pain. Gould's music spoke directly to her heart; his Bach wrapped itself around her like a soft winter blanket, until she was hidden inside it, its message coming through in a clear voice that reassured her that someone else, too, was lonely and vulnerable. And yet, friends and fellow musicians warned Batchen about the gangly Gould — he was a loner, a mysterious dreamer with all of his attention focused on becoming the world's premier musician. And didn't she know about his disrespect on the concert stage, always fussing with his handkerchief and threatening to pull off his tuxedo collar, fidgeting and moving his feet while waiting for the orchestra to finish *its* part? At times, Glenn Gould seemed a little nuts, or at least dark. Sure it would be grand to have a virtuoso on your arm for a concert, but at the end of the day, if you were not careful, he might drag you into his world of the pit and the pendulum.

Nevertheless, for a teenager, Gould certainly possessed maturity of musical spirit and, sitting there in the foyer of the Royal Conservatory on that fateful afternoon in 1950, Franny Batchen knew that he was one in a million. In those times, most young people looked like their parents down to the collar, hairstyle and the suit they had bought for them, but once Franny got to know Glenn, he stepped up and out of a much earlier era. With his gentleman's manners, lengthy coat, wool scarves and gloves in the winter *or* summer, his mind was so far away in another century, it seemed, that one only needed to find out what he was thinking by looking at his expression behind the long, light brown hair. Gould did not walk with a swagger, but was brashly confident and thought he could pull off practically anything. Facially, he had magazine looks with a milky complexion, dreamy eyes, soft lips and mouth, and that drawn, rebellious expression reminiscent of another mystery man from the 1950s, actor James Dean.

"To women, he was devastating," said Stuart Hamilton, a friend of Batchen's who had studied piano with Gould under Alberto Guerrero and once made a pass at Gould. "He was famous, he was a great musician, and he had that Hollywood look. He was very attractive in a cadaverous way because at times he seemed frail and bent over." Women ignored this, and even Gould's large ears, seeing only his sexiness when he sat down to play the piano and went into a trance. Yes, he was often dressed for a storm, but during his performance mode, he would launch himself into the eye of that storm and turn it into paradise. Spiritually, his music seemed to have religious themes, which was alluring to many women *and* men. If you liked Bach or Schoenberg, he could be a pied piper and you followed whatever crazy paths he chose. "His music was quite spiritual," Batchen would say.

In ways of the world, according to his friends and colleagues, Gould was a virgin or at least disinterested in the

bedroom, apart from sleeping until noon. He had even insin-
uated this to one of his pals at the conservatory, bassoonist
Nicholas Kilburn. When the subject turned to sex, Gould told
Kilburn, "My ecstasy is my music." Franny Batchen would have
something to say about that.

When Gould took her as his first secret girlfriend in the
early '50s, it was a coming together of two lovers of the same
music, but with largely different upbringings; Gould was an
only child, sheltered from many of the world's pricks and pains
by his parents and encouraged to live in a lively parallel universe inhabited by long-dead composers. Batchen needed
music as much as Gould; when your parents die before you are
six years old, you spend a lot of time searching for just the right
music and peace of mind.

That is what happened to Frances Elizabeth Batchen, born
with a sparkle in her blue-gray eyes in 1925 in Rouleau,
Saskatchewan (pop. 1,000), which became sixty years later the
setting for the fictional town Dog River in the successful CTV
sitcom *Corner Gas*. The depression was on the horizon and the
economy was suffering. "The crops had failed for eleven years,"
Barrault said. But there were happy times, too. "I recall playing
in the snow, walking knee deep in the snow and picking icicles
off buildings and licking them." The innocence of the idyllic
setting soon melted — Fran's mother, Elizabeth, a Russian
immigrant, died of complications relating to a nervous condition when Franny was four; her father, Scottish immigrant
lawyer William Tait Batchen, died when she was six, relating to
asthma. The destitute Frances and her two older brothers,
Alexander and Ronald, were taken in by their grandmother in
Prince Albert, Saskatchewan, but shortly thereafter in 1931, they
went to Scotland, their father's homeland. There Frances stayed
with her unmarried Aunt Bysshe in the tiny town of Peebles
while her brothers went to Edinburgh with their Aunt Agnes.
After three years, when she was nine, Fran moved in with Agnes

and her husband William, a bank manager, where she received a strict Presbyterian, Gouldian upbringing.

"When I was fifteen, I started smoking, lying in bed," she said, "and Aunt Aggie was sniffing from another room: 'Fran, are you smoking in there?' It was a Havana cigarette, quite strong." Batchen did not like Aunt Agnes, but her home had its benefits. "I grew up in a religious household and, in my teens, I thought about becoming a missionary."

Along the way, Batchen stumbled into classical music. One day, a young neighbor stopped by her aunt's house to play an upright piano and Batchen was transfixed. "She played something like Schumann and as soon as I heard it, I knew I wanted to play the piano," she said. Soon after, she was taking piano lessons and a new love was born. The music helped allay her insecurity and busy mind. "From the age of ten, I felt an overwhelming need for peace of mind, and it became a lifelong search."

When the Second World War exploded, her brothers Alex and Ronald enlisted with the Royal Air Force. While training for bomber flights with no enemy in sight, they were killed in separate accidents in 1941 and 1942 over Scotland and England.

By the time she was a teenager, the orphaned Frances had turned even more to classical music and to literature, not to mention smoking and some drinking, for guidance and comfort. During the war in Edinburgh, Batchen earned a master's degree in English Literature at George Watson's Ladies College. In the late 1940s, she returned to her native land of Canada to work for one year as an assistant at McGill University in Montreal to a professor of botany, Nicholas Polunin, a one-time Arctic Explorer. Then she moved to Toronto to study piano on a scholarship at the Royal Conservatory under prominent pianist Béla Böszörmenyi-Nagy and, of course, Alberto Guerrero. When she met Gould at the conservatory, Batchen had her own music, but it did not emote as much from her piano as it did through her. At the keyboard, she possessed a skill learned diligently in class rather than in nature, which did not flow quite as much as it was manufactured.

Her most attractive instrument was her personality — shy at first, but ultimately engaging and youthful. She was a full seven years older than Gould, but that was acceptable because he seemed at ease with mature women. "Our age difference didn't seem to intrude on the friendship; after a while, I just took it for granted," she said. Some acquaintances quickly suggested Batchen became Gould's surrogate mama — she agreed with this later in her life — and yet in many important ways, Franny was no Flora. Whereas Flora usually kept her hair under control in a bun, Batchen simply guided hers with a small wooden peg, letting it flow all the way down her back until it had a life of its own. Sometimes, when she dyed it pitch black, she looked like a geisha. Where Flora believed the world was already as set as a train schedule, Fran kept her tomorrows open and exciting. Musically, the two women were regional in their level of talent, compared to Gould's international gifts, but Batchen's desire and focus were anything but mediocre, and Gould liked that. He did not put up with boring people.

"Fran was vivacious, full of fun, extremely intelligent and very attractive," said her close friend Emily (Reid) Valleau, a young housewife at whose home Batchen sometimes stayed. "She was very athletic and could leap over a fence! She was a very fine musician and a wonderful photographer, and in a way she helped me raise my three kids. She taught my daughter sewing. Fran was a good sewer and a good cook. She made a lot of her own clothes." Gould friend and soprano Barbara Franklin described Batchen as "very small with long hair and longish skirts . . . she looked like a gypsy. She was not glamorous, but had a lovely, untouched personality."

At first, Glenn Gould was just not quite sure what to think of a relationship with Franny Batchen. Professionally, he was leagues ahead of her and most everybody else. By the early 1950s, Hugh Thomson wrote in the *Toronto Daily Star* that Gould "dealt a blow last night in Massey Hall to the assumption that the only worthwhile soloists for symphony concerts are those with foreign names and on the international circuit." If Franny wanted to become a concert pianist, her playing needed a lot of tuning. In other ways, however, she had things to offer the socially and sexually naive Gould.

It was the early 1950s and, as he entered his twenties while still living with his parents, Gould slowly discovered life outside the concert hall. Musically, he was mature, middle-aged, but he could not cook a steak or arrange a party and didn't have the first clue about taking a woman on a proper night out. Where some of his former classmates lost their virginity in high school, Gould seemed untouched — at least according to his friend, violinist Morry Kernerman. One hot summer's day, Gould and Kernerman were rehearsing together at the old CBC building in downtown Toronto when Gould spotted blood on the back of the violinist's shirt. "He screamed and stopped playing," Kernerman said. "I was pretty wild in those days and the night before a woman had dug her nails into my back. She was a very demonstrative woman. I told him what the blood was all about and he was fascinated. He listened like he was listening to someone who lived in another world. He didn't seem to know about such things. He was astonished." Until that point, Kernerman had noted, Gould "never discussed his intimate relationships, but he liked to show off with a pretty girl on his arm."

When he finally discovered women like Batchen and all they had to offer, Gould perhaps equated it to suddenly taking up Mozart, and the fairer sex probably aroused unusual or at least novel feelings for him. For much of his early life, Gould had felt his existence through his music, the beautiful strains of Bach and Schoenberg and Liszt; he listened to them, paid homage to them on his parents' record player, and they filled him with feelings of warmth, and when he played their works on his piano, he could even reach a state of euphoria or, as he told Kilburn, ecstasy. And so, one might say that his central nervous system became used to getting its fix, and even its climate internally, from musicians of long ago.

The world of music provided an escape and a parallel universe for Gould, as it does for many of us. He called it a "state of wonder." "The purpose of art is not the release of a momentary ejection of adrenaline but is, rather, the gradual, lifelong construction of a state of wonder and serenity," Gould would write a little later in his life. To him, the state of wonder was a place he could visit whenever he wished — which was every single day — a place that was reliable, safe, and comforting. Just listening to compositions of the great masters soothed his soul, calmed his nerves, and some days, he never turned off the television or the radio. In this world of music, he was an active, major participant, an explorer, and his talent blossomed at the piano to the point that, even when some critics bashed his often off-the-wall interpretations of old classics, Gould did not lose faith in his talent or his state of wonder.

However, the other world Gould lived in, the earthly world, could be termed the "state of worry." Just getting up and about in the morning, or, rather, the afternoon for late-sleeping Gould, could put one in an unpredictable environment of cold weather, people coughing or demanding things, such as conversation unrelated to Bach, his mother nagging and father wondering aloud why he did not try sports or other male activities. If he was not careful, his day could fall apart by teatime. Gould did his very best to control the state of worry: at home, he had his mother screen his telephone calls, he selected his friends and colleagues with kid gloves, he drove a car big enough to keep others at bay and the main staple of his diet became prescription drugs, especially tranquilizers.

Of course, there were some things that made Gould feel

good externally in the state of worry, produced by the immediate physical world: his pets, a motorboat ride in the calm and splendor of Lake Simcoe, and occasionally a New York strip steak at the Shangri-La restaurant near the cottage. But people tended to make Gould feel worse rather than better, particularly when they were in groups. Dealing with people could lead down the slippery slope of relationships, commitment and confrontations, which could leave a lemony taste in the mouth of the young man with the strong ego and thin skin — and yet Franny Batchen gave him enough warmth that he began to see her on a regular basis. For one thing, they shared their feelings and sensations about music, and she did not provoke his opinions or ego. When no one was around, she soothed him, stroked his thick hair on her lap, and so it seemed appropriate his nickname among family and friends was Spaniel. In fact, Gould was referring to Franny affectionately as Faun, like the forest creature. "His father was Possum, his mother was Mouse, he himself was Spaniel, and I was Faun," Barrault said. It was Franny who tagged him as Spaniel through his love for dogs, which was another thing they shared — once in Toronto, they found a stray dog, named it Sinbad, and turned it over to his mother, who sometimes found homes for strays.

Batchen had been pursuing a career as a concert pianist since she was an adolescent. In May 1950, at age twenty-four, she received a senior piano scholarship at the Peel County Music Festival in Brampton, Ontario. By September of that year, she was set up as a piano instructor and by 1951, she was on a committee organizing a recital at Toronto's Eaton Auditorium for her mentor Béla Böszörmenyi-Nagy, a specialist in late Beethoven and Liszt. It took courage for Batchen to strike up a friendship with Gould, who could be an intimidating, solitary figure, known for never having a girlfriend and shunning anyone who told him what to do. He had recently parted ways with his piano teacher, Guerrero, and was listening only to his manager Walter Homburger. According to his close friend Robert Fulford, Gould had no girlfriends in high school because he was so intent on becoming a wunderkind musician, but that did not stop Batchen, who was a risk taker. "From birth, I lived with an albeit naive, but incurable optimism about myself and the future," she would later write. "Creative in several directions, I felt I was a survivor."

And so she apparently made the first move with Gould in the early 1950s and very quickly, the dreamy-eyed pianist and the wide-eyed Batchen started sharing their passion for classical music, sometimes with a group of friends. Yes, believe it or not, in his late teens and early twenties, not long after he dropped out of Malvern Collegiate, the supposedly reclusive Gould hung out — well, sort of — with young artists, musicians, and filmmakers, such as George Dunning, Joyce Wieland, Michael Snow and George Gingras, all fresh out of school and now working for Graphic Associates, a small firm operated by Dunning and Jim Mackay, both formerly of the National Film Board. Television was young in Toronto and there was a growing demand for animated films. This group has been described as part-beatnik, part-Bohemian and part avant-garde. Another member of the group, animation cameraman Warren Collins, was surprised to see Gould get involved at all because he was known as such a lone wolf. Collins recalled that a few years earlier, while Gould was still enrolled at Malvern, he had spotted the piano prodigy walking down the street in a heavy raincoat, gloves and scarf in the warm June: "He seemed to be going over some music in his head and marking the rhythm by taking two steps on the road, then two steps onto the edge of the sidewalk. I could see his mouth moving to the imaginary music."

Gould admitted feeling uneasy in crowds; from all indications, this feeling bordered on a phobia or fear of people, which likely had a number of subcategories for him in the state of worry — fear of intimacy, fear of confrontation, fear of commitment, fear of touching, fear of catching germs, fear of having feelings and perhaps fear of people finding out who he really was. It would be difficult for anyone to diagnose this because he did not seek treatment for his phobias — and few people did in those days — but the circumstantial evidence, particularly his reaction to situations, was pretty solid.

The artists and musicians group would meet each Friday night at a modest brick rooming house at 46 Asquith Avenue in midtown Toronto — rented out by its co-landlords, Batchen and Hamilton — to play piano, listen to music and read some pretty heavy literature. The get-togethers became known as "Francesca's Salons," in honor of Ms. Batchen, and Collins is so absorbed by the memory to this day, he is writing a play, *Friday at Francesca's*.

The two-storey Asquith house was bubbling with creativity: upstairs lived CBC set designer Stan Sellen, CBC actress/singer Donna Miller and Hamilton, who taught opera in-studio to singers Joan Maxwell and Barbara Franklin, on their way to becoming prominent Canadian sopranos. Other visitors included brilliant minds like Snow, who went on to become an influential experimental filmmaker with *Wavelength*, *La région centrale*, and *Corpus Callosum*, which appeared in all the major film festivals across the world. Snow was also a painter, a sculptor and jazz musician, who would bang out jazz on Batchen's piano, although Gould, who professed a disdain for popular music, tried to look the other way. One artist, who stopped by occasionally, became known for painting pictures of women's undergarments.

"It was a nice place, a fun place, and I remember we had a garden at the back and put vegetables in it," Batchen said. Otherwise, Toronto the Good was not a rockin' town in the 1950s, prior to the influx of immigrants from all over the world, multiculturalism and extravagant festivals — it was, as someone once said, New York run by the Swiss. Much of the civic excitement was down at Maple Leaf Gardens, where the Toronto Maple Leafs were usually contenders for hockey's Stanley Cup.

As buttoned-up conservative as Toronto was in those days, it did manage to show an accepting side to musicians, artists and, to a degree, eccentrics — especially in the rooming house at 46 Asquith. "It became like a Bohemian lifestyle with colorful people flowing in and out," Hamilton said. "Nobody had any money, but people were screwing around with each other every time you turned around. Frances had other male friends besides Gould — artists and creative people. At one time, we had a woman living upstairs, May Kerr — I think that's what she called herself in a tongue-in-cheek way — and we eventually discovered she was a hooker. We had to evict her — actually, Franny did it; I didn't have the courage. And another woman had to have an abortion in the house." The other tenants became suspicious of May Kerr when street workers made a procession into her room, which was supposedly a drapery shop with the clumsily misspelled *Exculsive Drapery* on a sign on the door. "Bohemians? Yes," said Miller. "We weren't bound by any particular rules and were able to do our own thing. You could have who you wanted come in and people looked the other way."

One can only guess what Gould thought about all of this. (Did his mother know who he was hanging out with?) Over the years, as he did in his 1979 documentary, *Glenn Gould's Toronto*, Gould told a number of people that he was the Last Puritan:

> *When I was a child, and indeed until very recently, this city was referred to as Toronto the Good. The reference was to the city's puritan traditions: one could not, for example, attend concerts on Sunday until the 1960s; it was not permissible to serve alcohol*

in a public place on the Sabbath until very recently;
and now a furor has developed at City Hall over the
issue of whether Torontonians should be permitted to
drink beer at baseball games. But you have to
understand that, as an anti-athletic, non-concert-
going teetotaler, I approve of all such restrictions. I,
perhaps, rather than the hero of George Santayana's
famous novel, am "the last puritan." So I always felt
that Toronto the Good was a very nice nickname. On
the other hand, a lot of my fellow citizens became
very upset about it and tried to prove that we could
be just as bad as any other place.

Gould seemed to relate strongly to fictional characters such as Santayana's Oliver, who were gifted, lonely, perhaps antisocial, deprived of affection and sometimes puritanical in their out-look on life. Like Gould, Oliver had an internal struggle between his puritanical upbringing, devoid of emotions, and his worldly desires. (And like Oliver, Gould went downhill mentally, phys-ically and socially and died young.) And yet, perhaps as well as being repulsed by some of the goings-on at 46 Asquith, he was probably intrigued, even lured to an extent, just as he had been excited by Morry Kernerman's sexual exploits. The marquee attraction for Gould at Asquith was Batchen, the petite brunette with the subtle yet seductive smile, fair skin that earned her the nickname "Snow White" in some quarters and a personality that inspired the best in her friends.

"[Gould] saw her sparkle and her spirit and her musicality," Valleau said. Many described Franny Batchen as vivacious and yet she also had a girl-next-door wink about her, similar to those actresses who appeared in the television commercials that Batchen dealt with every day; like some of her friends, she worked for Sponsor Film Services and later Graphic Associates as a film librarian, filing commercials for insertion into television shows such as *I Love Lucy* and the *Mickey Mouse Club*. That was her day job — at night, she was a piano instructor working out of the studio in her rooming house, teaching children. But it was at the Friday get-togethers where Fran's personality blossomed as she would stand, arms outstretched, in the middle of her living room and put on her best exaggerated Scottish accent. "She was a great hostess and great at drawing people out of themselves," Collins said. "I'll always remember those informal parties. I had taken piano lessons and I'd try show tunes, *Oklahoma* or the theme from the *Wizard of Oz*, but Fran and Glenn liked classical music."

Collins wrote of that period:

> *She was a monument of sorts. The Fridays were long since established when I was introduced to the circle. Stan of Asquith was full of the mood of the place, and his room was full of paintings. He favored landscapes and portraits and was quite unfashionable, but well liked and sought after. He was actually eclipsed by the sparkle of her habitués, her long comfortable Fridays she took so long to destroy, the cold tea and stale biscuits, the earnestness and sweet intensity, the warmed over opinions, always varied but the lighting was constant, the mood warm as could be without a grate fire, and [Frances] Elizabeth was always there, the little bird lady with fragile, grateful ankles as she always paid fussy little attentions with blankets and biscuits. Her whole soul came to a worried little point midway between her eyes and tea-cup and one knew instinctively that she knew bookstores well.*

Franny Batchen even drew Glenn Gould out of himself occasionally, although he remained a work in progress; some nights, on his way over from his parents' home in The Beach, the unpredictable Gould would slink up to Batchen's window, decide there were too many guests (or the wrong mix of them), and simply trudge back home. "He would case the joint and, knowing how much he liked one-on-one encounters to parties, he would leave," Collins said.

When a piano was introduced, however, Gould would transform into quite a different animal and would eagerly help others join his state of wonder. One memorable Sunday night, he entertained a group at the home of Dunning — who went on to London, England, to become an animator and director of the Beatles' *Yellow Submarine*, 1968 — with a unique Clementi piano, which was a fragile, early transition from the harpsichord to the pianoforte. That night, a crowd of young people gathered around the Clementi in awe as Gould put on a bells-and-whistles show, even though, as a perfectionist, he kept stopping to re-tune the instrument. "I asked him to play Scarlatti [works of the Italian composer] and I sang or hummed along with him," Valleau said. The only thing that interrupted the magic of the evening, friends recall, was that two of the group of artists who had not been invited to the informal Gould concert scampered by the house and chucked stones at the window. (They could be a cheeky bunch and, in 1956, several of them were fired from Graphic Associates for goofing off.)

The group was so impressed with Batchen, some of them started making a silent, 16mm film revolving around her, *The Fabulous Francesca*, directed by Collins in the basement of his home, a few blocks from the house of Gould's parents on Southwood Drive. It was a free-form, mime flick à la Marcel Marceau, with a vague plot and exaggerated sequences. "It was kind of pretentious and silly," Collins recalls, "but it was one of our underground films and we were experimenting." Caked with thick makeup and wearing a tight dress to show off her shapely figure and smoking Lucky Strikes as she did in real life,

Batchen played an upper-class mistress who could have been mistaken for actress Gloria Swanson. "The Swanson angle was part of our fascination of her," Collins said.

In addition to the mime film, other likenesses of Batchen popped up, including several sketches and an oil painting by Stan Sellen. As well, he tried to draw a couple of sketches of Gould — "but they didn't work out. He was sort of always in the background," Sellen said. That was par for the course, Donna Miller conferred, remembering how Gould would "come over to the house, but then he'd come and go like a shadow." Batchen's friends respected him, though, affectionately calling him "Gouldie" behind his back. But Sellen recalls that "Gouldie" was not as sullen or reclusive as history seems to paint him — he recalls him coming to the house quite often to play piano with Batchen and to hang out with her. "They were very friendly with each other and I found Gould to be quite a friendly guy, but a little eccentric in his gloves and scarf . . . I used to sit and listen as they tried out some of his new stuff" (Sellen isn't sure, but it may have been Gould's composition String Quartet op. 1 and his interpretation of the *Goldberg Variations*).

But just who was pursuing whom? Collins suspected that it was Batchen who initiated the relationship, although he could not be certain. (After Batchen moved to New York in 1956, Collins drafted an unfinished script in which a character based on Batchen pursues a character based on Gould.) "I thought Fran was pursuing Glenn because her great desire always seemed to be trying to find security," Collins said. "She always seemed to be restless and moving around, although some of that could have been financial." Like during her tragic childhood in the Prairies, Batchen had troubles in her twenties, too. "Fran was always broke, always moving from one house or apartment to another," Collins said. "She had a lot of bad luck and there were bad winters and heating bills. She was always juggling things."

I put my arm around him and I thought he was going to jump out of his skin. He said, "What are you doing? Move over!" He was horrified and from that moment, I knew Glenn Gould wasn't gay. He turned out to be the furthest thing from gay.
— Stuart Hamilton after making a pass at Gould

SLEEPING *with the* PIED PIPER

Chapter THREE

Although Gould was seeing Franny Batchen on a regular basis, she was not the only woman in his life; he also went out occasionally on dates in 1952 and perhaps in 1953 with Elizabeth Fox, a cheery blond, who worked at the CBC. Mostly, they listened to music and discussed the literature of T. S. Eliot, playwright Christopher Fry and Russian and German authors, but not much else. "The really personal impression that sticks in my mind is that I didn't know what he was, sexually," Fox said. "I always felt he didn't even shave. He had really smooth skin and he looked sort of androgynous, though I didn't even know what the word meant at the time." Fox recalled going to Gould's parents' home and finding them to be very nice, caring people — "but they certainly deferred to him. I thought later of E. B. White's *Stuart Little*, about these people who have a mouse as a child. And he's dressed up as a human being, but he goes up and down the drains and all the rest. Well, when you were at the Gould's house, you'd think, these people have produced something that is not of them . . . they were constantly in awe."

Then there was Angela Addison, who was an intellectual like Gould, and in ways as much of a soul mate to him as Batchen was. Gould and Addison met as students of Alberto Guerrero at the Royal Conservatory in the late 1940s. She was seventeen and he was fifteen, and after classes, they hung out together, playing piano for one another. "He played things and tried to make me agree with his interpretations," said Addison. "When he was in a giving mood, he'd play music by Schubert. He played a lot for me in Mr. Guerrero's studio. He critiqued my playing a lot." When Glenn Gould was in his late teens and started driving a car, he drove Angela Addison for meals at a spaghetti joint on College Street — "or we'd just drive around town, talking." Gould liked to take his lady friends to his parents' cottage, two hours north of Toronto's rat race. It wasn't too much of a hike for Addison, whose family had its own cottage on nearby Grassy Point, but sometimes she and Gould would drive up to his cottage from the conservatory. "It became a normal habit for him; he was feeling very pressured in those days and it was a good release."

After leaving Malvern Collegiate Institute without graduating, it was here where Gould really prepared to kick-start his career, where he felt at ease among the maple trees and raccoons and waves lapping onto the shore, where the only thing to disrupt his thought patterns and the melody in his head was a sudden wind in the pines or a Jeep in the distance, where there was no one to tell him what to do (at least when his mother was back in the city), where he could be away from admirers, where he didn't have to touch anyone. Gould wrote, "Artists, as I see it, work best in isolation, where the outside world is under their control. You must leave the path of worldly ambition, listen to and heed your inner voice." Said Addison, "In private, Glenn could be himself — complex and many-faceted; as uninhibited as it was possible for him to be." He even got in some exercise — rare for him — if only riding around in a motorboat and waltzing through the woods with children and dogs.

Addison attended several of Gould's concerts, and so early in his career he was already bemoaning live performances. "We talked an awful lot about music. He tried to make me understand his dislike for playing in public," she said. "The most famous musicians onstage are hoping to find the perfect listener in the audience, but Glenn Gould was not interested in the perfect listener, but the perfect sound, and he was absolutely sure what the perfect sound was. He really didn't care about the listeners. It may have been he was desperately afraid of losing control. He needed to be in control." (However, throughout his career, Gould claimed he did indeed care about his listeners, especially with helping them make a connection with their music.) Addison found Gould to be not so much eccentric as contradictory. "I didn't find him that eccentric at all, but he didn't discourage the myth; he played it to the hilt. But he was complex. With someone like that, you're kind of walking on glass all the time; if you step the wrong way, you shatter it and yet you have to be straight and honest about the friendship."

Following Gould's death, Addison wrote in a tribute to Gould, "Friendship with genius can never be easy. It is perhaps the most fragile of human relationships. In Glenn Gould, I had a friend who was elusive, enigmatic, private and solitary. I also had a friend who was loyal, generous, courteous, fun and, of course, stunningly brilliant." Indeed, Gould had several different sides to him, Addison said, "that you would find hard to reconcile in a person. It wasn't all very nice; he was extremely judgmental, he could really come across with moral superiority. He wasn't like that with his close friends or colleagues. But in the ordinary course of life, he could be extremely critical, even cruel. At the conservatory, he was not overly critical about the musicality if people weren't as talented as he was, but he'd morally judge people." Addison recalls an incident in the 1950s at Gould's cottage with opera singer Jon Vickers: "Jon had a strong religious [Baptist] sense and he and Glenn clashed very much. I had just gone to one of Jon's concerts and it was lovely and well received. I think he sang Handel. At the concert, Jon was asked to do an encore and so he did 'Jesus Loves Me.' That upset Glenn. [Later at the cottage] in front of other people, he told

Jon that he'd prostituted himself by doing a religious song as an encore, which was ironic because Glenn himself adored the old hymns. Glenn had a very austere feeling about religion. You can hear it in some of the music he plays — it's very pure and austere. But I got angry with him that day, the way he spoke to Jon." Gould could also be outspoken to youths, Addison said. "Glenn got involved with young people who he felt were drinking or straying too much. He'd get in touch with their parents. I know he did that once in Stratford with one young man's parents."

Musically, Addison was fascinated by Gould's attraction to the northern Europe sensibility from Germany and Holland. "That shaped his life enormously, the simple, stubborn ways, the Bach, the whole northern European kind of ethics, which are very strong and simple, the roots of Protestantism, which were part of the backbone of his character. He was so married to that type of music."

Addison said she never went to bed with Gould. "There was never any sexual chemistry between us; he regarded me as a friend, a non-demanding friend. I posed no threat to Glenn on any level. In more intense relationships with women, there may have been emotional demands or commitment expected of him he didn't feel entirely easy with. He was very afraid of that. There's no doubt he had some controlling issues with some women." Gould was discreet about his close relationships, Addison said, and he expected the same from them. "If you are a true friend, you trust one another completely. You cannot shatter that trust."

Despite friendships with Addison and Fox, Batchen seemed to be number one in Gould's life with women well into the 1950s. (His mother should be kept in a separate category.) While on the surface their personalities appeared contrary, Gould and Batchen had lots in common: they were both intellectuals and deep thinkers who loved Bach and Schoenberg and contrapuntal music containing two or more voices heard simultaneously; they were both left-handed; they both loved animals; they both had a fierce drive to become successful pianists; both hated a particular color (Gould red, Batchen blue); like Gould, Batchen had a private side she rigorously guarded. They were both fond of literature and sharing quotes, such as: "There is my truth; now tell me yours," Nietzsche, or "There is no such thing as a difficult piece. It is either impossible or easy. The process whereby it migrates from one category to the other is called practicing," Louis Kentner. (For the record, Gould claimed he never practiced much, especially later in his career, but he may have been exaggerating.)

Like Gould, Batchen also had her moods. In photographs taken of her in the 1950s, she appears to show various emotions: of contentment, of optimism, as the life of the party and one photo of her sitting at a desk in a striped jersey with her hand on her chin, mouth slightly open, in which you would swear she was a soul lost in the woods. "I did feel lost at times," she said years later.

"Fran was very private, and she usually kept her moods to herself," Emily Valleau said. (Later, as Frances Barrault, she did not like going into details of her pain from those days. In 2008, I took the old rushes of the mime film *The Fabulous Francesca* to her home in Richmond, England. When I played the video for her, she seemed uncomfortable watching herself as a young woman. "When is it going to be over?" she kept asking. And when it was, I asked her how she felt. "Don't ask, Michael," she said grimly. "Don't ask." Two nights later, I asked the same question about her reaction to the video. "It's too difficult to talk about," she said.)

We do know that both Batchen and Gould suffered from stage fright. In his early twenties, he was already talking about quitting as a concert pianist for several reasons — he wanted to focus on composing to create a purer form of music electronically and also because he detested audiences, which he felt were waiting on the edge of their seats for him to make a mistake. As well, he was timid of catching their germs after his mother told him to stay away from crowds. Such nervousness can be poison to a pianist because when the body's fight-or-flight system kicks in, blood leaves the small muscles, particularly the fingers, and is transported to the big muscles, such as the arms and legs, in order to fight or run away, which is the traditional caveman response to a threat. Of course, Gould was always trying to protect his fragile body from his emotions and nervous reactions; he was already experimenting with prescription drugs to calm him, such as Valium and Nembutal. As early as age fourteen, Gould was taking prescription drugs, according to William Vaisey, who knew him as a musician and later as a neighbor. "In the old Royal Conservatory in 1946, he was taking pills for his hypochondria," Vaisey said. "I used to marvel how he wore his father's overcoat and leather gloves, even in summer."

Certainly, the pressures of performing were becoming more intense — up until 1954, Gould played just six to eight concerts a year, but that increased to fourteen in 1955, twenty-three in 1956 and thirty-six in 1957. In the end, Gould persevered onstage, thanks to his plucky ego and belief in his enormous ability, allowing him to trust himself in front of an auditorium packed with three thousand potential critics. On the other hand, Batchen did not trust herself enough. Although both she and Gould had a good memory recall of musical pieces at the piano, she was worse under pressure and her technique tended to break down; under stress, her rhythm and touch were affected and her fast movements became even faster. She also suffered from migraines, perhaps at least partly due to worry over performing. Another phobia they shared was the fear of being touched. Gould's history of this has been well-documented and there are many theories for it — a smothering mother who filled his head with an unnecessary worry of catching other people's germs to the point he took bottles of

Lysol disinfectant with him on road trips; a fear of intimacy or rejection and worry about hurting his fingers, which of course were his livelihood. Sometimes at his concerts, Gould would hand out cards to well-wishers backstage, asking them not to shake his hand for fear of injuring his fingers. He often wore gloves, he said, not to keep warm but to protect his fingers. In general, Batchen was more touchy-feely, but since childhood, she had had a fear of touching her own naval, or having others touch it — perhaps because she had been born with an umbilical hernia. "It was a sacrosanct spot," she wrote in her 1992 book *The Confidence Quotient*.

There were traits that Gould and Batchen did not like about one another. At times, Gould could be controlling and selfish and he detested Batchen's Lucky Strike habit. When she tried to quit smoking, Frances tended to be irritable and tearful, and she showed her temper. (Right next door to her rooming house on Asquith was the Institute of Hypnotherapy, which advertised a technique to stop smoking or to quit "other bad habits, social or personal.") Coming from the roots he did, Gould did not smoke or drink and would not curse unless his father's custom-made piano stool got damaged.

But one memorable afternoon in about 1952, Gould made Stuart Hamilton swear to himself. Hamilton, who had helped to introduce Gould and Batchen two years earlier, sauntered into the rooming house he shared with her. The sophisticated Hamilton walked past the studio through an unlocked door into Batchen's apartment to find Gould in a business suit and Batchen kneeling beneath him. "And there she was! She was giving him a blow job," Hamilton said. Oh well, so much for the couple's touching phobias. At that moment, it might have been appropriate for Hamilton to have calmly walked into a nearby washroom and hit a note his opera students would have been proud of. "Actually, I said, 'Oh, sorry,' and walked away," Hamilton said. "She should have put the lock on the door. I was embarrassed." A short time later, Gould waltzed sheepishly out of the apartment and asked to see Hamilton in the studio. Neither man dared to mention the fellatio, but instead Gould broke into a serious, lengthy discussion with Hamilton about music, perhaps to quickly change the subject. "I think he felt a little Presbyterian about what had happened, but I didn't judge him. Even before that, I knew he and Franny were having an affair. She didn't talk about it, but it was perfectly clear."

Presumably, Gould went home that night and decided he had to stop telling his mother *everything*. That sex act would remain a dark secret for decades; to many people, including some of his posthumous biographers, Gould did not seem to need sex. This is part of a larger fallacy still alive today — that deeply creative people and other geniuses ignore sex to pour all of their talent, drive and attention into their work, and yet as a species, even the geniuses among us are at best sophisticated animals with sex drives as well as needs for complex thinking, for writing scores and operas. The fact is, this was only the beginning of a sexual life — heterosexual — for a man who would so guard his privacy and his image that throughout his life, the world thought he was gay or asexual long after his death. "As a young fellow, Glenn was so neurotic about germs and what he ate — so afraid of everything — I just can't image that he ever took his pants off for a woman . . . but I don't think he was gay," said Peter Yazbeck, who was a conservatory student with Gould and knew him from age fourteen to thirty, then went on to become a music professor at the University of California at Santa Barbara.

Even after they were caught in a sex act, Gould and Batchen did not act like a couple when they were together in front of other people, Hamilton said. "Gould was especially prudent and secretive. That's why people thought he was gay." Hamilton, for one, is convinced that Gould was not gay. A few years earlier, the gay Hamilton had made his own pass at Gould while they were listening to Bach while sitting on a couch in the home of Gould's parents. "I put my arm around him and I thought he was going to jump out of his skin. He said, 'What are you doing? Move over!' He was horrified and from that moment, I knew Glenn Gould wasn't gay. He turned out to be the furthest thing from gay. He was very discreet about it, but he was a very highly sexual heterosexual."

Today, when confronted with the question, Frances Barrault admitted she had a sexual romance with Gould. Told that many people thought he was gay, she laughed. "Oh! Never, no way ... our relationship was physical. He was a sexy guy — sexy to women."

All of this stuff was news to most of the gang at Fran's Friday Salons. If anything, Gould's acquaintances thought his girlfriend might be Elizabeth Fox or perhaps Angela Addison. "We knew that Fran and Glenn were close, but many of us thought it was platonic," Collins said years later. "We never thought about them having a sexual affair, but it's quite possible. It must have been discreet. He was very sneaky, for one thing, about his [prescription] drug habits ... but we knew that Glenn was Fran's first big love. She once told me there were three men she could marry — Glenn, George Dunning and me. I said, 'Fran, I'm a gay man!'" As it turned out, so was Dunning. Collins once bought Batchen a turquoise and black full-length evening gown. "She looked stunning in it, especially with her attractive figure." Unlike many Toronto artists and musicians, Collins never thought of Gould as being gay. "I don't think he was; most of our group thought he was asexual. We thought if he was in love with anything, it was his music. He was so passionate about music."

Gould and Batchen did not reveal themselves romantically, or hold hands in public, she said, because that was the way Gould wanted it. "He was so very private and I had to respect that." But it was frustrating for Batchen, who, though discreet, would have liked to have been arm-in-arm in public with such a rising star. Unlike today, celebrities of the 1950s and 1960s were sometimes able to keep their sexual lives private — actors Spencer Tracy and Katharine Hepburn carried on a secret affair for years, President John F. Kennedy reportedly had prostitutes in the White House and the most macho Hollywood actor, Rock Hudson, turned out to be gay. A few of Fran's friends, like Emily Reid and Sylvia MacDonald, did know that Batchen was Gould's girlfriend, but they kept their lips sealed, and continued to do so for decades after Gould had died.

"[Gould] was very private, and so was Fran," Reid said. "We always protected her." And Reid did not interfere with the relationship, even though Gould would call Batchen at her home at all hours of the night.

In the small subculture of the classical music world, the Gould-Batchen relationship was known. "People knew about her in music circles," said Ben Sonnenberg, a New York writer, pianist and an acquaintance of Gould. "I remember [violinist] Alexander Schneider used to talk about her." Gould had his own close friends besides Batchen, although he rarely showed them off in public. They were mostly women, though he still chummed with childhood pal Robert Fulford and started a small concert company with him that featured Gould at the keyboard. Gould seemed to let his hair down more with women, perhaps at least partly because he had been closer to his mother than his father.

In 1953, Gould did something that might surprise Gould fans and researchers of today; he showed his teaching — or at least coaching — prowess. Throughout his life, Gould was largely a solo artist who never considered himself a teacher. When he was in his thirties, he told a University of Toronto audience, "I am, perhaps, in no position to talk about teaching. It is something that I have never done and do not imagine that I shall ever have the courage to do. It strikes me as involving a most awesome responsibility which I should prefer to avoid." On another occasion, Gould said he needed "a spinal resilience when I'm confronted with opinions not my own."

Yet teaching was one area in which Gould often sold himself short, because in 1953, just out of his teens, he showed the patience of an old professor in teaching Frances Batchen the slow, melancholic and oftentimes dark Berg Sonata, which he often played at concerts, and which would remain important to her for decades. It helped her keep an open mind about music because she was starting to lose her dream of becoming a concert pianist; besides teaching, Batchen was picking up a little money and exposure on the side recording music for dance troupes and their warm-up exercises. "In my twenties, I repeatedly made completely fresh beginnings, always ready to begin from scratch with some new viewpoint," she said. "But always the nervousness of playing in public, the stage fright, [that feeling of] being on trial, destroyed all the work." And yet just being with Gould, a rising star who selected his friends carefully, injected her with confidence. Gould enjoyed playing the Berg Sonata himself, as he did on CBC Radio in 1952; he thought the piece was so intense and complex, he went to great lengths throughout his life to explain it. He said that in it, the "fervently romantic" young Berg found the "perfect idiom both to accentuate his restless genius and to cloak his rather dissolute habits. This is the language of collapse and disbelief, of musical weltschmerz, the last stand of tonality betrayed and inundated by the chromaticism which gave it birth. It permitted Berg his ecstatic tensions, his sorrowful resolutions, his unashamed revelation of himself. It also indulged his weaknesses — the jacked-up sequence. . . ." For her part, Frances described the Berg Sonata as a "wonderfully somber fin-de-siècle piece."

And then, on February 18, 1953, at the tenth annual Kiwanis Music Festival in Toronto's Eaton Auditorium, the twenty-seven-year-old Batchen was entered in the senior solo competition for "modern" music, playing the Berg Sonata no. 1. Her twenty-year-old tutor, Gould, smiled like a Cheshire cat in the audience. Despite Batchen being unhappy with her performance, Gould was proud of his "pupil." "I came down from the platform and said to him, 'Well, that's the end of a beautiful friendship,' and he said, 'No, it isn't — you played well.'"

The judges agreed with him, awarding her the first prize. All of this was quite a compromise for Gould, who hated such competitions and once said that "competition rather than money is the root of all evil," even though he had captured a bunch of Kiwanis awards in the 1940s. Stuart Hamilton, who has seen hundreds of pianists come and go over the decades, reviewed Batchen as "okay" as a musician, "rather mechanical and not very expressive, but she was determined and she improved. Gould worked hard with her — when they weren't fucking — and he opened doors for her." Winning such a prize was usually a big deal for a budding concert pianist, according to Dr. Bruce Burns, who has been an executive of the Kiwanis Festival since 1958. "Anybody who goes through, they've got a musical career in store for them," he said, but noted, "some performers can be affected by nerves and anxiety." Burns was amazed to learn that Gould not only had a girlfriend, but that he was a teacher, at least once.

The Berg Sonata became an important piece for Gould in other ways; on November 3, 1953, just nine months after Batchen's prize-winning performance, Gould made the sonata his first commercial recording. It was done at the Bloor Street United Church in downtown Toronto and it earned Gould just $150, but it also gave him chance to publish his writing in the form of liner notes, which would become a popular means of communication for Gould in the decades to come. Gould also recorded the Berg Sonata for Columbia Records in 1958–59.

Meanwhile, Gould and Batchen became so intimate he took her a number of times to his parents' cottage, and there he shed his solitary side and made time for activities for two, such as playing piano, discussing Russian literature and putting around on the family's two boats, the *Alban B.* (after composer Alban Berg), and the *Arnold S.* (after Arnold Schoenberg). "He loved taking those two motorboats out onto the lake," she said. In the winter, the daring Gould drove his family's car across the ice with Batchen aboard. In the summer, Gould the animal advocate would sometimes try to scare away fishermen and other times would conduct an imaginary audience instead of steering the boats. Removed from his public, Glenn Gould showed a different side to Franny Batchen — he smiled and showed his teeth, for one thing, and wagged his big ears for fun to show he had quite a self-deprecating sense of humor to balance his big ego, and sometimes he hammed it up in his grandfather's raccoon coat. Yet he didn't reveal this side very often, she said. "He didn't communicate easily with people."

Gould even introduced Batchen to his parents as his girlfriend, she said. "I got very close to his parents. They were nice people, socially conscious and concerned with doing the right thing. Glenn adored his mom, but I think he was a bit afraid of her. Mrs. Gould bought me my first steam iron and his dad gave me a fur coat and Glenn hated that fact, since he was an animal lover and protector. I loved that coat. It kept me warm." (Batchen would not be the only girlfriend that his father presented with a fur coat.) "His parents were very kind to me. They assumed we would get married." In ways, Flora was like the mother that Franny never had.

Back in Toronto, Gould and Batchen made a cute if somewhat unorthodox couple when they showed up at places like the Coterie Café for a nighttime tea. "They were both artistic souls," said soprano and Gould friend Barbara Franklin, who had attended Guerrero's piano classes with Gould and was the winner of the CBC radio contest, "Opportunity Knocks," in 1950.

Actually, Gould and *Franklin* made a cute sort of couple, as well. In fact, Franklin was such a part of the pianist's life in the 1950s that in the years following Gould's death, rumors were that Franklin had been the one serious girlfriend of his life. "I went out with him a lot in Toronto in the 1950s and even in New York," she said. "We were very fond of one another and I knew him as well as anybody." She said that Gould would spend time with her at the rooming house on Asquith — sometimes in the company of Batchen and/or Franklin's voice coach Stuart Hamilton — as well as Gould's Southwood home and cottage, and Toronto hangouts like Diana Sweets Restaurant, "where we'd have sodas in the backyard with ducks swimming in a pond." Gould would phone Franklin up at all hours to chat, sometimes about his fears, from his parents' line, HO 9422. Gould was a good one-on-one conversationalist, especially on the telephone, where he did not have to be with a person face-to-face and could better control things — and who would hang up on Glenn Gould? "I thought he was a lonely person, a seriously lonely person. There were very few people he trusted enough to talk to."

Gould did not reveal his inner feelings much, Franklin said. "He released most of his feelings in his music, and when he did that, he showed *all* his feelings."

Yet Gould talked to her about his worries, especially of flying. "He hopelessly hated planes and traveling alone in Europe," she said. "At one point, he asked me if we could be two white swans who would fly around the world together. That's how lonely he felt. He needed someone to be a type of wife, to be family. He was so beyond the rest of us intellectually and musically, and he had some neurosis and didn't want people touching him, and yet he longed for the human touch." Less known in Gould's history was his fear of heights, but Franklin saw it up close one night when she went with him to see a concert of a harpsichordist at Carnegie Hall in New York. "He never liked to go to concerts, but I forced him to go," she said. "We were up in the balcony, all the way at the top, and I saw that he had a fear of heights. He was in agony." On other occasions, they had tea and "lovely sandwiches" in New York hotels.

"They seemed close in a spiritual way," Morry Kernerman said of Gould and Franklin. "He seemed to like older women." (Franklin was three years older than Gould.) After Franklin married, Gould continued to telephone her, but she started to feel uncomfortable. "I had to tell him to stop calling. I told him, "It feels strange talking to you when I'm lying beside my husband [in bed]."

From 1953 to 1955, with Franklin and Batchen as two of the witnesses, Gould composed his String Quartet in F Minor, the most significant composition of his life. With no training as a composer and no experience writing for stringed instruments, he agonized over it, sometimes just adding a few bars a day. Eventually, it received mixed reviews and to many it resembled a work of one of Gould's favorite composers, Richard Strauss. While Gould was writing the String Quartet, Franklin said, he had her talk, not sing, over the music. "We'd go to the cottage and rehearse and chat and laugh together. We never had sex, but we were tremendous friends. We'd call each other by our last names: Franklin and Gould, and Stuart Hamilton was Hamilton."

He did the same with Batchen. "He would agonize over it one bar at a time and play it to me, bit by bit," she said. On a typical evening after Batchen got home from work as a film librarian, Gould would call her at about eleven o'clock, put down the telephone and start playing portions of his composition to get her feedback. He also did this with the *Goldberg Variations*, which he was preparing to record for the first time. (He also played bits and pieces of the *Goldberg Variations* for Angela Addison to get her opinion.)

"I remember that [after Asquith] I moved into a house on Glen Road and it had a lovely big room, big enough for a grand, so I put a Chickering in it and Glenn really liked it," Frances Barrault recalled. "He used to come in and practice for his recording of the *Goldberg Variations*, the 'Gould-bergs,' and he would do it several ways and we would discuss the merits of the interpretations. And then, he practiced for his New York debut." Yes, the other member of the Glenn/Franny threesome had short, stubby legs and slightly square sides — Franny's Chickering grand piano, built in 1895 in Boston. It was actually a rental, a homely instrument of unfinished mahogany to some, but the great Glenn Gould was enraptured by its voice, similar to a harpsichord with a thin, Bach-like quality.

As a teenager, Gould spent a lot of time at the cottage, practicing and contemplating his future. Sometimes, when Gould and Batchen were together or when he would telephone her from the cottage, the sun would come up before she could fall asleep, but Gould did not seek out everyone for such advice. Usually, he was egotistical and stubborn and especially did not seek advice from those he felt were more qualified than he.

"The two years of isolation at Lake Simcoe had cut him off from the corrective influence of other musicians and taught him to be utterly self-reliant," said psychiatrist Peter Ostwald, an amateur violinist who played with Gould. Ostwald was in contact with Gould off and on from 1957 to 1977, but apparently did not know about Franny Batchen. (Gould was not in total isolation, however, as he visited his parents' home and was also giving concerts in those days.) "He no longer wanted to be advised by older musical colleagues," Ostwald said.

Gould likely played his music-under-construction for her, Batchen said, "as much to share it, as anything — he didn't like taking advice from anybody." Biographies note that Gould worked hard at the cottage with a tape recorder, tinkering with his unique style, which included unusually fast or slow tempi and a deliberate emphasis on inner or hidden voices. His dogs are noted as being nearby but the books make no mention of

Batchen's presence, which is hardly surprising considering the veil of secrecy around his inner life.

During this period, Gould was struggling over what type of music he should use for his debut coming up in the United States on January 2, 1955, in Washington, D.C., and his New York debut nine days later, and what might identify him as special. It was also during this time that he was becoming aware of his strange mannerisms at the keyboard. When they were pointed out to him by Batchen and others, he said, "I became extremely self-conscious about everything I did. The whole secret of what I had been doing was to concentrate exclusively on realizing a conception of the music."

But Gould was beginning to really spread his wings — from 1953 to 1954, he was involved with Ontario's Stratford Music Festival and on October 16, 1954, at the Royal Conservatory's concert hall in Toronto, he introduced his version of the *Goldberg Variations,* a relatively obscure, forgotten eighteenth-century piece written originally for harpsichord. Gould's interpretation would be his signature for the rest of his life and came after much fussing and experimenting. The concert drew only fifteen people who braved the torrential rains of Hurricane Hazel, but the "Gould-berg Variations" would soon have its own hurricane effect on the classical music world, beginning in 1955, when he recorded it for Columbia Records in an abandoned Presbyterian church at 207 East Thirteenth Street in New York. The *Goldbergs* were written by Bach about 1740, supposedly for a Russian count who was a sickly insomniac and asked for some soft, smooth and lively music to cheer him up during his sleepless nights.

Said Gould, "The *Goldberg Variations* is music which observes neither end nor beginning, music with neither real climax nor real resolution . . . it has, then, unity through intuitive perception, unity born of craft and scrutiny, mellowed by mastery achieved, and revealed to us here, as so rarely in art, in the vision of subconscious design exulting upon a pinnacle of potency."

"I really liked his [1955] version," Batchen said. (Gould re-recorded the *Goldberg Variations* in 1981, but she did not like the second version as much. "The first one seemed more spontaneous.") Gould sometimes took Batchen to concerts, but she learned quickly that she should stay alert if she was a passenger in a car being driven by Gould. One night she fell asleep exhausted on the passenger seat, awakening to find Gould driving erratically, with his hands not upon the wheel but furiously conducting an imaginary orchestra.

We should get married.
— Glenn Gould to Frances Batchen

A PROPOSAL

Frances Batchen had a front-row seat to an important crossroads in Glenn Gould's emotional life; due to his increasing concert schedule, he had to deal with people on a more regular basis, and it was causing him distress and physical problems. In 1955 and 1956, he told Batchen and others that he had developed an eating disorder, that he became so nervous around people he could not eat in their presence without later suffering from stomach aches, stomach spasms or diarrhea. It seemed as though it was a condition that had been slowly developing for some time because in the 1950s it was reported he would only attempt easy-to-digest foods while he was with others. "I remember eating an awful lot of spaghetti with him," Angela Addison said.

This is a common reaction in people stressed around others — their nervous system contracts their digestive system and does not allow for proper food digestion. Gould likely did not even have to eat with others to bring this on — just thinking about it can cause one's nervous system to react. And, of course, he was a full-time thinker and worrier. Gould often talked about death and dying and told Batchen he had been having recurring nightmares about being swept toward the brink of Niagara Falls. He believed a little in ESP and was superstitious to the point where he would cancel an airline flight if it had an "unlucky" number or sometimes rip up a check he was writing if he did not like the look of it — another of Gould's paradoxes as an otherwise-rational thinker. Naturally, he nearly begged Batchen not to mention any of these weaknesses to others, especially not to the media. According to her, he said, "'or it could have a negative impact on my career.'"

Beyond their lengthy discussions about music and their feelings, Gould remained smitten with Batchen, who, like he, was always searching for peace of mind (that would become a common trait among Gould's future girlfriends). "He didn't communicate easily, but we became very close," she said in 2008.

But perhaps they were getting too close. Addison remembers Gould sitting in her practice room at the Royal Conservatory in the early to mid-1950s in tears, pouring out his frustration over his courtship of a woman. He did not name her, but it was almost certainly Batchen, a woman Addison never met. "He was really upset and he was sobbing; I think they'd just had a breakup," Addison said. "He didn't confide in me so much as events caught up with him. He had to turn to someone."

Perhaps the problem was not so much that he was incapable of or did not want a real relationship or marriage, but that he could not reconcile it with his artistic needs and his belief that greatness could only be achieved through single-mindedness in his work. Perhaps he fretted that the state of wonder and the state of worry could not peacefully coexist. It seemed the same type of tearful reaction Gould had had before he met Batchen, when he had parted ways with his piano teacher Guerrero, a departure to which his parents had objected. "He never really cried, but there'd be tears — he'd get so angry," his cousin Jessie Greig said.

When Gould's career took off with his New York debut and the release of the *Goldberg Variations* in the mid-1950s, many of his friends were there to see it. In 1954, Gould performed the *Goldberg Variations* for the Montreal Ladies' Morning Musical Club. In the audience was twenty-two-year-old Carmel

Schwartz of New York, who was doing some research at McGill University for modern dance. "I was overcome by the performance," Schwartz said. Gould quickly became friends with Schwartz, a tall, blond, blue-eyed intellectual his age, who had varied interests. Six months later, Schwartz was in the audience for the most important concert in Gould's early career — on January 11, 1955, at the intimate Town Hall theater in Manhattan for which he received much-needed American media attention and good reviews. Sitting in the custom-made piano chair his father had crafted for him, Gould displayed his eccentric keyboard style and technical skills, and he was a hit. His mother was in the audience to see the fruits of her dedication to her son blossom even more, along with a woman who was quickly becoming his New York surrogate mother, Vienna-born actress Susan Douglas Rubes and her husband, opera singer Jan Rubes, who had met Gould years earlier in Toronto through music.

"It was a wonderful performance," Susan Rubes said. "We sat close to the stage and we could hear Glenn humming as he was playing. My husband said to me, 'You must stop him humming!' We relayed this to Glenn backstage and he just laughed. He was happy to see us there."

In fact, there was quite a large crowd of well-wishers backstage to see the Canadian pianist. "Glenn was very warm and normal and friendly and very humorous with everyone," Schwartz said.

Although he sometimes liked backstage partying, Gould did not like receptions; following the Town Hall performance, a party was held for him, but he left after just thirty minutes, feigning illness. (Later in the 1950s, he erupted at the thought of a post-concert reception in Montreal. One of the organizers, impresario Sam Gesser, recalls that two men came to Gould's dressing room following his concert. "I'm not going!" said Gould, his tuxedo drenched from the sweat of the performance. "I don't go to receptions. Go away! Go away!")

Franny Batchen was not able to make the trip to New York; she stayed back in Toronto to earn money to rent another apartment after she had to move out of the Asquith building. Her relationship with Gould was starting to get tense — he was calling her at all hours and she couldn't catch up on her sleep.

The morning after his Town Hall debut, Gould was offered a contract to record for the Masterworks division of Columbia Records. He signed the deal in the spring and remained exclusive with Columbia for the rest of his life. Meanwhile, Schwartz got a job as an executive assistant for the talent agency Columbia Artists and helped Gould to get some gigs at a critical time in his career — after the *Goldberg Variations* was released in the spring of 1956. "I remember concert executives wanted Glenn to audition for the Metro Museum concert series for young pianists, but I told them to listen to the *Goldberg Variations* and, once they did, no audition was necessary," Schwartz said. "After that, he got discovered and they started saying, 'This boy's a genius.'"

In the coming months, Gould would visit Schwartz in New York or call her late at night from Toronto and they would discuss literature, politics and everyday life. "He was just Glenn Gould to me, a person and not an eccentric or a big star," she said. "I was Jewish and he was very pro-Israel. He was very funny; if you were depressed, he would put you in a good mood. He had such a mind, but he didn't want to talk music with me and he was totally disinterested in my dancing." Schwartz recalls Gould showed up at her birthday party in New York, where she sort of set him up with actress Dina Doronne, who was playing in the original Broadway production of *The Diary of Anne Frank*. "I told him that I had this Israeli actress waiting for him and he came, and stayed until six in the morning. He thought she was charming and beautiful and I think they became friends after that. She went to some of his concerts." Otherwise, Gould never talked to Schwartz about his female acquaintances. "I couldn't imagine him having any girl-friends — he didn't want to touch anybody! He was so afraid of catching germs and he really was a drug addict," she said. "He could not do without — he got drugs for any ache or pain, and he talked to me a lot about it." Schwartz says she never became Gould's girlfriend. "I got busy with my own life."

Gould, Schwartz and Susan Rubes all became friends in New York. From 1955 to 1959, Gould stayed several times a year at the large, four-bedroom apartment of Rubes and her husband, Jan, on Seventy-eighth Street in Manhattan. "The New York hotels didn't have king-sized beds, but we did," Susan said. Gould and Jan would play four hands jazz on the piano. "[Gould] was fun and played games with our kids. He was a great clown and liked making fun of things, to provoke the adults," said Susan, who was appearing on Broadway and on television. "But his eating habits were funny — one night he wanted to know how fresh our ice cream was. Germs were his big thing. He wouldn't be around people who were sick, and his food had to be absolutely fresh."

Gould also visited the Rubes' family cottage in Collingwood, Ontario. "We'd be swimming in the bay and he'd be in his hat, scarf and gloves. My kids couldn't believe it. But he felt comfortable with our family and was able to relax."

Through the years, Gould sort of attached himself to other families and their children as well; violinist Morry Kernerman, who knew Gould from 1953 to 1962, said, "We had a lot in common and we were very close for a long time, and I think part of it was that he tried to be part of my life and he wanted to learn about my relatives."

But all was not hunky-dory. At about this time, Gould was seeking psychiatric help for pains he was having in his arms, his prescription drug use and other issues, according to psychiatrist Dr. Peter Ostwald. Apparently, Gould received consultation from a Toronto psychiatrist who decided to treat him with medication. Schwartz recalls Gould bringing up the subject one night at a party at the Rubes' home. "How long the treatment lasted or how effective it was I have been unable to discover," Ostwald later said.

Back in Toronto, Gould and Batchen continued their courtship, even though at times it was on rocky ground. Helmut Kallmann, a young CBC music librarian, recalls being invited to spend an evening with Gould at Batchen's apartment on Glen Road in Toronto's Rosedale district. "It was his lady friend's place," Kallmann said. "She was a pianist who was working on the big Brahms Sonata op. 5 with great diligence." Gould and Kallmann had a lengthy discussion about classical music, with Gould criticizing Mozart "as he often did. Glenn could not stand rivals," Kallmann said. (Gould also did not approve of Mozart's liberal Mediterranean lifestyle.) "This was only days or weeks after his *Goldberg* recording catapulted Gould into fame, but I don't think either of us made mention of it." After their discussion, Kallman said, "I was dismissed with the explanation that Gould had other important things to deal with that evening."

One can imagine that Gould and Batchen spent the rest of the night at the piano, then, following the Brahms, curled up in one another's arms as the snow fell outside the window. And one can also imagine the comfort and thrill of a woman earning Gould's hard-to-win touch, with him focusing on her for a moment, rather than his life's vision.

By February 1956, the snow in the window was no longer romantic and problems were continuing in the Gould-Batchen relationship. She was considering getting another job or moving out of town. But Gould wanted a more serious relationship, Barrault later said, even marriage. Just the thought of Glenn Gould proposing to a woman, never mind *marrying* one, seems far-fetched in the history of the eccentric pianist as we have known it until now. When interviewed in 2009, Barrault was eighty-three and her health was failing and she had difficulty remembering some details of her life and relationship with Gould. But Franny claims that he proposed to her in Toronto. As she recalls, she and Gould were sitting in her apartment when Gould said to her, "We should get married." That statement seems consistent with what we will learn about Gould's history of approaching things romantic or emotional — he would not speak of them directly. For example, when caught in a confrontation or deep discussion about feelings, he would often slip into one of his many comedic alter egos, such as Sir Humphrey Price-Davies and Wolfgang von Krankmeister, who could broach such subjects with light dialogue. Barrault recalls that she did not respond to his "proposal" that night, but in the ensuing weeks and months, she considered the possibility of becoming Mrs. Glenn Gould.

Apparently, not everyone trusted her intentions with the young pianist. "She struck us as a lost soul and he was so young and naive," Peter Yazbeck said. "We invited him to parties and his mother brought him — at age eighteen! When Glenn came in, everything stopped. Suddenly, you couldn't mention sex or have dark humor. . . . I think that Frances may have taken advantage of him."

Yazbeck was not the only one suspicious of Batchen's intentions. After Gould died in 1982, a note was found in his apartment from Gould's manager Walter Homburger. It did not name anyone, but seemed to be aimed at Batchen. "Watch yourself — I think that she'll be poison," Homburger wrote. "She is a piano teacher and obviously is trying to obtain publicity for herself."

However, by most accounts Batchen put in solid hours and effort with Gould — long, long hours, when they were together or when he was calling her late at night from the cottage. There is no evidence she tried to exploit their relationship and she never talked about it publicly, preferring instead to keep her memories of her relationship with Gould to herself.

The decades since Gould's death in 1982 have proven those wrong who thought that Frances was out to make a name for herself while courting Gould. She never tried to exploit their relationship and, in fact, she told no one, except for her close friends, about her courtship and proposal from the world's most famous pianist. When interviewed by a writer in 2001, she mentioned nothing about being Gould's girlfriend, although she did talk about their friendship. She and her friends talked to me about it only after I located them in 2007–2008. In any event, Gould and Batchen never married. She said she ultimately turned down his proposal, partly because he was stifling her with his late-night telephone calls.

"He'd be up all hours on the telephone and that would overwhelm her," confirmed Donna Miller, who had lived in Batchen's rooming house. "He could afford to do what he wanted to do because he didn't have a regular job like the rest of us."

"We had fallen in love, oh, yes, and he told me he loved me ... but I refused to marry him because I knew he was such a powerful personality," Barrault said. "It would have been destructive for me. He would have smothered me. He would have been too difficult to live with. Not an easy person. . . ." She said Gould was surprised by her rejection: "He didn't realize that what he was doing to me was so serious that I would not marry him."

Warren Collins, who continued to correspond with Barrault through the years, heard that she and Gould "had a falling-out."

Their painful disagreements were sometimes seen in small details, like one night when Gould asked Batchen what she would do if they were both trapped on a melting ice floe. Apparently Batchen said she would stay on the floe with him and that irritated Gould, who had hoped she would say that she would jump off into the water, allowing him more time to live. "I think they both got upset over that," said Batchen's niece Jane Varnus. "In fact, it could have been one of the things that led to their breakup."

Toward the middle of 1956, Batchen was struggling with her career. Some of that progression came through lessons with Gould and then Alberto Guerrero, but it had already cost Batchen her rooming house at 46 Asquith. "It was costing us $200 between Frances and I to rent Asquith, which was a lot of money in those days, and it was always a struggle to pay the bills from month to month," Hamilton explained.

Gould was continuing to call Batchen late at night and she had a hard time dealing with it because she was exhausted and under financial pressure to keep a day job and pay her bills. Gould had his own pressures; after the release and success of the *Goldberg Variations* in early 1956, he was becoming an international star and was the subject of photo profiles in major magazines, both musical and general interest, including *Vogue*, *Glamour* ("Men We'd Like You to Meet") and a feature in the prestigious *Life* magazine of March 12, which called him the "Music World's Young Wonder." Writers called him hip and cool, but while his professional career was booming, his personal life was teetering and he felt as though he was losing control of the Fran affair.

In March 1956, due to these issues and his impending breakup with Batchen, Gould did something he rarely did before or after — he took a two-week vacation to Nassau in the Bahamas. Tagging along was writer/photographer Jock Carroll, who was to publish a feature on Gould in *Weekend Magazine*. But Gould wasted the sun and the sea — he would not go into the water even though long gloves and a diving mask were arranged for him. (One photo Carroll took showed Gould sitting on the seaside rocks, looking forlorn.) In fact, he rarely came out of Room 421 at the Fort Montagu Beach Hotel, telling Carroll that he was agonizing over an opera he was composing. The opera was likely based on Franz Kafka's novella *The Metamorphosis*, in which a traveling salesman, Gregor Samsa, awakes one morning to find that he has transformed into a "monstrous vermin," likely a roach. He is treated like an out-cast by his family, who are horrified by his transformation, and they keep him in his room, even though he still wants to go to work. It's possible that Gould — in this transitional period in his life — strongly related to Samsa and his sister, Grete, who fed and took care of him while he was in his insect state. (Gould seemed to relate to women who, like his mother, were care-givers.) Perhaps at age twenty-three, while spending less time with his parents, breaking up with Batchen and hoping to shift careers, Gould was going through his own metamorphosis.

On the Bahamas trip, when Carroll ventured into Gould's hotel room, he found a book on meaning in the visual arts, which Gould and Batchen had shared, along with an assort-ment of vitamins and pills for allergies, insomnia and circulation problems. One night, the non-smoking pianist playfully, or perhaps neurotically, began pulling matches out of a box and lighting them, one by one, slowly watching them flame out. Another night, when the local entertainers had gone home, Gould went into the empty lounge to play piano with a cheesy string of colored lights overhead and bongo drums at his side. During the trip, a daring Gould actually told Carroll he had two girlfriends, which was something of a scoop:

Carroll: "Do you have many girlfriends?"

Gould: "I have a couple I phone regularly. One in New York, another in Montreal. We talk about literature and music and philosophy . . . you are not, Mr. Carroll, going to pry into my sex life the way you apparently do with everyone else."

Then Gould forbade Carroll to use the information about his girlfriends. (When the *Weekend Magazine* article was printed, there was no mention of them, but long after Gould's death, Carroll published a book on their trip, *Glenn Gould: Some Portraits of the Artist as a Young Man*, which was pre-dominantly a picture book featuring the pianist in various musical and personal poses in the sun-drenched Caribbean. In it, Carroll used the above quote. From my research and some speculation, I believe the girlfriend in New York was Frances Batchen, who was commuting from New York to Toronto at that time (to this day, Barrault believes it was her). But who was the mystery girl in Montreal? Was she a true-blue, romantic beau or just an intimate soul mate, a nighttime phone caller?

One month after the Bahamas trip, Gould continued to socialize with Carroll in Toronto and told him that some of his fears were growing, especially of being trapped with people, which resulted in tightening of his throat and nausea. He said he was taking a lot of tranquilizers and seeing three doctors, one of whom told him there was "nothing wrong with my sexual development, nothing physically wrong." When Gould suspected during a telephone call that Carroll was writing this information down for the magazine article, he stopped the conversation and never spoke to Carroll again.

Back at home, the disagreements with Batchen became the norm, and the late-night phone calls were taking their toll on her psyche. Batchen realized their relationship was over, and she called it quits. In the late summer of 1956, she moved to New York where she got a job with Canada's National Film Board for two years, then set up her own film distribution company, Batchen Films, and traveled across the United States to sell children's films to television stations. "I wanted to develop as a person, and I had to earn a living," she said. From New York, Batchen sent letters to Gould, updating him on her activities.

Friends say that over the ensuing months after their breakup, Gould was distressed, but he was not too upset that he could not go out and buy himself a brand new Plymouth Plaza automobile for $2,000. (He loved big cars and the independence they gave him.) And there were always concert audiences to love him — from Mount Lebanon, Pennsylvania, to Montreal, to Spokane, Washington, and overseas. In December 1956, though, Gould was in a foul mood. Usually even-tempered to a fault, he was said to go into a rage with officials of Steinway & Sons in New York, complaining that his Steinway CD 90 was too loose in its action. He threatened that, if their technicians did not fix it, he would start playing a Heintzman piano. They fixed it.

Although Batchen and others later largely blamed Gould for their breakup, at the time, she seemed to be remorseful in a letter she mailed to him from New York. She wrote as "Faun": "Having learned a kind of dogged optimism in the face of adversity, I imagine the next thing to learn is how to grow up, and to find out who I am, which I really don't know yet — not just professionally but in every way. I know you must have wondered many times all spring whether I was going out of my mind, behaving the way I did. I have been going to write to you *so* many times, but diffidence, and not neglect, stopped me . . . many times I would have given anything to undo some of the hurt I caused you — and I didn't know how to do that either." Later, Batchen told Gould about getting mugged in 1957 for the fur coat that Bert Gould had given her. "I was walking along Seventieth Street West toward my flat and a guy followed me into my building," she said. "He punched me in the mouth and stole the coat." The incident left Batchen with a type of post traumatic stress disorder and for years after, under some pressure situations, she would have flashbacks and fear for her physical safety.

Meanwhile, back in Toronto, Barbara Franklin was surprised to hear that the couple was in splitsville. "I don't think [Gould] could have forced his intentions on any woman. I loved that guy; he was such a good person," Franklin said. "Marriage is a hard thing for many musicians — the traveling, the lifestyle, the pressure."

After Batchen and Gould broke up for good, he rarely responded to her friendly letters, she said. And yet he helped her — and her piano students — indirectly from an experience he had while playing a concert in Tel Aviv in 1958. Batchen came across this anecdote in Geoffrey Payzant's biography, *Glenn*

Gould Music & Mind, in which Gould talked about playing a piano with an uneven action, which he described as having "power steering" and the tendency to play the pianist, rather than the other way around. According to Payzant, "Full of anguish [Gould] went forth alone, driving a Hertz rental car into the desert to think. There on a sand dune, he sat for an hour, rehearsing in his head the concerto he was to play that night, not upon the mental image he had of the Tel Aviv piano, but upon his mental image of the familiar old Chickering back home at the cottage in Uptergrove. Every note was rehearsed mentally, as if upon the Chickering with its characteristic feel, sound and surroundings. Desperately clinging to this image, he went onstage that night and tackled the piano as if it were the Chickering . . . when the performance was over, he left the stage in a state of exaltation and wonder." Batchen used this quote in her book *The Confidence Quotient*. Her time with Gould had helped her understand her nervousness — and his. "He never liked being a concert pianist, even though he was a marvelous pianist," she said. "He was too self-conscious." Batchen named Gould in her book, but made no mention that they had been lovers!

In 1960, Batchen sent Gould another letter, addressing him as "Spaniel," in which she talked about constantly living in transition and believing that "the state of *flux* or *transition* or *becoming* is one of the most permanent conditions and that the concept of 'normal peaceful living' is a hoax invented by a malignant satirist."

Eventually, Gould became estranged from Batchen and her Bohemian pals and filmmakers. As is the case with many people, perhaps it was just a matter of drifting apart from old friends as one gets into their thirties and forties, but it is believed that Gould slowly became more reclusive or at least more private into the 1960s and especially the 1970s. "He withdrew into his music as he got older," Barbara Franklin said. But

Gould did not necessarily forget what he had learned from his friends and acquaintances of the 1950s. He became a maker of documentary films and radio shows in the 1960s and 1970s and he wrote to a friend that the making of the two 1959 National Film Board documentaries about his life, *Glenn Gould: On the Record* and *Glenn Gould: Off the Record,* "has done more for my morale and indeed enthusiasm for life in general than anything else within memory." It is hard to gauge if any of the filmmaking skills of Dunning, Michael Snow and others had rubbed off on Gould because he rarely gave credit publicly to those who helped him. When the film *Thirty Two Short Films About Glenn Gould* was released in 1993, the *Canadian Encyclopedia* noted: "Michael Snow's minimalism could have inspired the sequence in *Thirty Two Short Films* composed only of extreme close-ups of piano hammers hitting the strings."

I always felt that I was his link to the "real world" — the world outside that he had no interest in joining.

— Gladys Shenner

GLADYS *and* CYNTHIA

Chapter FIVE

In the spring of 1956, another woman breezed into Gould's life, even while Frances Batchen was still there — Gladys Shenner, a freelance writer assigned to do a story on Gould for *Maclean's*, Canada's national magazine. Gould agreed to meet Shenner at Batchen's apartment and the twenty-three-year-old writer showed up with her notepad and enthusiasm for an exciting project, expecting to find an eccentric pianist dressed like a monk, but what she found practically made her gulp — Gould laying on a sofa with his head resting as a pet poodle on Batchen's lap. "She was stroking his hair," recalled Shenner, now Gladys Riskind. ("Stroking is essential for survival," wrote Batchen in *The Confidence Quotient*.)

On the sofa, Batchen may have been comforting Gould because she — or both of them — knew that their romance was on the rocks. And Gould may have chosen to let Shenner see him like this because he wanted or *needed* her to help. Otherwise, why would such a private, sensitive, image-conscious man have invited a national magazine writer to his girlfriend's apartment, allowing her to find him in such a vulnerable position? There were many other venues where the interview could have been conducted, like Union Station at rush hour. Certainly, Shenner was surprised to walk in on such a situation. Her early research had suggested Gould was shy, a loner with few friends who left his piano stool only to talk to the breezes along the shores of Lake Ontario.

"It was none of my business, so I didn't ask about the details, but I got the impression they had a sexual relationship," Riskind said. "They must have been close because I think she gave him her Chickering piano, and he took it to his cottage up north." (Actually, Gould took over rental of the piano when Batchen could no longer afford it, then bought it outright in 1957 for $555. He described it as one of the last classical pianos in America: "It had extraordinary qualities — a tactile grab and immediacy that I had always believed pianos could have." Batchen, on the other hand, remained miffed for decades afterward, upset that he would have bought her piano rather than help her out with the payments so she could keep it. "He had no conscience about that," she said in 2008.)

"Not long after I first saw them, she left him," Riskind said. "I think he wore her out, took so much out of her with his lifestyle. She was working and he would keep her up until two or three in the morning on the phone. She knew a great deal about music and I think she was a frustrated musician."

Although Shenner was a writer/researcher, those were the only details she could discover about Batchen, for it was common for Gould to keep the women in his life in the dark about his other female friends. That, actually, was a lot for Gould to tell her about another woman. "He had a great way of keeping people's lives separate from one another," his assistant Ray Roberts would say, years later.

And so it was that Gladys Shenner took over the stroking of hair, or at least the ego, in Glenn Gould's life, becoming his close friend over the next seven years. The torch officially passed when Batchen emigrated from Canada to the United States in the fall of 1956, after she turned down Gould's marriage proposal.

In the first few weeks, as Shenner got to know him, Gould was a very cooperative interview for her story:

Glenn Gould is now accepting engagements for $1,250. He has hit the musical scene with a volcanic impact . . . he is far too thin for his five feet eleven inches and looks almost emaciated. His face is nearly gaunt.

"Glenn called me every night at midnight and we would go over things with the story," she said. "I was a young writer and my first draft of the story was not very good, but he helped me, gave me a lot of confidence."

He dresses outlandishly . . . when he practices he wears a flowing striped dressing gown or a baggy blue sweater cut deep at the neckline and armholes. Gould's only hobby is reading – heavy Russian and German prose and obscure poetry. He's always been too old for his years. . . .

The writing was buzzing along until just before deadline, when Gould inexplicably got cold feet and wanted to back out of the story, but Shenner convinced him to stay part of it. In the end, it was an impressive 4,000-word article, entitled "The Genius Who Doesn't Want to Play." It painted a portrait of Gould as a sensitive, eccentric genius putting up with concert audiences for financial stability until he could become a full-time composer. Although Shenner's article revealed some of Gould's idiosyncrasies, he said he liked it and he allowed himself to become close friends with Shenner, a pretty, sharp-minded brunette. "I became his conduit to the outside world," she said. They talked on the phone almost every night and he took her to his parents' house in Toronto. "I got to know his mother and father. He adored his mother, a nice warm lady who had a funny way of saying 'piano.' She said something like 'pian-a.' I don't think Glenn and his father were very close. I think he wanted Glenn to play sports, but he didn't want to."

Sometimes Glenn Gould took Gladys Shenner for dinner at the Benvenuto and Windsor Arms restaurants. It was stimulating for a young woman barely out of university, but Shenner was an open personality with a hungry mind. She was born Jewish in Saskatoon, Saskatchewan, to a "very peppy, tenacious sales lady," and a father who owned a small store and a ladies ready-to-wear store. "I was brought up to make something of myself," Riskind said. The family moved to Brandon, Manitoba, when she was four. There, she started freelance writing for the *Brandon Sun* at age fifteen and later attended the University of Manitoba, graduating with honors with a bachelor of arts in political science in 1953. She worked for *United Press* in Winnipeg, Manitoba, for one year before moving to Toronto in 1953, where jobs for aspiring writers were more attainable. "I think I was ahead of my time. How many girls at twenty-one in the 1950s went to Toronto to find a job?" In 1954, Shenner was at first reduced to writing things like the crossword puzzles for *Liberty Magazine*, owned by high-profile businessman Jack Kent Cooke, but later she was invited to do some editing for *Chatelaine* magazine and reported on an international fashion show in New York. After her article about Gould appeared in *Maclean's* in 1956, Shenner struck up a tight bond with Gould — and yet over the next few years, he invited not Shenner but at least two other women to go on tour with him.

At about the time Shenner and Gould were developing their friendship and shortly after Gould returned from the Bahamas, he continued his music with women. He went to Ottawa, to the house of an eighteen-year-old piano student, Cynthia Millman, whom he had met the year before at the Morning Music Club in Ottawa, where he had played the *Goldberg Variations* and several other pieces. Like Franny Batchen, Millman had just won the Kiwanis Music Festival, which was known in Ottawa at that time as the Ottawa Music Festival.

"I had been criticized because I played an esoteric piece off the beaten track, but I still won," said Millman, who is now Cynthia Floyd. After the session, Millman asked for Gould's autograph, which was usually a no-no because Gould disliked giving them, but he was receptive toward her. "For some reason, he took a liking to me," she said. Cynthia Floyd recalls Gould saying, "'Oh, you're the girl who plays Hindemith I've been wanting to meet.'" Gould was impressed when he discovered that Millman had questioned a statement in a composition about the Berg Sonata, which had been central to his relationship with Batchen. "'You should be an editor!'" he said and they forged a relationship where Gould was her unofficial mentor, she said.

At Easter in 1956, Gould went to Ottawa to play again and this time, he stopped at the house where Millman lived. She played Bach's Concerto in D Minor for him while Gould sang the orchestra part and flipped the pages for her. "He thought I had talent as a pianist," she said. At the time, Gould was preparing to record Beethoven's Concerto no. 1 and he asked Millman's advice about what style he should choose. "He wanted to know which I thought was better, a sophisticated approach or a naive playing approach, then he played for me and he wanted to know how I would do it . . . I told him I could see him doing it both ways. I was being protective." Gould asked her opinion on other occasions, as well. "One time he phoned me and played a recording of a violinist to see what I thought. I think when he was young in the 1950s, he asked people advice more than he did when he got older."

Gould and Millman sometimes had lunch together and once he offered to drive her to Sudbury "but he had lost his license." Another time at a restaurant, Gould made suggestive comments about a waitress — "so I knew he wasn't homosexual." He rarely showed his emotions to Millman, except that he got upset when his friend and fellow pianist Van Cliburn won the first International Tchaikovsky Competition in 1958 in Russia and received a ticker-tape parade upon his return to New York. Gould had performed in Russia the previous year, but had received no such welcoming committee. "He thought it threw Cliburn into the limelight," Cynthia Floyd said. Also in 1958, Millman won the Bach Prize at a competition at the Canadian National Exhibition in Toronto, but failed to win the overall piano prize. Gould consoled her. "He said he understood because Van Cliburn was sort of stealing his thunder."

Gould was interested in trying to learn German, she said. "He asked me if I was fluent in German. He liked to read [German author] Thomas Mann. He couldn't speak German, but he could mimic it." In 1960, Millman told Gould she wanted to leave Canada to study music abroad. In September that year, he wrote to her that her intentions were at the same time "encouraging and frightening . . . while I do not expect to be held to account for my advice if it should be inadequate, I realize that it is tremendously important for you at this stage to have some sage words or counsel and I just wonder if I am the proper person to give them. I think it is true . . . that the atmosphere of a place in which you reside can have a great deal to do with the expansion of the musical disposition, though it doesn't always work this way and certainly no one place can possibly be right for everyone."

Gould tried to shoot down the idea of Millman studying in the United States with famed Austrian teacher Eduard Steuermann. "Such an influence would be absolutely disastrous . . . from what I have heard [he] is a very unpleasant individual." Gould suggested several other teachers for her, including Bruno Seidlhofer in Vienna. She took his advice and studied in Vienna for eight years.

"It was a big turning point for me," Cynthia Floyd said. "I liked to be solitary and he encouraged it. In Vienna, I had no phone or doorbell, so we wrote letters to each other." In the early 1960s, Gould was impressed by Millman's rendition of Beethoven's Ninth Symphony and he wrote to the Canadian Council on her behalf to try to get her funding. The council gave her $4,000 for two years, and Gould also got her a concert with the Kitchener-Waterloo Symphony Orchestra. "I saw a very generous side of him," she said. "He guided me where to go, he sent me places."

Floyd said it was possible that Gould thought about having a deeper relationship with her. "I'm not sure what he expected, probably more [than music]. But did I want to give up my career? It's possible it could have developed into something more, but I wasn't ready. I was a slow developer." According to Floyd, at one point Gould invited her to come to his apartment on St. Clair Avenue, but she did not go. "I knew then that he needed mothering. I don't think [a romance] would have worked. I'm a fairly strong personality. It would have been a catastrophe for me." But she said their relationship remained healthy in its platonic state and they got along well, partly because they were both intellectual and liked to be alone — and Gould seemed to like both those traits in a woman. "Our musical backgrounds were similar, although I didn't start [piano] until I was ten. He enjoyed sparring with me, but he respected my opinion and Glenn seemed to want to protect me as a person. We were both puritanical and we had a mutual friend, who slipped some gin into my lemonade. Glenn became incensed and very angry. He told the man he had no business doing that."

At about the time he was chummy with Millman, the twenty-three-year-old Gould was talking about quitting the concert stage. He told CBC interviewer Eric McLean on April 25, 1956, that he wanted to shift his career from concert performances to composing. "I'm a little afraid if this career keeps on going, it's going to seriously interfere with what I really want to do, which is composing . . . I'm longing to retire [from performing] at twenty-six. I have a lot of projects for two years and an opera. I'm a very slow composer." This, despite the fact that McLean said Gould's album of the *Goldberg Variations* was selling marvelously.

He really needed someone
to take care of him.
— Mezzo-soprano and Gould friend Joan Maxwell

Overlapping VOICES

Chapter SIX Gould may have been in his own state of changeover, but, with smoke from Franny's Lucky Strikes still on his coat, he dragged some of his hang-ups along with him, including his briefcase chock-full of prescription drugs. Apparently with the signature blessing of doctors and pharmacists, by 1956 Gould was taking myriad drugs, which would come to reach legendary proportions. He consumed drugs for everything from performance anxiety to sleeplessness, to colds, to poor circulation, to headaches and depression — even though some of these maladies may have been imagined. In his pocket, he carried Valium pills and would pop one into his mouth if he had to deal with someone he felt uncomfortable with. Gould sometimes joked about it. He told Jock Carroll in early '56, "This pill complex of mine has been grossly exaggerated. Why, one reporter wrote that I traveled with a suitcase full of pills. Actually, they barely fill a *briefcase*." But Gould's friend, mezzo-soprano Joan Maxwell, saw little to laugh about. A chunk of their late-night phone calls were consumed with Maxwell trying to get Gould to stop his pill habit, which she worried was becoming an addiction.

Maxwell and Gould had forged a friendship from the time Gould was a student at the Royal Conservatory of Music in 1949 while Maxwell was a student at the University of Toronto's

67

Faculty of Music, which was housed in the same building. She was a stunning, intellectual, personable blond who would become one of Canada's leading opera singers. Maxwell believed that Gould used drugs as sort of a protective wall to keep him safe from what he viewed as a harmful world. "He had a family doctor who lived near him on St. Clair and would give him prescriptions for far too many drugs," she said. "I suspect that his doctors, perhaps intimidated by their patient, over-prescribed in deference to his wishes . . . and he seemed to be unaware of the side effects of these drugs. He couldn't bear any kind of disagreement, not even a subtle hint of discord, and if an interviewer asked him an upsetting question, his stomach would start to bother him — and out would come the (drugs)." There was Butazolidin, an anti-inflammatory, Valium to reduce anxiety, and Seconal for a good night's sleep. Whenever the effect started to wear off, Gould would increase the dosage, Maxwell said, and there would be consequences. Gould was usually punctual, but while doing a television special in New York one day he was nowhere to be seen. "The orchestra was waiting, the whole crew was there — but no Glenn Gould!" Maxwell said. A search party was sent to his hotel room, where Gould was in a deep sleep and had to be wakened.

All of this is ironic because Gould did not fall prey to other addictive habits like drinking and smoking to ease his pains. For one thing, alcohol interfered with his piano playing. In April 1956, Maxwell was at a small gathering hosted by CBC producer John Roberts. It was following Gould's performance at Massey Hall in Toronto, and Gould was entertaining them with his playing, but suddenly he put down a glass of wine he had been sipping and announced, "That's it. I'll never drink again." He made a similar claim on another occasion, at a party at the home of New York conductor Leonard Bernstein.

Maxwell was one of the first people to try to get Gould to face his drug problem. Her husband, insurance man Harvey Rempel, recalls that "she chastised him frequently and vigorously about it, and was really not surprised when this self-indulgence took a more sinister turn and Glenn became, in many ways, an addict."

Part of Gould's problem, according to Maxwell, was that she considered him a loner lacking a support system. "For the most part, he lived like a hermit, and must have experienced tremendous loneliness," she said. "I think this is why he was so fond of dogs. Glenn felt that every child should have a dog, that it was a very important part of a child's life. I think he must have been very lonely as a little boy because he was an only child." When Gould visited the Maxwell home, he would lie on the floor with their big poodle. "Strange," she said, "that some-one so concerned with germs would be so comfortable hugging a dog and letting him lick his face."

Gould did report some physical ailments in the 1950s — aches in his arms, hands and back, flu, sinus pain, fatigue and depression — and admitted that he had "a horror of catching colds, an absolute horror."

"His back problems were legitimate; his posture leaning over the piano was atrocious," said Dr. Herbert Vear, Gould's chiropractor from 1957 to 1976. "But he was an oddball who didn't like change . . . he was always humming a little tune that was going around in his head. But he could be friendly; in the waiting room he would blend in, talking to people."

"He was preoccupied with his health and he always wanted to find out what was wrong," Gould's friend Morry Kernerman said. "At one time, I thought I had stomach problems and he took a vicarious interest in how prescription drugs affected me. He wanted to try the drugs I was using."

Gould did not suffer these issues in silence and he was not as alone as Maxwell believed — indeed, not as much as some Gould biographers would lead us to believe. Part of this fallacy was the fault of Gould himself — he often kept his friends apart or in the dark, particularly his female friends. The fact is that during the 1950s, Gould had at least seventeen women and at least eleven men he regularly confided in or had lengthy discussions with in person, but mostly over the telephone or by mail. One wonders if all of these people would make up for one *real* mama in Flora Gould? Glenn still lived with his parents in the late 1950s, but he was getting out more, going to the cottage, touring on the road and seeing much less of the mother who had been the bedrock of his early life. He certainly needed people to talk with, seeing how he was finally in the mental preparation of moving away from home, feeling high stress over his concert career and perhaps feeling his sexual hormones kicking in at a higher rate. The more people he had to talk to, the more bearable was the "state of worry."

Among his female friends in the 1950s were Batchen, Shenner and Maxwell; Angela Addison; Barbara Franklin; Elizabeth Fox; his cousin Jessie Greig; Susan Rubes; Carmel Schwartz; his Columbia Masterworks publicist in New York, Deborah Ishlon; Quebec dancer Susanne Hamel; students Cynthia Millman and Anahid Alexanian of St. Catharines, Ontario; Russian teacher Kitty Gvozdeva; Walter Homburger's secretary Verna Sandercock; and two Austrian-born harpsichordists, Silvia Kind and Greta Kraus. And he had many other female friends who were more fleeting or casual, like Elizabeth Barry, who worked for CBC Radio and once helped Gould pick out furniture on a shopping excursion.

His male friends in the 1950s included childhood buddy Robert Fulford, Morry Kernerman, Harvey Rempel, Leonard Bernstein, CBC producer Howard Engel, New York writer Ben Sonnenberg, CBC producer John Roberts, composer John Beckwith, pianist Anton Kuerti and two amateur musicians who were professional psychiatrists, Dr. Peter Ostwald and Dr. Joseph Stephens. Many of the men knew one another and that was fine with Gould, according to Paul Myers, one of his New

York producers. "He wanted them to know one another."

Some of these friends, of course, were closer to Gould than others, such as Frances Batchen and John Roberts. Later in life, Gould brought some of these pals along with him, but added some new friends and acquaintances, as well: soprano Roxolana Roslak; pianist Monica Gaylord; Columbia secretary Carol Hodgdon; Columbia record producer Andrew Kazdin; his piano tuner Verne Edquist; philosopher Marshall McLuhan; Catholic priest and theology teacher Father Owen Carroll; television producers Judith Pearlman, Margaret Pacsu and Janet Somerville; CBC technician Lorne Tulk; Gould's assistant Ray Roberts; *Piano Quarterly* editor Robert Silverman; music student Sonia Marie De León; CBC public relations rep Linda Litwack; conductor Victor Di Bello; Columbia public relations rep Susan Koscis; writers Richard Kostelanetz and Tim Page; and Swedish vocal coach Birgit Johansson. In 1966, Gould had at least 250 people on his Christmas card list. In the 1970s, Di Bello believed he was one of the few people in Canada who had Gould's phone number, but there were likely many others.

At one time, Gould would juggle eight to ten friends, phoning them, corresponding with them, talking with them about everything from politics to Kafka, although reportedly he only kept one close girlfriend at a time. This montage, these overlapping voices in Gould's life, would come to parallel not only his contrapuntal style of piano playing, but also an art form he would invent in the 1960s: "contrapuntal radio," in which several people's voices would be heard over one another. Perhaps it takes a village to raise a genius, or to keep him sane in a world that at times demanded more than he could give. Gould was able to juggle them and keep them compartmentalized because he had a puzzle-solving brain that was second to none. Perhaps his personal life at times reflected the way he wove the themes of his music together. As producer Bruno Monsaingeon wrote of Gould's music, "Very few people are able to work in segments and still give a unity to all these segments. Gould could keep a complete view of the total work and an abstract one, very coherent from the first to the last note, and still do one segment at a time."

Most of Gould's friends were acquaintances, those he chose to communicate with from a distance over the telephone. These calls could go on for hours and seemed to be a type of "people fix" for Gould, almost an addiction in itself that he went back to again and again. If he did have trouble finding people he could immediately connect with, as some biographers and therapists have speculated, Gould certainly spent enough time engaging with and gabbing to those he found. Then there was the very small group of close friends he had tighter relationships with, such as Batchen, Greig, Roberts, Sandercock and Shenner.

Most of the female relationships were platonic, according to Howard Engel, who went on to become a mystery writer, but was not considered part of Gould's inner circle. "Oh, he was very private, but was he terribly interested in sex or the urge to procreate? Most of his relationships were pragmatic, a meeting of the minds of mutual interest. He got a lot of fun out of playing on words and rubbing ideas together, rather than bodies." Gould needed a woman to take care of his daily needs, Engel said. "He wore very heavy clothing, baggy trousers and jackets, un-pressed and out of shape. Nobody was looking after him, encouraging him to comb his hair and brush his teeth."

Sometimes Gould just needed somebody to talk to about things other than music. Cousin Jessie Greig recalled phone conversations which included "every topic imaginable — sciences, technology, music, philosophy, education, world situations and even his current and future projects . . . he read me the whole of his favorite book, *The Three-Cornered World* [by Natsume Soseki]. Perhaps these hours served as a buffer and a release from the pressures of a world that seemed intent at breaking down the wall of isolation that he had so studiously constructed over many years."

His platonic pals did what they could for Gould, mostly from a distance. Deborah Ishlon was close enough to Gould that he nicknamed her "Shorebird," which was quite an honor, seeing how he only gave close family members and Franny Batchen monikers of animals. Rumors have always swirled in Gould cult circles and recently on the Internet that he had an affair with Ishlon, but there is no evidence to suggest that. However, besides being somewhat responsible for his eccentric image in the media as his United States public relations representative, Ishlon was always looking out for Gould's health. In 1956, she sent him an article about actor Robert Cummings, a fellow pill-popper who maintained his youth and vigor with a high-protein diet and food supplements; then, in 1958 when Gould was depressed and sick with the flu during a European tour, Ishlon recommended yoga exercises. Mind you, some of Gould's fans chipped in, too, like an Atlanta, Georgia woman, Mrs. A. King, who donated an electric heater to Gould in 1959 after he complained of cold drafts.

Friendship with Gould was not always a one-way street, however. As we will see throughout this book, he often did favors for people without fanfare or media attention. For example, when Joan Maxwell suffered back pain, he recommended a new remedy — acupuncture — which she tried. When she suffered from tonsillitis, he talked her out of having an operation, which might have altered her voice. And when she did extensive traveling for her musical career, Gould begged her to curtail her frequent flying; he suffered from aviophobia and stopped flying in the early 1960s.

Silvia Kind and Greta Kraus were like a Viennese tag team — both much older than Gould — who tried through telephone and correspondence to help him with his health problems, recommending massage, yoga and even hypnotism.

Kind was also concerned about his tendency to get lovesick. One night in Toronto, Kind and Gould went to dinner with another friend and his fiancée. Kind said, "I had the feeling that he was in love with the friend's fiancée, but his decency and his shyness would never have permitted him to reveal in the least his feelings. I felt sorry for him. He kept his private life under lock and key and I would never have dared to open it." However, Kraus, as a confidante to some of his female friends and lovers, was more privy to his romantic thoughts and predicaments, as we shall see later in this book.

One of Gould's issues with women was that he could be impulsive. Following one of his concerts in Quebec in February 1957, he met Susanne Hamel, a striking Francophone harpist and ballet dancer with braided hair down to her knees. Having been seduced by his Beethoven, the student from Laval University in Quebec City, who was four years older than Gould, managed to get backstage to chat with her idol. The whole scene was enthusiastic and awkward, since she knew little English and he barely spoke French. Hamel was a poet and a dreamer who wanted to share her love of the world, but during her student years she was a little coy. She did, however, get to touch Gould's famous ragged piano chair, crafted by his father. Hamel remarked to friends, "I love the beauty of Glenn's soul." At first blush, Gould was interested in her as well, and she said Gould invited her to go on his tour to Russia later that year as a sort of translator, even though she knew virtually no Russian. This offer was confirmed by a letter Gould wrote to Hamel shortly after:

Dear Susanne: I regret very much now that we did not have a chance to speak after the concert . . . I am sure that your reluctance with English was surpassed by my embarrassment with French. Let's hope that when we meet again, we shall both be able to be more

*communicative. In two weeks I shall be off for Russia;
now that it is so close it seems rather hard to believe.
But if my stomach holds up with the Russian food, I
imagine that I shall have a really fascinating time. I
really wish that you were going along as an
interpreter – providing that you do know more than
one phrase, of course.*

In Russia, his official interpreters were Kitty Gvozdeva and
Henrietta Velayeva. Gould referred to the latter as "a marvelous
girl. . . . really a charmer as a human being . . . I remember one
day in Leningrad, we were taking a walk through the summer
gardens which were part of the palace of Catherine II on the
banks of the Neva." The only reported incident in Russia
involving a woman was that the wife of a Russian diplomat
allegedly made a pass at Gould; he ignored her.

After Gould returned from Russia, Gould and Hamel did
meet again and she says they became friends. During Hamel's
visit with Gould in Toronto, he commented upon her newly
shorn looks, "What happened to your long beautiful hair?" But
she says she never became his girlfriend. "I wanted to have a
closer relationship with him, but I was too shy, and I think he
was too busy to have relations with women." After his death,
she wrote a romance/poetry book, *Glenn Gould, My Lovely and
Tender Love.*

Gould was not too busy, however, for a one-night stand with
another woman, which he carried out sometime in the late
1950s, according to Ray Roberts, who was his assistant from
1970 until 1982. "Glenn told me that he'd had a concert somewhere in the Midwestern U.S., Chicago or somewhere," Roberts
said. "She was a musician who had her face on an album cover.
Glenn went to watch her concert and they went at it in her
dressing room — he described it as a 'wild affair, a wild event.'
Then he went on to order me never to mention it to anyone."

And Gould never mentioned it again to Roberts or presumably to anyone else. "Glenn liked to call himself 'the last puritan,' but if you knew about the women in his life, you could hardly call him that," Roberts said.

One wonders if there were other adventures while Gould was on the lonely road during his concert career. In 1957, while he was in Florida, a forlorn-looking Gould was picked up by police while sitting on a park bench, in his usual mismatched socks and long, unshaven face, on the suspicion of being a vagabond. They let him go when he explained he was a concert pianist.

He never had romance
in the open.
− Gould's manager Walter Homburger

The EMPTY SEAT
in the AUDIENCE

Chapter SEVEN

Verna Sandercock was hired in 1958 as secretary for Gould's manager Walter Homburger, a dream-maker for the stars and an arts administrator. Sandercock could type a clean business letter, meet deadlines and bowl you over with her black page-boy haircut, friendly brown eyes and ruby red lips, even though she referred to herself as "no raging beauty." She was a trim five-foot-two, three months younger than Gould and could nearly match him in wit and wisdom. Their relationship quickly became more than business as she earned the status of one of his "close-up people." According to Verna, whom Glenn sometimes referred to in his letters as "Angel" or "Puss," the pianist wanted to give her the business. Gould began taking her to the same restaurants he had gone to with Gladys Shenner. In the late 1950s Gould did not display the finicky eating patterns he had suffered with Frances Batchen, although he would exhibit it once more in a later part of his life. "When I knew him, he ate regular food and was certainly not a vegetarian," Sanderock, now Verna Post, said. But that did not mean he did not try to control the climate around him — "He had all the eccentric mannerisms about the cold — whenever we were in his car he'd roll up all the windows and when we got to a restaurant he'd ask them to turn off the air conditioning."

To be associated with a rising superstar was unexpected for

a young woman from the Prairies (that was three flatlanders in a row for Gould if you consider Batchen and Shenner before Sandercock). Verna was born in 1932 in Cupar, Saskatchewan, the second youngest of five children to Charles Sandercock, operator of an eighty-acre homestead with swaying fields of golden wheat. "We had a piano, but no musicians in the family, except for me," she said. Verna had no false expectations about having a career because most women, like her mom, were destined to be housewives and raise young'uns. "It was a very different social milieu in those days and as a Prairie farm daughter, you didn't have big dreams." And yet, the bright Sandercock went on to attain a degree from a business college in Regina, where she also worked as a secretary for IBM. In 1955, she received the highest mark in Canada for voice studies at the Regina Conservatory, and that year she moved to Toronto to continue her music studies as a mezzo-soprano at the Royal Conservatory of Music "singing a lot of heavy lyrics." Verna Post recalls seeing Gould "whipping around the halls" at the conservatory, but she did not meet him until landing a job as Homburger's secretary in 1958, and thus she never met Batchen or had even heard about her.

Sandercock helped Gould through an important crossroads in his life; in 1959, at nearly twenty-seven years old, he finally moved out of his parents' house in the Beach and for a short time sequestered a room in the Windsor Arms Hotel in Toronto, where he found a sympathetic switchboard operator to screen his telephone calls and visitors. Then in December of that year, after hearing that his friend Van Cliburn, an up-and-coming American pianist, had bought a house, Gould invested in a mansion fifteen miles north of Toronto with a regal name — Donchery — on a wooded property along the Don River, a country estate away from everybody, boasting twenty-six rooms, a dog kennel for his beloved mutts, a tennis court for the athleticism he was never interested in and a swimming pool. Gould wrote to a German acquaintance he had met on a tour of Europe, Edith Boecker: "The view from down below looking up and especially at night with floodlights was like looking at Salzburg Castle from your own strawberry patch." But paradise crumbled before it began — the press found out about the extravagant mansion and Gould was embarrassed and he never moved in. "Anyway, the house was too big — it was overwhelming for him," Post said. "I had to phone and cancel his furniture."

Also in 1959, Gould was in a reflective mood about marriage. When writer Dennis Braithwaite of the *Toronto Daily Star* asked him if he had ever thought about getting married, Gould responded: "I have thought a great deal about it. That again is the unfortunate side of this life, not that it can't be combined with marriage, but that is all part of the lacking of roots and goes with being a concretizing person. Though I must say that I do have friends in much the same position."

Braithwaite's follow-up question: "Are you engaged or do you have a steady girlfriend?"

Gould: "I am not engaged."

Braithwaite: "Getting back to your music . . ."

That was typical of a Gould interview; very little was requested of his private life because writers knew how he would react and were nervous about their interviews being sabotaged, and Gould managed to dance around tricky questions without lying. Notice that Gould did not deny having a steady girlfriend in 1959; perhaps he considered Sandercock his girlfriend by this time.

For the first six months of 1960, bachelor Gould lived at the Algiers Apartments on Avenue Road in midtown Toronto, but he complained about the heating and that someone was spying on him and shining lights into his window from a nearby apartment building. Gould's unofficial therapist, Dr. Peter Ostwald, speculated that Gould sometimes suffered delusions, even paranoia, possibly from taking too many prescription drugs, or a certain mixture of them. Post agreed that Gould was taking such drugs, "but he seemed to be functioning fine . . . and yet he allowed himself to get suckered with prescription drugs."

Later in 1960, Gould moved into the nearby Park Lane Apartments at 110 St. Clair Avenue West, where he would live for the rest of his life. The brown brick, U-shaped depression modern building in a quiet neighborhood suited Gould in many ways: the walls were thick, the residents elderly, the management security-conscious and his six-room penthouse with a garden terrace offered him a sanctuary for his music. In other words, the place was hardly a barrel of laughs, just liked he wanted it. "He took me there and it was nice," Post said. "It wasn't messy at first and one bedroom was still usable."

The couple shared their love of music and would often *talk* in lyrical voices, similar to recitatives, a type of singing conversation sometimes heard in works by Mozart. Post recalls such ditties with Gould: "Oh, Mr. Gould, you have a letter from that la-la-la-ady, so-and-so in Montreal, and she wants an autographed record a-a-a-album." And he would reply, in a less-than-talented singing voice: "Oh, I know, Miss Sandercock, but please tell her to buy the a-a-a-album, ship it to me and I will consider my John Hen-n-n-nry at that time . . . time, time. . . ." Sanderock would also "sing" such recitatives with Homburger.

Gould did not become a hermit on St. Clair Avenue, as has often been written; rather, in the coming years he would establish several offices and studios around town, including Homburger's office on Adelaide Street in the downtown core, which secretary Sandercock described as "a funky little place with a desk and a manual typewriter." Her job, she quickly discovered, became substantially more than fielding Gould's fan letters and juggling his concert schedule. "We weren't very busy, so I started doing a lot of his personal stuff." She sent Gould's mail and holiday cards, took his laundry to the dry cleaners and bought his dress shirts, but she never told her boss about it — "I didn't want to be seen mixing work with pleasure."

Oh, it was pleasure, all right, at least behind closed doors, where Gould transformed into Don Juan and they would often kiss "like a couple of flirty teenagers." But wasn't this the same Glenn Gould terrified of touching people or attracting germs? "Oh, no, no, no — heavens, with him kissing was in the books," Verna Post said. "He was a passionate kisser." She said that on a number of occasions, Gould wanted her to go to bed with him, but she balked. "We didn't have protection in those days and I didn't want to get pregnant. I couldn't handle that. I don't know if he could have been a father, because of his commitment to his music. I don't think he was the marrying type. He told me that once."

And yet Gould's father Bert seemed to think Sandercock would make a splendid wife for his son. "What Glenn needs is a wife," Bert told her, to which Sandercock replied, "Oh, Mr. Gould, I don't think Glenn will ever marry." But Bert would not give up and he crafted Sandercock a Persian lamb jacket with a gray mink collar — and she bought it from him at a discounted price. It was similar to the fur coat he had given Frances Batchen, his son's former girlfriend, in the mid-1950s and this seemed to be Bert's gesture for potential daughters-in-law. For her part, Gould's mother Florence gave Sandercock a crystal perfume atomizer.

Other than Gould's parents, few people knew that Sandercock was Gould's secret girlfriend. In fact, Post says she was Gould's secret beau for several years to the point that even her boss was kept in the dark. "I wonder if Walter's onto us?" Gould once chuckled. And, in a letter he sent to Sandercock in 1959, Gould quipped, "I can't help but think that that cantankerous little man suspects something!"

To this day, Homburger says he knew nothing of Gould and his secretary having a romance. "Verna was a wonderful girl and a great help to me, but Glenn was very private; I think because of his personality. I didn't want to know about them — I couldn't have cared less. If they did things, it wasn't out in the open. He never had romance in the open."

Gould apparently was not happy that Sandercock would not go to bed with him. "He accepted it, though, and we continued to see one another," Post said. She went with him a few times to the Lower Rosedale Shakespeare Society, taking along "Mascot," a stray cat she adopted, but she didn't take part in the quizzes and tongue-in-cheek discussions about Shakespeare's works with Gould and his sophisticates. Of course, she became a regular for his late-night phone calls. "He'd put on false voices like a little old lady — 'Hello, this is the overseas operator, will you accept a collect call from Mr. Glenn Gould?'"

Gould sometimes made light of Sandercock in letters to Homburger: "The reviews of [Gould's interpretation of] the Brahms, which are now beginning to arrive in force, are almost unanimously glorious — so glorious indeed that Verna chokes on most of them when reading them."

In late 1959, Sandercock helped Gould through a crisis — or a would-be crisis: while visiting in New York the company that manufactured his concert piano of choice, Steinway & Sons, Gould claimed that one of the Steinway employees was over-exuberant in greeting him with a slap on the back. In a delayed reaction, Gould later claimed his shoulder, arms and left hand had been injured. After consulting five doctors, who could find no real injury, Gould insisted his nerves had been damaged and he talked them into putting him into an upper body cast for a full month. He sued Steinway and settled out of court, even though some doctors believed the injury was imagined. A number of concerts were cancelled and Gould became depressed. For emotional support he leaned on people like Sandercock and Dr. Joseph Stephens of Baltimore, a harpsichordist and psychiatrist, whom he had met in 1957. But many Gould associates, including Sandercock, thought Gould had overreacted to the Steinway incident, perhaps looking for sympathy.

And yet Gould often sympathized with the needs of others; for instance, in 1960 in New York, Gould offered help to Toronto-based singer Jacqueline Gooderham, a stranger to him. Gooderham found herself stranded with baggage at Grand Central Station and her scheduled car had not arrived to pick her up. "I was upset," she said. "In fact, I was in tears." Suddenly, a polite man who had been on a train with her showed up. "I've got a ride; let me take you wherever you want to go," he said. On the way to her hotel, the man showed interest in Gooderham's work, which included everything from Broadway musicals to operatic arias. "He wanted to hear all about my gigs on the Mediterranean and Caribbean cruise ships, singing for the passengers. When he mentioned that he was also a musician, I suggested he might like to try out for the band." But the stranger only smiled and said he wasn't up to that kind of work. It took her some time to realize the stranger was international pianist Glenn Gould. "He was a nice guy," she said.

Back in Toronto in 1959–60, Gould introduced Sandercock to what she would call her and Gould's music — Brahms' *Intermezzi*. It was an intimate, personal album he was preparing to record in New York and he had only played samples of it in live concerts. "We were at his St. Clair apartment one night when he played it all for me," Post said. "He was going to New York the next day to record it and he was excited. When he finished playing, he said to me, 'God, wasn't that sexy!' I thought to myself, 'This music is mine!'" What she didn't realize was that the Chickering piano Gould used for the seductive music had once belonged to his former girlfriend Frances Batchen.

Later he told an interviewer that he played the *Intermezzi*, "as though I were really playing for myself, but left the door open . . . I have captured, I think, an atmosphere of improvisation which I don't believe has ever been represented in a Brahms recording before." Gould never said that Verna influenced his music, but he was usually slow to credit people and the influence they had on him. Critics noted that Gould's version of the Brahms *Intermezzi* created an atmosphere of nostalgia, intimacy and melancholy, although John Beckwith in the *Toronto Daily Star* dismissed it as "supper music."

At the height of his touring career, in the late 1950s and early 1960s, Gould asked Sandercock to travel the world with him. In December 1958, he crafted a handwritten letter to her from the Sharon Hotel on Herzlia on Sea, Israel, where he was performing (he did not mail the letter, but hand delivered it to her upon his return to Toronto):

> *Angel –*
> *Your note received and contents fully savoured. The card is fine and I am eternally grateful for your efforts.*
> *I am sending back the list with additions. Where I do not specify the address it will likely be in your files. I suggest using five cents stamps – prestige, you know, prestige!*
> *As you may gather, I love it here (not the pianos, though). Think I might even come back for a holiday sometime. On the second day here, I moved out to this hotel where I have a room overlooking the seashore – than which there is nothing more inducing to contemplation. The reason for the move was that the philharmonic guest house does not have central heating. Guspidan Gomburger remained at the guest house where I still go for most meals because the hotel cooking is frightful.*
> *I rented a car and hence I have explored certain out of the way nooks. Just returned from getting lost in the Arab quarter of Jaffa – also lost one of my chrome plates in a collision (sic) with a blind Arab*

truck driver (keep that to yourself).

*Guspidan has a cold at present (wouldn't be sur-
prised if I am catching it) and his social activities
have been sharply curtailed. He still talks vaguely of
calling up some blond that he met at a party last
week but as you know he's getting on in yrs. and he
doesn't act upon these impulsive notions as once he
did.*

*Ah, if only you had come too. Then all would be
right with the world. How about officiating as tour
mgr. beginning Dec. 25. I am so spoiled from having
such an excellent aide-de-camp all yr. that I don't
know how I will manage without. Do think it over.
Salary $100 a week − travel expenses − exposure to
my stimulating conversations − vacations in the
Hawaiian Islands with pay. All these and other benefits. Truly the chance of a lifetime. Hurry, Hurry!
Think of seeing the fog in San Francisco, the smog of
L.A., of roasting in Houston and freezing in
Minneapolis. What other job could offer so much?*

End of salestalk.
Affectionately,
G-G-
*P.S. If any other names occur to me, I shall send them
along tout de suite.*

The card Gould refers to in his letter is a stock Christmas
card that Sandercock had picked out for him to send to his
friends and colleagues. "It was a very sedate card, nothing
whimsical and not religious," she remembers. "Something like
'Best Wishes for the Holidays.'" Gould suggests that
Sandercock put five cents on each envelope and seal it, rather
than send them with the envelope unsealed at two cents apiece.
"He wasn't cheap," she said. Guspidan Gomburger is Gould's

manager Walter Homburger. Post said that the offer of $100 a week plus expenses was generous for those days, more than she was making with Homburger.

The letters and the offers of globetrotting with a famous pianist sounded thrilling, but there was a slight impediment to this "job" offer — Gould would not allow Sandercock to actually *attend* his concerts. And if his concert was at Massey Hall or some other venue in Toronto, Gould had the audacity to ask her to leave town. In 1960, Sandercock was prevented from flying to Vancouver for his performance with the Vancouver Festival Orchestra, but Gould went a step further. According to Post, "He phoned me from backstage and said, 'I just realized they're broadcasting this concert. Turn off your radio!' On another occasion in Stratford, Ontario, Sandercock had already bought a ticket when Gould ordered her out of town, leaving hers as the only empty seat in the auditorium.

Dr. Ostwald speculated that Gould did not like it when people he knew were in the audience: "It made it very uncomfortable for Glenn when someone he knew personally was in the concert hall; it was a real distraction. Often he would beg friends not to come to his concerts. He preferred strangers, and that was agonizing enough."

After 1960, even Homburger was banned from Gould's concerts. "He felt there were three thousand pair of eyes watching him and it made him nervous," Homburger said.

This was not the Gould of earlier in his career when he welcomed friends and relatives to his concerts, even his demanding mother. "At that time, maybe he allowed her to attend because her approval was more powerful than his disapproval — he was looking to her approval as his mother and teacher — but after that maybe he didn't want anybody to decimate him," said Toronto psychotherapist Rebecca Rosenblat, a relationship expert. "It seemed that whatever he did wasn't good enough for him. He was God, but also a child, perhaps, in her eyes. It sounds schizophrenic; how do you make sense of that? He was likely confused." Rosenblat said there might have been an additional reason that Gould dismissed Sandercock from his live concerts. "If she was withholding something from him, this could have been his way of evening the score."

Gould didn't care much for working with friends, either, such as his New York producer Paul Myers. "When we became good friends, it was harder to work together," Myers said. "He said it was too hard to work with friends in a control room." In the overall concert picture, Gould said that large crowds and performing in public made him so nervous, he didn't even like attending other musician's concerts. "I always get very nervous at other people's concerts," he said. "It always distresses me to feel that they have the same sort of responsibility I have on other evenings."

In any event, Sandercock felt self-conscious and even guilty about the situation. "He didn't like the reason I liked to go to concerts — I found them a very exciting experience and he thought that was a terrible reason for me to go. After he quit in 1964, I started to worry, 'Was I the reason he quit concertizing?'" Eventually, Sandercock had to send Gould a telegram: "I, Verna Sandercock of the city of Toronto, hereby swear that in future I shall not be a member of a visual or listening audience of any Glen [sic] Gould performance without his specific sanction. Signed, Your Affectionate Hex." From then on, she had to listen to his records and tapes. "It was sad, crazy," she said. But they stayed together.

Sometimes, Sandercock fantasized about being Mrs. Glenn Gould, but she did not know if he was in love with her. "He was attracted to me, certainly. I knew he liked me. But if you got too close to him, he set up the wall and he backed off. He was a totally complex man, very opinionated. He had a good sense of humor, but he wanted everybody to laugh at his jokes. And he was pretty private. If you said the wrong thing at the wrong time, he would cut you off. It happened to other people, and some of them never knew why he did it."

In 1959, Gould was making plans to go to London to play with the London Symphony Orchestra under conductor Josef Krips. When Sandercock caught wind that Gladys Shenner was going to be in London at the same time as Gould and wanted to do another magazine story on him, she got jealous. "I knew they were close . . . he'd met her a few years before I did," said Post. In the end, it was neither sexy Francophone Susanne Hamel nor Sandercock, nor that unidentified musician in the midwestern United States, who got to see Gould in concert in England, but rather Shenner — for four performances. "I always suspected they were involved," Post said. "I think he had an affair with her, especially during his tour in London; he was with her a lot. I could sort of tell, and it upset me. I was really upset with him. I felt like a woman scorned." Post also suspected that Gould was having an affair with Deborah Ishlon, his publicist in New York. "It was the way he used to phone her, the way he talked to her, with lots of giggling and laughing. It was the same way he talked to me." But there is no evidence to suggest the late Ishlon and Gould were lovers.

If it was any consolation to Sandercock, Shenner was not exactly *invited* to the London performances by Gould, but happened to be working in England at the time for a women's magazine. When he realized that Shenner would be in London; however, Gould would spend a lot of time with her.

*He talked about his fears, about how he really
hated performing and the dreaded traveling.*
— Gladys Shenner

That SPRING *in*
BERKELEY SQUARE

The music hiccupping from the piano in the foyer of the Grosvenor House irked some of the graybeard guests. It was "Jailhouse Rock" by Elvis Presley, pounded by a cheeky but hardly stupid Cambridge student, who turned a quick about-face with "A Nightingale Sang in Berkeley Square" when threatened with no more iced wine by the concierge. This was May 1959 and worlds were colliding, especially up the road in Liverpool where the working class was starting to conspire with the Beatles. Back in the Grosvenor, there was a gap with several minutes silence until a very different tune came from the Steinway grand, drifting throughout the posh hotel, across the British gardens and out onto the Thames. It was Mozart, so wonderfully played that everything else came to a halt — the busboys, the blooming of the roses, the tourists and the Cockneys filing out of the football matches, not to mention the chaps standing atop wooden soap boxes proclaiming the end of civilization.

Filing into the foyer during this serenade at the permission of the concierge men were a dozen journalists, gathering in restrained amazement around the piano where Glenn Gould was holding court. He looked and played like he was not from the Commonwealth of Canada, but the dark side of Mars in his winter overcoat, mittens with holes for the fingers and a cloth cap. Photographers couldn't get enough, but he took his sweet time with his glass of orange juice while his left hand kept working the keys. One of the writers dared to ask about his gloves. "I have to protect my hands," he explained. "They're sensitive to this pressurized air — this pushed and cold air that you get in these air-conditioned buildings." Another rush of air came from so many brows being raised in unison.

Just three years earlier, Gladys Shenner had written in *Maclean's*:

> *For, at a time when prima donnas are not in fashion and the artist is supposed to act like the boy next door, Gould is, above everything, an individual . . . he dislikes advice and never follows it. A mere youngster among concert pianists, he won't accept instruction and dislikes practicing. Yet the Goldberg Variations, which has established his position as a pianist, is a work that takes most artists a lifetime to master.*

Shenner smiled at the reaction of the British press. By this point in Gould's life, she was chummy enough with Gould to be allowed to touch the historic chair he carried around to sit on while playing. Gould was in London, staying first class at the Grosvenor for a couple of fortnights of Beethoven concerts at the Royal Festival Hall with world-class conductor Josef Krips and the London Symphony Orchestra. Working for an English women's magazine, Shenner got to see Gould every night. She rushed home from work to see him at the Grosvenor, otherwise known as the "Grande Dame of Park Lane" with its palatial suites and imposing forecourt graced by Lutyens wrought-iron gates. "We ordered in a lot, served by a man in tails and white gloves," Shenner (Riskind) said. Thus, she made the transition from one of Gould's acquaintances of telephone and letter communication to one of his close friends.

"One time, I talked him into going out for dinner. Glenn

wasn't cheap and always picked up the tab," Riskind recalled. On another occasion, American pianist Van Cliburn, a friend whom Gould tabbed the "Texas Troubadour," came to Gould's room to visit. Gladys was there and recalls the two sophisticated pianists talked a lot about, of all things, psychic powers and ESP: "They were kibitzing in dialects and talking crazy stuff. [Cliburn] said he could tell what kind of person you were simply by walking into a room and seeing you. They laughed a lot and played the game Twenty Questions." Gould chided the younger Cliburn for recently accepting the top prize at the first International Tchaikovsky Competition because Gould hated awards and competitions. "Van was intuitive and a very sweet person," Riskind said. "A few years later, I went by myself to one of his concerts and visited him backstage. He still thought Glenn and I were a couple and he asked how he was doing."

While Gould would not venture over to Shenner's nice, expensive one-room flat at Regis Park, nearby on London's west side, or to the dance hall, where she loved to waltz, he did join her one sunny afternoon to feed the starlings at the Japanese garden near her hotel. "People were impressed by my apartment, especially for a single young woman who came all the way from Canada and was making more money at writing than the men!" she said. One day, Gould and Shenner went to Bath to watch Gould perform with violinist Yehudi Menuhin, but Gould backed out of the recital when he discovered that the hotel he and Shenner were about to check into did not have central heating. "I was very disappointed," Shenner said. "But I understood Glenn by that time."

To her, Gould hardly seemed as reclusive as his press clippings, but, years later, *Toronto Daily Star* writer Martin Knelman wrote of this period in Gould's life: "In 1959, Glenn Gould was a charming, playful and engaging young man who was still eager to succeed and had not yet grown weary of the world's attention."

During those foggy London nights, there was lots for Gould and Shenner to chat about — Communist rebel troops had just taken over in Cuba, making Fidel Castro the new president; Charles de Gaulle had been inaugurated as the first president of the French Fifth Republic; a chartered plane carrying Buddy Holly, Ritchie Valens and the Big Bopper had crashed during an Iowa snowstorm; the St. Lawrence Seaway had opened, linking the Great Lakes with the Big Pond.

And a young man in Bournemouth, England asked Gladys Shenner to marry him (she would not name him for this book). "I went to his house and couldn't understand a word his father said to me; I said I wasn't ready for marriage and Glenn agreed it was best for me to take my time." Gould told her that, he, too, was not interested in getting a spouse. "At that point in his life, he felt he could never marry," she said. "He wouldn't have touched marriage with a ten-foot pole." Gould did, however, take joy in some other people's families, especially their children. "He was very close to a family in Vancouver and talked about their children a lot."

One night, Shenner and Gould discussed passages from the novel *Of Human Bondage* by Shenner's favorite author, Somerset Maugham. Very rare for Gould, he even talked to her sometimes about his emotions: about how he was afraid of dying and it was great agony for him to get on airplanes to fly to concerts. "He talked about his fears, about how he really hated performing and the dreaded traveling," she said. "He was reading Nietzsche and talked about death. That was depressing. For somebody in his twenties, that was young to be talking about dying." Shenner's presence seemed to lighten Gould's loneliness on the road; on many of his tours, the only comfort he would receive would be letters and cookies from his beloved Mama.

When it came time for Gould's four Beethoven concerts at the Royal Festival Hall on the south bank of the Thames,

Shenner was with Gould backstage, both before and after each performance, which netted the pianist a hefty $3,500 per concert. "We had an electric kettle and someone would boil the water so he could soak his hands in a basin," she said. Prior to a concert, Gould would roll his shirtsleeves back over the elbows and completely immerse his hands and lower arms into a deep basin to increase circulation and relax muscles. For three of the four concerts, she watched from the wings backstage, through the window of a door that Gould used to get to the stage. As with Verna Sandercock, Gould did not like people he was close to being in the audience. "He told me that Arthur Rubinstein and other pianists couldn't play when their wives were in the room," she said. "He didn't want anyone he knew interfering with his career." But for the fourth Beethoven concert, Shenner tricked Gould and sat among the audience of 2,900. "Sitting out front with thousands of people, I was so overcome by Glenn's performance and the whole experience that I started to cry — softly. There was a young man sitting next to me and he turned to me and said, 'Is he your husband?' so there obviously were sparks that made observers feel our closeness. In fact, everybody thought we were engaged or married. Sir Josef Krips would always say to me, 'You take care of him; he's so delicate and fragile.'"

Shenner found out firsthand how fragile Gould was. One night in his hotel room, when she said she wasn't feeling well, Gould produced the case he carried with him from city to city. It was a big case with three sides and shelves and when he opened it up, it was full of prescription pills. He said, "Gladys, what do you need?" Gladys was not shocked; she'd already written about his drugs in her *Maclean's* piece:

> *He takes vitamin pills and stomach tablets to counteract nervous indigestion. He takes pills to stop sweating so his hands won't stick to the keys. He*

takes more pills to stimulate his blood circulation. He claims that practicing harms the circulation in his hands. He has had them insured with Lloyd's of London for $25,000.

During the concerts, Shenner's description of Gould in her *Maclean's* article seemed to stand the test of time:

Gould crouches over the keys, his shoulders high, his head pushed deep into his chest, his legs crossed. His elbows and wrists hang below the keyboard and his lank blond hair falls over his forehead and often brushes the piano keys.

All of this meant precious little, of course, once his long fingers took over and began a dance across the enamel keys that had even the demanding Brits in awe. Yes, he irritated them with his humming and conducting himself while he played, but Gould did not mind the criticism so much anymore; he was playing like the young maestro who had just sold out Massey Hall in his hometown, who had become the first North American to play behind the Iron Curtain in 1957. After Khrushchev, what formidable bears remained? The only bear was on his side: conductor Krips, with his vigorous gestures to the orchestra, referred to Gould as "one of the greatest musicians of our time, if not the greatest." The audience agreed with warm applause and sometimes standing ovations, which turned into encores. "He made Beethoven Concerto no. 4 sound like a celestial music box," said *News Chronicle* music critic Charles Reid. "Never before have I heard such a thistle-down touch."

Backstage, fans clamored for the Canadian star, especially one young woman who pursued him romantically. "She went through the line backstage and Glenn got a little worried,"

Riskind said. "He made me stand beside him and pretend we were a couple. He told her I was his fiancée, that we were to be married." And why not? Miss Shenner was a very pretty brunette — above average height at five feet seven with short, dark hair and brown eyes a model photographer could spend an afternoon trying to capture. In a dress of purple sequins, she looked like she had a season's pass to the Royal. At times backstage, she almost looked, or at least felt, smug, knowing that her article in *Maclean's* had been justified. Indeed, she was starting to feel at home with the elites: "Being with Glenn, I rose above myself. His brilliance, his persona, motivated me to become better. He brought out the best in me."

Meanwhile, all through the civilized commotion backstage, and despite his usual performance anxiety, Gould was winding down beautifully. (A photograph later showed him dressed up to snuff with a nice suit, vest and tie and a smile, gloves back on, sipping water — or was that wine? — and a little happiness, like he not only came from money but was willing to earn more.) He told a reporter that the audience had been "quite wonderful" and that he was impressed with the concert hall. While managing to avoid most handshakes extended to him from across the room, he gave Gladys a peck on the cheek. It sneaked up on her. She had a boyfriend three thousand miles away, but romance was in the air and Glenn Gould was the prince.

The British press gave Gould's performance mixed reviews. They didn't like his animated behavior and lack of concert hall etiquette, but they adored his subtle interpretation of Beethoven; he played it not as some pianists did, with aggression and power, but with refined introspection, even poetry. Overall, Shenner and Gould had a blast during their month in London. "We had fun, we laughed, we had a good time. Part of it might have been because of me. I think that was a good period of his life. He was a dear friend. There's no doubt about it, he loved me affectionately. When he wrote me, he always signed *Love Glenn*. He always kissed me on the cheek, hello and goodbye. I think it was because our relationship was close. I wasn't pushing. He felt comfortable with me."

He even showed normal streaks to Shenner. "I never saw his paranoia. When I was with Glenn, he never seemed that extreme to me. Yes, he wore the heavy clothes, and sometimes he thought and talked about death a great deal, but I was so used to him, he didn't seem nuts. When you knew him the way I knew him, he was extremely smart, so lucid and made good sense. I would've noticed if he was nuts."

The tour wasn't without its hiccups. Because of Gould's fear of germs, people would shake his elbow instead of his hand. Shenner caught a scoop when she noted that early in the tour, one admirer shook his elbow so hard, it damaged his nerve, partially paralyzing Gould's little finger. "He had to rephrase portions of Beethoven's C Major Concerto to avoid using the finger." Another night in London, she recalls, Gould came down with something and his temperature rose. He claimed it was European flu and that he was too sick to play the fifth and final concert. He was replaced by British pianist Louis Kentner. Said the *Daily Express*: "There's Ills in That Thar Gould." As well, in August of that year, Gould wanted to cancel another concert in Salzburg so he had Shenner call officials to do the dirty work for him. (Over his career, Gould routinely cancelled about twenty-five percent of his concerts, due to real or imagined illnesses, costing him thousands of dollars in fees, but he did reschedule and play the concert in Salzburg.)

Back home in Toronto, if Verna Sandercock was suspecting that Glenn and Gladys were in bed together (Shenner said they were not), he was not showing it in his letters. He wrote Verna a letter from the Grosvenor House about his illness (referring to Walter Homburger as "Gomburger," "Gomburg" and "W.H."):

Dear Puss,

Once again I greet you from a sickbed. Saturday I contracted (sic) the ache-all over feeling we hear about in the Alka-Seltzer ads. Yesterday my temperature began a modest climb (in the 99s) and I summoned a doctor. He didn't entirely agree with me that the symptoms indicated a minor grippe because he could not find any respiratory trouble. This morning he came again (my temp. is now just below 101) and suggested that his inclination lay toward assuming it a focal infection, possibly a resumption of what I had in Hamburg.

Needless to say, tonight's appearance cancelled or, rather Messrs Harold Holt are busy finding a substitute. I had to assure Homburger that I was not suffering Emperoritis since this is the second cancellation for that in as many months.

A pathologist has just been in and has done the blood tests of which we will have the results by this afternoon. If it is focal nephritis, I think I shall give up Europe as a bad job.

Gomburger has taken it with more equanimity than customarily. In fact he became quite hilarious on the phone last night − accused me of being a master fabricator and said with my capacity for deceiving people I'd be a natural for Army Intelligence. "Why," he went on, "every time you phone the office from on tour we hear the same (censored) complaints. Even Verna thinks it's a big joke." To which I replied without hesitation, "Well, what the heck do I care what Verna thinks." This produced a great guffaw from the other end. I can't help but think that that cantankerous little man suspects something!

Otherwise, Gomburg has been pursuing his

characteristically cavalier existence and seems to be living as energetically as always. Ah, for the life of the "Blond and Blue-eyed" as Thomas Mann says. Funny what a chameleon I let myself become. To W.H. I pose as the archtype [sic] of severe and stone-hearted sobriety. And then I appear to you — Inconsistent creatures, aren't we?

Has my Israel cheque come yet? Can certainly use it.

Have been exposing what I believe is a genuinely cinematic formula for the Nat. Film Board. They may well throw it out, but I'm getting hot, I think. Wanta be an extra?

Take good care of yourself, puss.

Love,

Postscript

3 days later, Thursday. It is not nephritis. Just a troubling virus. Can't shake the last remnants of fever though and I am trying to make up my mind whether to go to practice today or not.

Your letter arrived this morning. Macduff [Verna's cat] *sounds like a worthy mascot for the LRSRS* [Lower Rosedale Shakespeare Reading Society].

Re: the Star, do you mean they printed only the Manchester Guardian — Cardus review. I haven't seen it myself but Walter told me of it. I gathered from what Gerhard wrote to Walter that the Globe, at any rate, reprinted the Times. Gladys Shenner is preparing an article on the more hilarious aspects of this trip, of which there have been many.

Following Gould's London tour, Shenner left England for a writing assignment in Paris, but before she did, she received a letter from Gould, confirming that he had enjoyed his time with her in London. He is responding to a number of letters she had sent to him in the preceding weeks:

Dear Old Shenner:
Many, many thanks for your letters. As I warned you, I am a very haphazard correspondent but please don't let that compromise your maidenly pride and write as often as you can.

Your description of your first day on the job was very sad and affecting but I think not really unexpected and I am equally sure that by now you have found a greater security in the work and are getting along famously. I would love to know how your interview with Julie Andrews came out. By the way, your fame as foreign correspondent reached its zenith with a picture on the front page of the Globe & Mail, in which, doggoned, if you didn't look glamourous as hell! I assume that your mother saw it and sent it to you. If not, let me know and I shall try to dig up a back issue of the Globe for you — it was the one at the UNESCO conference or whatever.

When I arrived home at the airport on Friday afternoon, I immediately phoned Gordon Spears and told him about the indiscretion about the two hotel suites (in London). He sounded rushed off his feet and we only spoke for a minute but he did say that he was not sure about the fate of the story and did not seem to want to elaborate beyond that. I was rather puzzled by this and didn't notice until the following day that in Friday's paper, they devoted an editorial to me, a very flattering and gracious editorial, but written in the manner of an apology. It took the tone that the London press had overstated my mannerisms and that all good Canadians would rise with irate displeasure at the slighting inference that I was anything other than the archtype [sic] *of the well scrubbed, gentlemanly boy next door. It seemed odd that it was also the* [Toronto Daily] *Star that reproduced the Manchester Guardian to the exclusion of all others. I still think that your story struck a sane balance between the two poles and was, moreover, entertaining, and extremely well written and I think it would have done much more to straighten out the misconception of the Neville Cardus reproduction than the editorial, which most people probably missed seeing anyway.*

For the past week I have been on top of the world. I have been luxuriating in the glow of the NFB [National Film Board] *movie spotlight and I believe that I have finally found my true place in this world. I am, forsooth, an actor, something my public has long suspected anyway. We have been doing sequences in New York this past week and tomorrow we begin the scenes at Uptergrove. I will tell you about the thing in detail when I see you in August and I only hope that I am still supported by this lofty cloud of ego on which I ride at present. This movie-making has done more for my morale and indeed my enthusiasm for life in general than anything else within memory.* [Gould is referring to the filming in the summer of 1959 of two documentaries about himself by the National Film Board of Canada, *Glenn Gould: Off the Record* and *Glenn Gould: On the Record.*]

Finally, let me say what a great pleasure, a really great pleasure, it was to see you and talk with you so much in London. I hope that you found our talks of some benefit; I know that I certainly did; and I also hope that you are finding the desired balance between

your social and business life and that your enthusiasm
for London is unwavering.
Affectionately,
Glenn

Gould recovered from his illness to give what would become the final public performance of his career in Europe later that summer at the Lucerne Festival in Switzerland. Although he would never return, Gould left a lasting impression on the Europeans and they bestowed him with awards and millions of adoring fans.

From Switzerland on September 5, 1959, on the letterhead of the Palace Hotel Lucerne, Glenn Gould wrote Gladys Shenner a four-page letter, which read in part:

> *I am writing now . . . in the hope that my sad story*
> *will add just the right touch of bitters to your idyll in*
> *the sun and will force you to contemplate however*
> *briefly those whom life has seen fit to serve her as*
> *Naturkinder. Perhaps in the quiet shadow of some*
> *beach hut soothed by the lapping of the surf, you will*
> *spend a moment reflecting on those of us who are*
> *chosen to run against the tide. . . .*
>
> *. . . I arrived in Lucerne last Sunday afternoon by which*
> *time my fever was on the way up and the cold had*
> *arrived in full force. Nevertheless, the concert on*
> *Monday was a huge success – much the finest Bach D*
> *I've done and [Herbert von] Karajan and the*
> *Philharmonic were just superb. By Tuesday the cold had*
> *added the complication of sinusitis with which of course*
> *I will not fly so I have been canceling and re-scheduling*
> *my departure every couple of days. . . . Right after the*
> *concert last Monday, I phoned . . . only to be told that*

*you had already checked out . . . I have been
speculating . . . whether you are already on Onassis'
yacht exchanging "santes" with Sir Winston. I feel quite
sure that the seductive allurements of the Riviera set
are being handled expertly and discriminately.*

It seems Gould was eager to keep their relationship intact
when Shenner left Europe and returned to Canada because
Gould mailed her another (undated) letter on two pages on his
personal letterhead and two pages on the Fort Garry letterhead
of a Winnipeg, Manitoba hotel.

It read in part:

*It was awfully good to know that you arrived home
unchanged from the Riviera and its social climate . . .
my season begins next week and so I'm getting
depressed as usual. My piano I fear is languishing at
the docks in New York. It arrived this week a couple
of days before a longshoreman's strike began. This
could ruin it and I'm rather helpless to do anything
about it. Please do keep me informed about your
plans. I'm sure you would like Israel if you get there.
I was there in December of last year and the weather
was still marvelous . . . my roles as actor-commentator
become more interesting. I am gone to do a "Close-
up" for C.B.C. with the Texas troubadour − Van −
probably filmed in December. I may soon retire into
my new role of the musicians' Ed Murrow.*

At about the same time, while staying with a friend in
Winnipeg, Shenner was surprised to receive a telephone call
from her favorite pianist — "how he found out where I was
staying, I'll never know!" What Shenner did not tell Gould was
that she had become engaged to a doctor in Toronto and was

wearing his diamond ring, but that the relationship was already on the rocks and lasted only three months. One of the last letters Gould sent on the stationery from his parents' home was to Shenner (he refers to his upcoming concert schedule):

October 21, 1959
Dear Gladys:
Our letters crossed, as you will see, and I am happy to know that your plans for Israel have become more definite and are permitting your stay there for some months. I think it is a wonderful idea and I should also imagine that there are a lot of excellent story possibilities there.

The season has started and, as I said a few weeks ago, I am terribly depressed about it. In the morning I have to go but at least it started well. I did not see Mrs. Secter in Winnipeg but I hope that she managed to get to the concert. This was the first time that I had played the Brahms D minor and I was extremely happy about it.

As for the reformation of Shenner, there isn't much more that I can add. I am terribly touched that you acknowledge me for having had some small part in it and I only hope that in the long run it finds you happier and more secure.

It wouldn't surprise me at all, by the way, should you find Israel so enchanting that you decided to remain indefinitely. But what are the possibilities of working there without becoming a citizen? That might be a formidable obstacle.

Please don't be offended that I can't sign this letter. It doesn't imply neglect, only absence.
Love
Glenn/vs

vs was Verna Sandercock, who, in Gould's absence, had to type his correspondence for him. It's probably safe to say that after reading this letter, Verna — who was still Gould's girlfriend — had an inkling that something had gone on in London with Shenner.

His fan mail was very important to him —
he'd be shattered if he didn't get any.
— Gould secretary Naomi Lightbourn

Lots of
FEMALE FRIENDS

Chapter NINE

Back in Toronto, Gladys Shenner got to visit Gould's new penthouse on St. Clair Avenue. She found it to be well kept and not cluttered, like some future visitors would report after Gould fired his cleaning lady for gossiping about his personal life. "It was a very nice apartment with a waiting room and a big piano. We talked a lot there and he played for me, Bach and Mozart," Shenner said.

Gould also talked occasionally about becoming a composer, but he did not seem to be able to deal with emotional issues. One day, following a disagreement with her mother, Gladys showed up at Glenn's apartment in tears. "He wanted to help, but he didn't know what to do, so he took me over to his piano and played for me until I calmed down."

By 1961, Shenner was living in Montreal and working in public relations and marketing for Trans-Canada Consultants. There, on the company's letterhead, she wrote Gould an intense, lengthy letter that could be interpreted as romantic, tongue-in-cheek or humorous — or all of the above.

From your playing of the [Brahms] *Intermezzi, I am convinced that you feel life and love as deeply and sincerely as I. I am convinced that only we, two, amongst this world of cold hard ruthless people see the true inner romance of love – in all its shimmering beauty . . . we have that inner perception, that fine sensitivity, that communion with the gods which gives an added insight into the real meaning of life.*

The fact that you are famous, and probably terribly wealthy, means nothing at all to me. It's your soul – your beautiful, penetrating, other-worldly soul – that draws me to you . . . I'm sure that a man of your keen perception can readily tell from this letter that I would, indeed, have much to offer a man of your talents.

You need someone who understands you as you really are; someone to look after you and protect you from the buffetings of the harsh world about you . . . you need the love and understanding of a good woman. And I am prepared to give this to you.

So, my dear Glenn, I await, impatiently, your verdict. I do hope that it will be favorable.
Your humble servant,
"Ever constant" Shenner.

Gould did not respond to her letter. Meanwhile, also in 1961, Verna Sandercock's relationship with Gould began to wane somewhat, although part of it had to do with his constantly being on the road. "Our relationship could be quite involved and intense, and then there would be nothing," Verna Post later said. Some of the problem might have been Verna's continued reluctance to go on the road with him and become his full-time aide de camp.

In the fall of 1960, Gould had arranged to play two concerts with the Honolulu Symphony Orchestra in Hawaii for December 11 and 13. Publicity arrangements were made and Sandercock ordered the music from Luck's Music Library in Detroit. But late that fall, while they were having tea at his apartment on St. Clair Avenue, Gould abruptly informed Sandercock he did not want to go to Honolulu unless she would go with him. She refused, and the next day he canceled the concert, giving a phony excuse to the crestfallen organizers in Hawaii. "I felt kind of strange about it, but there was nothing I could do," she said. "He always wanted someone to go with him on his tours as an aide, to get everything done for him, and sometimes I thought that was all I was in his life," she said. "But then we had those other moments together. . . ."

Sometimes, Gould's absence on the road seemed to upset Sandercock; Morry Kernerman recalls one night when Sandercock came to his home while Gould was on tour, and he had to console her. Nothing happened that night except a long conversation, he said, but Kernerman wonders if that liaison subsequently affected his friendship with Gould, who returned from his tour and was not as warm toward the violinist. "[Sandercock] was very pretty, awfully pretty, and she had a teasing manner with men, but she seemed very possessive of Gould and I had the impression she was his girlfriend," Kernerman said. "It wasn't my style to take a man's woman away from him." According to Kernerman, Gould was romantic toward women "in a broad way. He had a need to idolize them, to make them into something special."

If Sandercock had known that Gould had shared his Brahms' *Intermezzi* with Gladys Shenner, she might be jealous all over again. Sanderock once said that the *Intermezzi* was *their* music, which was personal between them because he practiced it with her in his apartment before recording it in New York, and yet Shenner received an autographed copy of the record from Gould with a warm signature: "To Gladys, after her unforgettable reading of Arden — from one romantic to romantic. Affectionately, Glenn, May 27/61." Gladys is proud of that record cover because Gould rarely gave away his signature; he once told her, "If I started giving autographs, there would be no end to it."

When Sandercock left Homburger's office, taking over her job for two years was Naomi Lightbourn, a former editorial assistant at the *Toronto Telegram*. During that time, Homburger moved from the small office on Adelaide Street to another downtown Toronto location on Sheppard Street, where Gould was given his own little space. Lightbourn and Gould developed a good professional relationship and a friendship. "I admired him, especially for his great sense of humor," she said. "He'd come in, take his shoes off and put up his feet on a desk, showing the holes in his socks. We kidded him a lot and we joked that we'd take them and darn them for him." Lightbourn found out that Sandercock had had a type of romance with Gould, but she did not follow the same route. "He would call me late at night and we'd talk about lots of things. Sometimes he would read letters to me from his fans." Gould had now become popular worldwide for his music and his sex appeal and in 1962 he received a fan letter from Margaret Avison, one of Canada's finest poets. "I remember one young student at the University of Toronto who had real crush on him," Lightbourn said. "Very few people knew about his apartment on St. Clair Avenue, so all the mail would come through our office. His fan mail was very important to him — he'd be shattered if he didn't get any."

Being associated with Gould could be a coup for a young woman. "He often drove me home at night in his huge, white Lincoln. I always hoped I'd be seen in this gorgeous car with Glenn Gould." Lightbourn saw Gould's eccentricities up close in the office. "When we moved to Sheppard, we had to find an office which had heating controls because he always wanted the air conditioning turned off," she said. "When we'd have tea and cookies, he'd always ask if the cups had been sterilized and he'd want to know if anyone with a cold had touched the phone on his desk." One day, while Gould was wearing his trademark winter coat and gloves with the fingers cut out, Lightbourn accidentally touched his fingers while going over his "atrocious" handwriting with him. "They were cold as ice!" she said.

Sometimes, while they were working on radio scripts, Gould invited Lightbourn to his St. Clair apartment. "It was such a dark and dreary place. The walls and the living room were almost midnight blue." As mentioned earlier, Gould had become infamous for not wanting people he knew in the audience, but he expressed some disappointment that Lightbourn had not joined him backstage following a concert in Stratford. "He obviously saw me in the audience because, later, he said, 'Why didn't you come backstage?'" But their relationship did not extend beyond a professional one in the two years she knew him, perhaps because she had a boyfriend at the time. "[Gould] wasn't the sort of person I would confide in, and I think I wasn't the person he would want to confide in," Lightbourn said. "If I had had a secret love affair with someone at the time, I would have never told him about it. I would have been worried he wouldn't keep it to himself." And yet Lightbourn was fascinated with how Gould dealt with his emotions, or did not. "When my mother died suddenly, he asked me a lot about her death, how I reacted to it and how my father reacted to it. I thought that maybe Glenn didn't experience the same emotions as other people did, that he had to rely on what other people told him about emotions. I found his reaction very interesting."

Another young woman Gould spent a lot of time with in the 1950s and 1960s was concert pianist Anahid Alexanian, who lived in St. Catharines, Ontario. Like Gould, she was a child prodigy, or at least a juvenile prodigy. They were both students of Alberto Guerrero, a decade apart, and they had parents who had money to keep them in music. Some details of their relationship are not known, but they likely met through the Royal Conservatory in Toronto. Alexanian was born in Canada to parents who were survivors of the Armenian Massacre in the First World War.

Alexanian's mother was from a talented family of musicians and writers. While Anahid Alexanian's parents were Christian evangelicals, Anahid was a puritan like Gould. At some point in the late 1950s, Gould tutored her, taking her under his wing musically as he had done with Frances Batchen and Cynthia Millman, but without much fanfare or publicity.

"I didn't see Glenn as a teacher," Sandercock said. "I couldn't image him having the patience to be a teacher."

Alexanian developed traits known to both Gould and Guerrero. "She held [Gould] up as her example," said her sister Armine, a cellist. Nevi Palvetsian, who studied piano with Anahid, added, "She was the same ilk as Gould, they were a lot alike. They were brought up not to be worldly. She had that fey quality that Glenn had."

The Gould and Alexanian families became somewhat close and Anahid and Armine visited Glenn's cottage on Lake Simcoe. "His parents had a hard time understanding why he was eccentric," Armine said.

Anahid was pretty, but not stunning, and had a bright mind, flashing black eyes and intense concentration for the things she loved. "She was extremely intelligent about many things," said family friend Syraun Palvetsian. "She was Canadian, but spoke and wrote Armenian beautifully."

Anahid could also be shy. "She was extremely talented and good at school with marks in the high 80s and 90s," said her cousin Haig Semerjian. "Her father made her quit school [to concentrate on her music]." In 1959, Anahid performed at the Canadian National Exhibition as part of a group of Royal Conservatory students and graduates.

That same year, critic John Kraglund watched one of her performances and was stunned by the similarities in style between her and Gould. He said her performance showed "too much of a Glenn Gould influence."

"My sister had a low chair and she sung out loud while she

was playing," Armine said. "I think eventually, she would have got her own style as she got older."

Gould and Alexanian corresponded quite often as friends, usually talking about music or their mentor/pupil relationship and Gould sometimes wrote to her when he was lonely on the road. Here is a sample of a letter from Gould of September 23, 1960:

> *After receiving your itinerary for the fall season I can only say "Wow!" It is, as you undoubtably know, a fantastically large amount of repertoire to survey in such a short time but I am sure that you will do a wonderful job with all of it. I hope that I shall be able to hear some of the broadcasts though, unfortunately, I will be on tour during most of that period but do let me know how they go. It occurs to me, however, that some of the broadcasts would leave very little time for commentary. It may be that they look longer than they really are but I do hope that you will have a chance to get off a few remarks.*
>
> *I am happy to say that the right shoulder was nothing serious, merely the result of thoughtlessly carrying a suitcase. I guess I am just too delicate for this world. Anyway, the arm is fine now and I did a long stint in the television studio yesterday putting a Beethoven show on tape.*

In the beginning, Alexanian performed largely in Toronto, but later had concerts in New York and Washington, D.C. On December 4, 1960, she performed at Massey Hall with conductor Walter Susskind and the Toronto Symphony Orchestra, and was hailed as a promising young Canadian pianist. In 1962, the *Toronto Daily Star* proclaimed, "Miss Alexanian, 21, is known as 'The Female Glenn Gould' because of the way she bobs and weaves while playing. She has received excellent notices from the critics." Alexanian performed "a versatile program ranging from Scarlatti to Bach to Liszt to Barber. Miss Alexanian is no novice on the local musical scene. She has a respectable number of solo recitals to her credit and made the headlines last spring when she introduced to this city Schoenberg's masterwork 'Pierrot Lunaire' . . . she has established herself as a musician of great sensitivity, intellect and courage. She has been known as one of the few young local pianists who has the curiosity and mind to tackle works by Schoenberg, Boulez and other sophisticated contemporaries."

Star music critic Udo Kasemets noted that when Alexanian "projects dark poetic moods (as in the last variations of Beethoven's last sonata), or spins a sustained lyric line (in the Andante of Bach's *Italian Concerto*), one can sense the great interpretive potential of this young musician." But Kasemets saw flaws: "Regrettably, this deepness of Miss Alexanian's soul is not paired with other necessary qualities needed for successful piano playing . . . if she wants to make a success of her concert career, her first task is to bring her technical and rhythmical abilities to par with her feelings and intellect. Hers is too valuable a talent to be wasted."

Alexanian gave a lot of her credit to Gould. "I think theirs might have been a meeting of two souls," Morry Kernerman said. "She was crazily in love with him. He was like a god to her."

"I know she had a crush on him," said her cousin Haig Semerjian. We do not know if Gould returned the favor.

Sometime in the early 1960s, Gould was going on tour and suggested to Alexanian that she get tutoring from Kernerman, whom Gould respected as a musician and friend. "She had studied with him and received his teaching, but I don't think he wanted her around anymore," said Kernerman, who found her to be "talented, highly intelligent and cerebral. She was really into twelve-tone music." He worked with her on several occasions, but became annoyed when she seemed more interested in talking about Gould. "She couldn't stop talking about him — she gleaned from me any information, personal and professional, about him . . . his habits, what he ate, when he slept, every detail until it was quite extraordinary. She even started to act like him. She drove me crazy."

Kernerman said he did not know the depth of the Gould–Alexanian relationship, but today he wonders if it had anything to do with the fact that Gould ended his eleven-year relationship with him as a friend and musician (his aforementioned meeting with Sandercock was another possibility). When he returned from his tour, Gould would not talk to Morry ever again, and he refused to give the violinist an explanation. One day, Kernerman tracked down Gould at a rehearsal for a Brahms trio. "I walked in and, when he saw me, he hit the piano keys hard with his hand and stopped playing," Kernerman said. "He said, 'Excuse me, we're rehearsing right now' — like I was a stranger. I said I wanted to talk to him, but he said he was too busy and that he would write or phone me to explain what had happened."

Gould eventually did write to Kernerman. "He said, simply, that I would never know his reasons and that he didn't want to discuss it further. It was very traumatic for me, but at first, I thought nothing had happened. I felt completely bewildered and had no idea why he did it. I harbored feelings of guilt; I thought I might have caused him pain." Then, through a mutual friend, Gould said that if Kernerman ever showed up at one of his concerts, he would get up off his piano stool and walk away. "I was so devastated when I heard that. What if he had showed up to play and I was in the orchestra?" Kernerman was upset enough that he moved his family to Montreal. "To this day, I don't know why he cut me off, but I wonder if it had something to do with [Alexanian]. Or it may have had something to do with Sandercock, or something else." For many years, Morry refused to tell his story, but now, he says, "My feelings have changed."

Meanwhile, Alexanian's career was taking a tumble as her parents' money waned. "Someone was embezzling my father's [carpet] business and Anahid lost her financial support," Armine said. November 6, 1963, was a traumatic day for Anahid and her family: they were forcibly evicted from their St. Catharines' home. The headline in the *Toronto Daily Star* the following day read, "Screaming Girl Pianists Handcuffed." The story described how Anahid, twenty-two, her eighteen-year-old sister Armine and their fifty-one-year-old mother were hauled screaming from their home in handcuffs. "For three hours, they fought off sheriff's officers, policemen and three policewomen," wrote the reporter. "As they were handcuffed and led struggling to cruisers, they shouted, 'Nazis! Fascists! Gestapo!'"

"When the family got thrown out into the street, Anahid never got past that," said Palvetsian.

"She was very brilliant, but she didn't get the right breaks," her sister Armine said. "And her teacher Guerrero died when she was still in her teens."

Eventually, Anahid went to New York to study music. Syraun Palvetsian remembers seeing Anahid perform in Washington, D.C., in the late 1960s. "She wore gloves and had a low stool, like Gould — I was shocked," Palvetsian said. To this day, Anahid Alexanian has not talked about her relationship with Gould.

*At the age of four I started very studiously
to draw rain. Just rain, page
after page of it.*
— Cornelia Foss

The BEGINNING *of a* TRIANGLE

Chapter TEN

The odd man out in what would become the secret triangle of the classical music world was Lukas Foss — by most accounts a cheery, cerebral maestro with boundless energy. Long before the sweet, salty breezes of the Hamptons blew his wife Cornelia into the arms of Glenn Gould, Lukas was *somebody*, who played a major role in shaping the face of American music in the last half of the twentieth century. Foss collaborated and summoned lightning bolts from the sky with the Olympians of the orchestra — Leonard Bernstein, Aaron Copland and Glenn Gould, as well as famous poets like Carl Sandburg. Although the humble Foss, who was short in stature, never attained their height of fame, some of those stars considered him their equal. In fact, when they first met in Los Angeles in the late 1950s, Gould called Foss "the greatest pianist in the world."

Foss was born on August 15, 1922, as Lukas Fuchs, into a cultivated Jewish family of a Berlin philosophy professor and a mother who was a painter. Unlike other lads in Berlin, Luke did not boot a soccer ball or march in lockstep with the German youth movement, but studied piano and theory with Julius Goldstein, who introduced him to Beethoven, Mozart and, dearest of all, Bach. By age six Lukas Foss was copying songs; the following year he invented variations on pieces he learned with Goldstein; and by eight he even tried his hand writing an opera, based on a story his mother told him about a devil.

The family escaped the Nazis to France in 1933 and they sailed to the United States in 1937, where his father changed the family name because Fuchs "sounded like a dirty word in English." After having breakfast with composer Aaron Copland in 1937, the two musicians became friends for life.

During that first year in New York, Foss composed his first published works, writing them on the subway on his way to school; by sixteen, he was earning money playing for dance companies and giving piano lessons. In 1940, he earned national headlines when *Time Magazine* reported that "Nazi Germany's record in music has been as shoofly as in the other arts: there are today more good German composers outside the Fatherland than in it. Not all exiles are veterans. Last week a phenomenal 17-year-old popped up in Manhattan. His name: Lukas Foss." He enrolled at the prestigious Curtis Institute in Philadelphia to study composition with Paul Hindemith, a renowned German composer. Serge Koussevitzky, the legendary Russian conductor of the Boston Symphony Orchestra and a champion of contemporary music, also mentored Foss. Young Lukas had a cocky streak and he was in love with the work of Russian composer Igor Stravinsky. When Foss enrolled in a class at Yale, Hindemith wrote a letter to Koussevitzky: "I can't teach Foss. He wants to know everything but he won't follow anything." Koussevitzky showed Foss the letter and laughed: "That's what I want in my students — they want to learn, but to do things their own way."

In 1941, Lukas had just become an American citizen when he wrote *The Prairie* from a poem by Sandburg, even though he had never set foot on the prairies. He did, however, become a friend of Sandburg. At about the same time, Foss became a prominent student at the famous Tanglewood Estate and summer music festival in its second season of 1941. Nestled on an idyllic two hundred acres of impeccable lawns and formal gardens in the Berkshires of Massachusetts, Tanglewood quickly became a greenhouse for blossoming talents of classical music, including German refugees like the highly driven Foss, who were giddy with their freedom following the suppression of pre-war Europe. The atmosphere crackled with inspiration, creativity and thick accents. "If ever there was a time to speak of music, it is now in the New World," said Koussevitzky, who also taught at Tanglewood. "So long as art and culture exist, there is hope for humanity."

Foss was the youngest buck in a group studying composition and conducting over the summer, which included rising star Mr. Leonard Bernstein. Years before he became the face of classical music, Bernstein was the face of young professionals at Tanglewood, and he would also become an instrumental character in the life of Glenn Gould. Bernstein was an exhibitionist, hugging the men and kissing the women, addicted to life, cigarettes and halvah at the deli. Everybody wanted to be near him for one reason or another, to take part at least briefly in the rhapsody that appeared to be his life. When he ran his fingers through his thick black hair, he could have been a movie star. Whereas Foss was comfortable using the long, traditional conductor's baton, being a servant to the music as well as a leader, Bernstein refused to use a wand, preferring to conduct with a wave of his hand; he liked to *feel* the beat, as well as his pulsating ego.

Bernstein and Lukas took to one another quickly. "Lenny was four years older than I was," Foss said. "He was a Harvard graduate and I didn't even have a high school diploma when I arrived from Paris. . . . I liked Lenny enormously and I thought he was not really a student because he had all the answers already. He was like an older brother to me because I was naive and he was not a bit naive. I looked up to him and . . . I think I was aware that he would go far, that he was the real thing."

Tanglewood was suspended from 1942 to 1945 because of the Second World War and some of the upstart musicians tried to avoid the draft to keep their careers on track. A few years later, Samuel Adler conducted Foss's first symphony and first piano concerto. "Lukas was a model for all of us," Adler said. "I can't think of anyone besides Bernstein in our time who was a composer, a musician and a conductor."

As he collected mentors along the way, Foss became less rebellious and more cooperative. "Influences are enriching," he said. "And they can be found in every work of art, even the most original." Foss developed a wide-ranging style and took chances in his work. "My music is consistent in its inconsistency, a welding together of things that usually you would not find together, namely tonality and the wildest kind of innovation, the deadly serious and the pop," he said. "I feel like the way to advance into the new musical territory is to advance rear first, waving to the disappearing past, but I also want to know where I'm going." Foss won two prestigious awards with the Boston Symphony, allowing him to spend time in Italy at the American Academy in Rome. There, in 1949, he met seventeen-year-old Cornelia Brendel who was, like his mother, a painter. She had her own tale to tell.

Cornelia Brendel was born in Berlin in 1931 to father Otto J. Brendel, a scholar, poet, philosopher and painter, and Maria Weigert, a woman ahead of her time. Weigert broke through the "boys only" tradition of German gymnasiums, but was prevented from finishing her doctorate at the University of Heidelberg when her father found her slippers under the bed of her husband-to-be Otto.

When Cornelia was still an infant, the family moved to Rome, where her cigar-smoking father was named an executive at the German Archaeological Institute. In 1936, he was dismissed through Hitler's racial laws as being married to a non-Aryan. While her father searched for a job and a place for them to live, Cornelia and her mother moved back to Berlin, living under a false name to protect their identity. The family was reunited in the United States in 1939, where Otto landed a job as an assistant professor of art and archaeology at Washington University in St. Louis, Missouri, and in 1941 they moved to Bloomington, Indiana, where he taught at the University of Indiana. While there, Otto wrote for a volume on erotic art, later published by the Kinsey Institute, and Cornelia developed her talent in drawing. The attractive, energetic Maria went on to become a writer and scholar in her own right.

In 1949, the family moved back to Rome where Otto was named as a distinguished American scholar. "I grew up among the beauties of Rome and was taken to museums from an early age, so I was drawn to art from the very beginning," Cornelia said. It was at the academy where the beautiful, blossoming Cornelia won awards while studying sculpture and there she met another Fellow, Lukas Foss — they were introduced to one another by none other than Aaron Copland.

They were both blue eyed, bushy-tailed intellectuals, who quickly fell in love and married two years later, in 1951. "He was a Fellow and I was the child of a Fellow," Cornelia remembers. "We eloped. We had a secret wedding at the Campidoglio. I came home afterwards and my mother asked, "Where have you been all afternoon? I wanted to say, 'Oh, out getting married,' but I didn't. I was young and had to get the American Ambassador's permission for the marriage, but he said to us, 'You are obviously very much in love.'" Her parents were angry when they belatedly found out about the verboten wedding. "But then they saw him play his piano concerto and they very much changed their minds," Cornelia said. The Fosses, who moved to Manhattan and then Los Angeles, rose quickly as a glamorous couple in high society. A photograph snapped in the early 1950s shows them at Tanglewood, performing a Piano for Four with Bernstein and his wife Felicia.

In 1953, Lukas Foss was named to succeed Arnold Schoenberg, one of Gould's must-have composers, as professor of composition at the University of California at Los Angeles (UCLA). There, the open-minded Foss began probing and questioning the musical ideas of tonality, notation and fixed form. In Los Angeles, Lukas and Cornelia first lived in actor John Barrymore's old house and held parties for the heavyweights of the American music scene. "They were very social and we had fascinating evenings," said Cornelia's close friend, Edith Wyle. "Cornelia was always charming."

One night in the late 1950s, they were driving to dinner near their Los Angeles home when Bach's *Goldberg Variations* came on the car radio as though it had never been played before. Lukas was so enraptured by the unusual interpretation, he asked Cornelia, who was driving, to pull over to the side of the road so that he could listen and discover who the pianist was. There, Lukas sat in a trance, listening to the recording and the Bach broadcast for so long, the couple were late for their dinner. It turned out the pianist was Glenn Gould up in Canada and, not long after, the Fosses met him in Los Angeles, where Lukas was rehearsing for a show with Leonard Bernstein. That day, a blond, baby-faced Gould showed up unannounced in winter clothes, despite the balmy weather. "My husband looked up and saw a hat and scarf coming toward him," Cornelia recalled, chuckling. "[Gould] said to Lukas, 'Hello, I'm Glenn Gould. I came here on purpose to hear you, the greatest pianist in the world.'" That was a huge, perhaps tongue-in-cheek compliment from Gould, who by that time thought *he* was the greatest. Lukas was in his mid-thirties at the time and his wife and Gould in their mid-twenties. It was the beginning of a long relationship for all of them.

Glenn Gould was in awe of Lukas Foss, especially since the latter was proficient at conducting, composing and piano playing. Gould wanted to become notable at all three, but at the time, he had developed only his playing to an international level. The Fosses were strikingly handsome, intelligent and creative.

What Lukas lacked in height (five inches shorter than Gould's six feet), he made up in strong, dark looks, bright blue eyes, personal magnetism and a dashing demeanor. Cornelia was blond, with blue eyes and a graceful presence, yet an independent streak for a married woman of that era. It is hard to say whether Gould was attracted to Cornelia immediately, but she was certainly fond of him. "I was drawn to his handsome looks and his huge intelligence," she said. "He had an original mind, was extraordinarily canny and had an enormous sense of humor."

A short time after their first meeting, the Fosses saw Gould perform live in Los Angeles. The Gould concert experience was a true novelty, both for the couple and the classical music world: he sat sidesaddle at the piano in a trance, often crossing his legs to stop his feet from stamping, swooning and swaying his upper body, allowing each of his fingers to have a mind of its own and humming while conducting himself with his free hand as his hair became storm-tossed. By that time, according to Tim Page, a writer and Gould friend in the early 1980s, "He was the James Dean of classical music . . . he made Bach swing." And, ah, the sound of his piano — so fluid and many-voiced; every now and again like a train whistle off in the night and other times touching everything in the concert hall like a massage.

After meeting Gould in the late 1950s, Foss did some collaboration with him and Cornelia would often join in when an evening turned social. It did not take long for Glenn Gould to win Cornelia Foss with his looks, intelligence and dry wit. For his part, Gould was attracted by her striking looks, intelligence and independent streak, as well as the stability she fostered as a mother of two children. Gould and the Fosses soon became close friends and Gould visited their second house at 555 Greencraig Road on a Brentwood Hill in the Santa Monica Mountains where, on a clear day, you could see the Pacific Ocean. Both Cornelia and Lukas worked at home in those days and many of her abstract paintings and sculptures graced the walls. She called her work "studies" and did not give them titles, but she was already established as a professional artist.

One of the many possible reasons Gould took a fancy to the Fosses was his fascination with all things German — his favorite composers, such as Bach, novelist Thomas Mann and his manager Walter Homburger. Gould loved to apply a thick German accent to his conversation, especially when he was pretending to be one of his alter egos, Dr. Karlheinz Klopweisser, a fictitious composer and critic. When playing Klopweisser, as a satire of German composer Karl Stockhausen (1828–2007), Gould would don a long wig and wave an enormous electric wand. Gould also was fond of the Fosses' children, Christopher (born in 1957) and Eliza (1961) and their pet dog, an Australian Puli, shorn for the warm weather. "In this family, everybody is a live wire," Lukas Foss told the *Los Angeles Times* for a feature story in 1961. Gould even rollicked on the floor with the kids, which was not unusual because he turned into a different person around children and pets, chortling and playing as his fear of germs and being touched vanished remarkably.

Musically, Glenn Gould and Lukas Foss were soul mates; both were tireless and witty Bach disciples unafraid to add their own touch to the classics. Gould admired Foss's experimental work in forming an improvisation ensemble for a clarinet, cello, piano and percussion. Also in 1961, Foss won the New York Music Critics Award for his song "Time Cycle," a work for voice and orchestra that premiered with Gould's friend and colleague Leonard Bernstein and the New York Philharmonic. However, Foss, who was also a professor of music at UCLA, was falling behind in his composing and had canceled a teaching engagement at Tanglewood for the summer. In Canada, Gould was showing his own leadership qualities from 1960 to 1963 as co-director of music at the Stratford Festival, and he arranged for Lukas to play a successful stint there.

In November 1961, the drama continued in the Fosses' lives

as tragedy swept across the California paradise: hundreds of homes were destroyed by a fire in the Santa Monica Mountains. "Eliza was still a baby," Cornelia recalled. "Christopher was three or four and my mother was staying with me, but Lukas was in New York working with Leonard Bernstein." As flames began to engulf their house on Greencraig Road, Cornelia desperately scrambled to save precious things. "I got one of my husband's scores out of there and a couple of my watercolors, and I put our dog in our Jaguar. Fifteen minutes later, the house exploded. The city had not turned off the gas." In the fire Cornelia lost about twenty-five large, semi-abstract paintings, the result of four years' work, and some of Lukas's manuscripts were destroyed. "UCLA had acquired a place to have a show of mine; they chose me to be the first young artist there, but it was a crookedly run gallery and UCLA pulled out of the project," Cornelia said. "I hired a trucking company to have all the paintings brought to our house. But I should have taken them to a studio. . . . We lost everything, including our house."

Gould had a history of comforting his friends who suffered losses and it was no different with the Fosses. "He was very kind to us," Cornelia said. After the fire, the Fosses moved across the country to a furnished apartment in Manhattan, owned by composer Elliott Carter, and established a summer dwelling in the fashionable Hamptons. It wasn't all bad for Cornelia, who said, "I hated living in Los Angeles beyond belief. If the devil had to invent a city, he'd make Los Angeles — no sidewalks, no feeling of place, no indigenous plants, everybody driving — it's a nightmare. Every morning, you wake up and find the same morning you had the day before. Hellish."

In the Hamptons, the Fosses quickly became part of a group that included the high-profile Bernstein and artists Fairfield Porter, Larry Rivers and Jane Wilson, poets John Ashbery, Kenneth Koch and James Schuyler and musicians Ned Rorem, John Cage and Morton Feldman, who all took turns hosting feasts. "How good it was to be young and in the Hamptons!" wrote author/photographer John Jonas Gruen. "And how very seductive and exciting to live where some of the greatest American art was conceived and executed . . . oh, how sexy a hot sandy beach is, and how foolishly designed swimming clothes are. Relax: life has just begun, anything can happen."

Cornelia agreed: "It felt like one endless artists' party."

A type of musical triangle evolved among Gould, Lukas and Bernstein. Sure, it was largely Elvis and the Beatles who changed pop music, but during the same era, the individualistic Gould challenged convention and allowed classical performers to usurp power from composers and conductors. In fact, in 1962, Bernstein noted to a Carnegie Hall audience that the only times he had to give up "being the boss" to a performer was when he played for Gould. The bisexual Bernstein and Gould collaborated on several concerts and records, which fuelled speculation in some quarters that Gould was not heterosexual. Few people knew about Frances Batchen, Verna Sandercock or that "wild time" Gould had experienced with the singer in Chicago. To many, his sexuality was a non-entity, something a genius didn't have to bother with.

Bernstein was introduced to Gould the same way the Fosses had been — through Gould's recording of the *Goldberg Variations*, and for a while he and his wife, Felicia, called it their song. The Bernsteins met Gould in 1957 and the relationship lasted for most of the pianist's life. Of course, the Fosses were already friends with the Bernsteins and the four of them loved hosting parties. They partied together, they ate together (Gould was still getting over his eating disorder), they hugged and kissed (all those germs), they flaunted all that Mozart stuff (well, at least Bernstein and Foss did; Gould *said* he disliked Mozart) and the Fosses still had that old-world, German thing going about not being affectionate toward one another in public (which Gould *could* relate to). Although Gould at times bought into their glamorous little world, it was a little too hot for him; one night with everyone huddled around the piano at Bernstein's apartment, Gould accepted a glass of wine, but it made him woozy and a little out of control and he vowed never to drink alcohol again. "I couldn't play the piano properly for the rest of the night," he complained.

The Bernsteins inhabited a type of Bohemian world, similar to the one Gould had sampled back at 46 Asquith with Batchen in Toronto in the 1950s. He put up with such groups, as long as he really liked the music and the people, but in general terms, Gould preferred intellectual conversations in small groups, preferably one on one, preferably on the telephone, preferably with him doing most of the talking, and yet, he enjoyed the smarts and insights of the Fosses and Bernsteins. Like him, they were philosophers and risk-takers.

Gould likely learned of Bernstein's bisexuality early in their relationship, although biographers are not certain when. At a party, following one of their performances together in 1959 at Carnegie Hall, in which they played Mozart Concerto in C Minor, Bernstein invited Gould to his home for a party, along with David Oppenheim, director of Columbia Masterworks, and thirty other notables. According to Gould friend and fellow pianist Anton Kuerti, in front of many people Bernstein put his arm around Gould's shoulder and said, "You played so beautifully during the cadenza, I almost came in my pants." The young Kuerti, who had met Gould the previous year, was stunned. "I was a little taken aback by that type of talk, although I learned that Lenny often swore and said the F-word. I don't remember Glenn's reaction, but he probably laughed." In the years that Kuerti knew Gould, from 1958 to 1962, they never discussed Gould's sexuality. "I took him the way he was," Kuerti said.

There is no evidence that Gould had a homosexual tryst with Bernstein. "There was a lot of gossip that [Gould] might be homosexual, but I tried to dispel that notion by telling people that he was not, including Jock Carroll," Morry Kernerman said. "Some people might have thought he was gay because while he played you saw some effeminate gestures on his hands and his loose wrists. [Gould admitted his piano style was more feminine than masculine.] But he didn't seem to mind people were talking about him being different. He did have an image to maintain; he didn't mind the eccentric persona, but he seemed to be above all things of sexual nature."

On other occasions, Gould had shown some disdain for being linked to gay or bisexual men. Remember his sour reaction to Stuart Hamilton's pass at him at his parents' home in the 1950s? In those days, gays and bisexuals were not out of the closet to the same extent they are today, but it was already known in tight music circles that Bernstein had had sexual relations with Copland and other men. When Gould visited Bernstein's New York apartment in the late 1950s, his wife Felicia took the crumpled-looking Gould into the bathroom to shampoo and cut his long, matted hair. "He emerged from the bathroom looking like an angel," Bernstein later wrote. "I've never seen anything so beautiful as Glenn Gould coming out of that bathroom with his wonderful blond clean hair." And then, when Bernstein returned the visit to Gould's Toronto apartment in the 1960s, the conductor asked for a tour. "I wanted to see his apartment and said, 'Oh, this must be the bedroom,' but he wouldn't let me go in," Bernstein said. He theorized that Gould kept him out because it was as messy, or messier, than the rest of the place, but maybe Gould had other reasons. As far as we know, Gould was not threatened by Bernstein, partly because he respected him so much as a musician. The musically finicky Gould even liked Bernstein's popular music, calling *West Side Story* a masterpiece.

"Lenny really admired Glenn," said Gould's producer Paul Myers. "Lenny might have made a pass at Glenn, but Glenn never

*Glenn Gould appears pensive while vacationing in the
Bahamas in 1956. His romance with Frances Batchen
was unraveling.* (PHOTO BY JOCK CARROLL)

A painting of Frances Batchen in the 1950s by Stan Sellen.
(COURTESY STAN SELLEN)

(OPPOSITE, TOP): *Frances Batchen takes a serious pose during
the time she was dating Glenn Gould in the 1950s.*
(PHOTO BY WARREN COLLINS)

(OPPOSITE, BOTTOM): *Frances (Batchen) Barrault in her home
in England in 2008 with former student William Morris.*
(PHOTO BY MICHAEL CLARKSON)

*Filmmaker Warren Collins, a friend to Gould and
Frannie Batchen, in the 1950s.* (COURTESY WARREN COLLINS)

Warren Collins today. (COURTESY WARREN COLLINS)

Magazine writer Gladys Shenner in the late 1950s when she was close to Glenn Gould. (COURTESY GLADYS RISKIND)

Glenn Gould
32 Southwood Drive
Toronto 8, Canada

Dear Gladys,

I was awfully good to know that you arrived home unchanged by the Riviera and its social climate. Would not your distress with all it represents (which is as evident in your letter as I felt it would be and ought to be) be conducive to creating the sort of incriminating article we talked about — There is in your letter just the right quantity of resentment at having been cheated of an expected idyll. Please make it vital and do a great piece — I'm sure you could —

Glenn Gould's 1959 letter to Gladys.
(COURTESY GLADYS RISKIND)

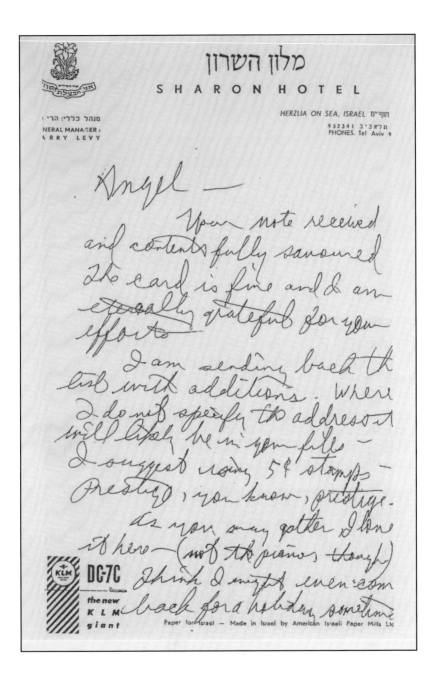

The first page of Glenn Gould's 1958 "Angel" letter to his secretary Verna Sandercock. (COURTESY VERNA POST)

Verna Sandercock in 1955, several years before she became Glenn Gould's secretary and girlfriend.
(COURTESY VERNA POST)

Verna (Sandercock) Post in Hawaii in 2007.
(COURTESY VERNA POST)

Cornelia Foss at Flying Point Beach, N.Y., in 1963.
(PHOTO BY JOHN JONAS GRUEN)

*Cornelia and Lukas Foss admire one of her paintings
in their summer home in the Hamptons in 2007.*
(PHOTO BY MICHAEL CLARKSON)

Soprano Roxolana Roslak singing in the 1970s around the time she met Glenn Gould. (COURTESY CANADIAN MUSEUM OF CONTEMPORARY PHOTOGRAPHY, OTTAWA)

Roxolana Roslak in her Toronto home in 2007.

*Pianist Monica Gaylord hides behind a mask in the
1970s. Her relationship with Gould remains a mystery.*
(COURTESY CANADIAN MUSEUM OF CONTEMPORARY PHOTOGRAPHY, OTTAWA)

Swedish music teacher Birgit Johansson in her youth, before she met Glenn Gould. (COURTESY OF MAGNUS TORDEUS)

Columbia Records' public relations representative Susan Koscis, who became close to Gould. (COURTESY SUSAN KOSCIS)

Superintendent Marilyn Kecskes examines in 2008 the damage done to Glenn Gould's mailbox decades before by curious fans. (PHOTO BY MICHAEL CLARKSON)

mentioned it. Glenn often talked about his severe Presbyterian upbringing when such things were mentioned." Ray Roberts, who became Gould's assistant in the 1970s, doubts that Bernstein ever made a pass at Gould. "I think, like many men who had male colleagues, Glenn would have seen such a thing as changing their relationship." But Gould did mention once to Roberts that he knew Bernstein "went both ways" sexually.

And yet, Gould could never really shake the rumors about his own sexuality, partly because while on tour he traveled with a massage therapist, Cornelius Dees. "Every time I visited Toronto, Gould had a Dutch masseur," said Gould's friend, Dr. Joseph Stephens. "And I would sit there with him while he was being massaged. And I thought what is this all about? Because my theory, which is absolute theory, is that everybody must be starved for human physical contact, and since he had no other physical contract that I knew of, he had physical contact with this masseur, and these sessions would go on and on." Stephens added that Dees "continually rubbed Glenn's shoulder, arms, chest and his back and Glenn seemed to enjoy it — he talked and laughed all the while. . . ." In 1960, Gould had more than one hundred visits from Dees at his apartment, which included long chats between the two men, according to Dees' daughter-in-law Elizabeth.

In his book *Beethoven's Kiss: Pianism, Perversion, and the Mastery of Desire*, author Kevin Kopelson suggested Gould was a closet gay, along with Horowitz, Pogorelich and Van Cliburn. The latter, a good friend of Gould, *was* a closet gay and, like Gould, closely guarded his sexual life and the media did not pester him about it. (In the 1990s, a longtime male lover filed a palimony suit against Van Cliburn, which was dismissed because of a lack of a written agreement.)

Gould's writer friend of the 1950s and 1960s, Ben Sonnenberg of New York, once asked him what he told people if they asked he was gay. Gould responded: "I always quote

[Vladimir] Horowitz, that there are three kinds of pianists: homosexual pianists, Jewish pianists and bad pianists. And, I add, pianists who play better than Horowitz." Yet Sonnenberg, and likely many other men, found Gould sexually attractive. "I remember being very curious about him sexually, even though I was not homosexual," Sonnenberg said. "I found him very, very attractive — he was an extremely warm and compelling person, talented, intense, all of those things.

Naomi Lightbourn believes Gould was heterosexual. "There was a lot of speculation about whether Glenn was gay," she said. "He just didn't seem that way to me." She noted how enthusiastically he reacted to fan letters from women.

At the same time, Gould was not worried about gays or bisexuals, CBC producer John Roberts said. "Glenn was strong in his shoes; he knew who he was."

Still, into the 1970s, rumors were out there that Gould was gay. "A newspaper reporter asked me if Glenn was into the same sex and I told him I had no idea and no interest in finding out," said Gould's CBC publicist Linda Litwack. Fans may never know if Gould had a gay liaison, but there is no evidence that one ever occurred and no reason to believe it did.

In any event, Gould's sexuality was not as important as the public perception of it, according to University of Toronto music professor Robin Elliott. "There's a theory that all great stars are bisexual in their performance mode," he said. "[Gould] was appealing to both men and women sexually. It's an attraction fans have for Hollywood stars, leading musicians and celebrities."

Along with his friendship and collaboration with Bernstein, Gould let his relationship with Lukas and Cornelia Foss blossom into the 1960s. Gould expressed an interest in performing a concert in Buffalo after it was rumored that Lukas Foss would be appointed conductor of the Buffalo Philharmonic Orchestra. Despite the orchestra material being sent on his behalf for a performance in January 1963, however, the concert was never held.

Through this exciting, transitional early period with the Fosses, Gould was winding down his long friendship with journalist Gladys Shenner who was living in Montreal. "Glenn was still calling me faithfully a couple of times a week and we'd talk for two hours," she said. "He loved hearing about my social life. He wanted to know about my boyfriends and what I was doing, although it didn't go over too well with one of them. He used to tell me he didn't concertize that much in New York and when he made records there he had to drive all over the city because he didn't like the hotel beds there. We didn't have much talk about music. I always felt that I was his link to the real world — the world outside that he had no interest in joining. . . . He didn't want to join the real world because I think he got what he wanted from his music." Gould was also deep in thought about finally retiring from the concert stage, she said.

Suddenly, as he was about to turn thirty-one, his relationship with Shenner crashed. "He stopped calling and I never heard from him for a while," Riskind said. "When I called to find out what was going on, he said he didn't have time to talk, that he was getting a massage. He said he'd call me back, but he never did. I guess that was par for the course. He's controlled relationships and done that to other people, cut them off all of a sudden." Shenner never heard from Gould again. After his death in 1982, a document was found in Gould's Toronto apartment, apparently a draft of a letter written in the early 1960s. It read:

Dear Gladys:
I gather you tried to call me yesterday, so this letter
– though difficult – is necessary.
*   You are as well aware as anyone by what intuition*
I am sometimes governed; upon what "unreason" my
decisions are sometimes based. And this intuition in
the business of human relations is a force which I
serve quite without question; and when it seems to

*demand isolation from one person or from everyone –
that too is obeyed. However illogical and unpredictable, and infuriating this may be to others, I have
found in this obedience – however arbitrarily I may
have used it – a source of immense strength.*

*And I can only ask you to be charitable and forgive
me, and believe me when I tell you that you are in
no way responsible for this – except in the sense that
we are all of us responsible for the world's becoming
– to try to understand when I say that the one thing
I will not do is to analyze – to explain my reactions
– except to myself, and once again to believe me when
I tell you that I hold you in as much affection as ever.*

Gould biographer Kevin Bazzana said that Gould sometimes cut off women if he felt they were becoming a threat to
his emotions or his career and yet he wanted to spare their feelings. (A similar good-bye letter was found after Gould's death,
addressed to a woman named Eliza sometime in the 1960s: "Of
course we parted friends — why shouldn't we? However much
I may have upset you it was, at worst, the result of a thought-
lessness sometimes characteristic of me but never the intent of
deliberate malice. So you must believe that I could not but
think of you kindly." Eliza was never identified.) To this day,
Shenner says she never pressured Gould to have a sexual relationship with her. "I never talked about going further than we
did; it was what it was. We were intimate friends, but not intimate sexually."

Shenner would come to believe that Gould's blossoming
relationship with Cornelia Foss in the early 1960s had an
impact on her. "Their relationship began about the time Glenn
and I no longer kept in touch so maybe that had something to
do with it," Riskind said, adding that she never received a kiss-
off letter from Gould. While they had been friends, she had

received four letters from him — "they were caring and warm ... and I have his autograph." But she remains disappointed he cut her off. "I was hurt, but at first more angry than hurt. He never gave me a reason," she said. She never saw Gould after 1963, although she considered contacting him several times, "but I got married, had children, my life changed and I got very busy. In retrospect, I realize that at the time Glenn ended our relationship, he was seriously re-evaluating his life, and he did stop concertizing within a year. Also, his actions with me would foreshadow a lifelong pattern of suddenly walking away from friendships for no outward reason. But Glenn never wanted to get close to any one person — although he needed people on his terms, and usually over the phone."

Also in 1963, Gould contacted one of his old protégés, Cynthia Millman of Ottawa, who was in Toronto while on holidays from Vienna. "He wanted us to get together, but I was hesitant," she recalled. "By that time, I was under the spell of his playing and his personality. I became almost afraid to get in touch with him again. I still regret that I didn't, but being in his presence could be daunting. His intellect was powerful." (After returning from her studies in Vienna in the late 1960s, Millman remained hesitant about renewing her friendship with Gould. When she got married in 1970, her husband encouraged her to contact Gould, but she never did. "I always felt guilty that I never really thanked him for helping me. I really admired him. He was my idol.")

It's possible, of course, that Gould simply wanted to renew his teacher-student rapport with Millman. Shortly before he contacted Millman in 1963, he had told the *Globe and Mail* that he saw himself partly as a teacher and a lecturer, "yet I feel that teaching, which tends to dissect the teacher too closely, is bad. There's always danger in speaking of self in the teaching forum. If one can maintain objectivity, then teaching can be satisfying and successful." Following an American concert tour in 1963,

Gould delivered several lectures at universities and music organizations.

When Lukas Foss officially became conductor in Buffalo in 1963, the Fosses started spending more time with Gould, who lived just a ninety-minute drive up the Queen Elizabeth Way highway in Toronto. In early September, the Fosses moved briefly into a motel in Buffalo, then bought a big old Victorian house in that city. Highly industrial Buffalo was a hardly a garden city or cultural Mecca, but it boasted friendly, home-grown people and, Cornelia noted, "wide streets and so many trees." Buffalo, known for its chicken wings, beef on weck sandwiches and its professional sports teams more than its classical music, still went out of its way to embrace the Fosses. Just two weeks after they moved to that city, the *Buffalo Evening News* featured an article on Cornelia and her family, complete with a photo showing a glamorous-looking Cornelia in lipstick and medium-length, Mary Tyler Moore hair (a style Gould loved), holding her two children, Eliza, eighteen months, and Christopher, six. It looked like a happy young family, although Lukas was not in the photo and was not quoted in the article. "Mrs. Lukas Foss is a petite blond with blue eyes, a warm smile and a quiet composed manner," the article opened. "The wife of the new conductor of the Buffalo Philharmonic Orchestra, an artist, mother and homemaker, emits a calm and casualness which disguise her demanding roles and busy schedule . . ." Despite losing most of her paintings in the Los Angeles fire, Cornelia continued her career as a painter and sculptor, exhibiting in Buffalo. In her work, she said, she was "trying to give a valid expression to all my most moving experiences." She explained her art: "It is not non-objective art. The object may not be clearly definable, but it is there."

Part of Cornelia's busy schedule soon involved an eccentric pianist in Toronto. "Glenn phoned my home a lot. It started out as a friendship with Lukas and Glenn and me," she said. In

January 1963, Gould and Foss were still buddies, as Gould wrote a letter to a CBC executive, recommending Lukas for a television show: "You might wish to keep him in mind for a CBC engagement sometime in the future . . . he is a marvelous musician and a very lively personality." But Gould and Foss's wife were starting to make their own music together — on the heels of one or more affairs that Foss himself had with other women, according to mutual friends. Gould felt at ease with the well-traveled Cornelia's broad view of the world; around this time he was quoted in a documentary that he liked associating with people who had a general view of society rather than artists who may be narrow-minded and egotistical.

"Slowly, Glenn and I began a love affair," Cornelia Foss said when she finally broke her silence in 2007. "Our life together moved slowly forward and was carefully planned, over many years." Suddenly, she found herself caught between two blue-eyed pianists with strong faces that looked deeply into life, enthralled by the magic that music did to them and *through* them. But their personalities were different: Gould sometimes bordered on reclusive, whereas Lukas was more animated. Both were highly driven in their musical careers. "They were very passionate, had enormous ability and had great love for what they were doing," Cornelia said. "I think Lukas was even more passionate and driven than Glenn."

Apparently, Lukas began to get suspicious of Gould's developing romance with his wife when Gould would telephone their home, pretending to be someone else, as he often did for fun, introducing himself as one of his many alter egos — Sir Nigel Twitt-Thornwaite, the dean of British conductors; Theodore Slutz, a New York cabbie; or Herbert von Hochmeister, sage of the Arctic. Gould would sometimes have his calls answered by the Fosses' "Chinese maid," not realizing that the maid was actually Lukas, returning the joke (or perhaps getting revenge on the suitor of his wife).

Even before their marriage got shaky, Lukas and Cornelia were not public lovebirds. "They never seemed that pleased to see one another," one friend said. "They were German, not touchy." Other friends noticed that Lukas was chasing other women, and it was this, some believe, that drove Cornelia into the arms of Gould and put their marriage on the rocks at Flying Point Beach in the Hamptons, where the Fosses socialized in the soft winds of summer. Cornelia should have seen the affairs coming; later, she would reflect in a 2002 biography of her friend Caroline Blackwood entitled *Dangerous Muse*: "You have to remember this was the 1960s, when everyone was cavorting around like mad. There was just something in the air that made it possible. No one frowned on it — the possibilities seemed endless. No one understood yet what harm it could do, not simply to oneself and to one's partner, but to the children."

One would have thought entering into an affair with a married woman would have been the last thing for Gould, raised in a strict, religious home, the Last Puritan himself, but in the early 1960s, he was going through a transition stage and beginning to look at his work, and perhaps life, in a different light. For years, he had talked about walking off the concert stage for good and becoming a composer and producer of documentaries for radio and television. In his personal life perhaps he could enter a serious relationship, perhaps marriage, perhaps fatherhood.

In his early thirties, finally living on his own, Gould *looked* like a man, having put on a few pounds with his hair starting to lose its battle with time. His expression seemed to be getting more intense, more lived-in, sucking in all the thoughts and issues and pain of the world and holding them tight, deciding what to do with them, his eyes more mature, like they had seen more than they had bargained for. Yet to Cornelia, Gould showed flashes of a little boy with many needs, dressed in ruffled shirts and odd socks, with sunglasses from the lost and found.

She knew how to handle him.
— CBC producer John Roberts,
on Cornelia Foss's relationship with Glenn Gould

The MUSIC
INTENSIFIES

Chapter ELEVEN

To this day, Cornelia Foss remains reluctant to provide details of her early romance with Glenn Gould, but her friend and Gould biographer Otto Friedrich said it began while the pianist was still on tour prior to 1964, which made it difficult for the lovers to get together. They met when they could in New York, Buffalo or Toronto. Sometimes Gould carried black-and-white photographs of Cornelia with him, from hotel room to lonely hotel room, to remind him of what new and exciting life might lay ahead for him — one of them showed Cornelia sitting on the sand at Flying Point Beach in oversized sunglasses and a loose top, a breeze sifting through her long blond hair, arms around her knees in a vulnerable pose, looking away from the sea, smiling as though she had just spotted someone she liked. In his thirties, Glenn Gould was a teenager in love with the Face That Launched a Thousand Fugues.

At one stage, while the Fosses were living in Buffalo, Cornelia came to visit Toronto with her two young children and their two dogs to stay in an upscale downtown hotel, according to Gould's close friend, opera singer Joan Maxwell. "They had naturally planned to leave their two huge St. Bernards at home," Maxwell said. "Glenn became very upset, insisting that the children had to have their dogs with them; he could be very persuasive, so in the end the family came, animals and all. The noise of the dogs and the mess from their hair caused complaints that prompted the hotel manager to ask them to leave. Glenn was irate at this irrational justice and went on at great length about how unbelievable it was."

And so it began — the sophisticated Hamptonite artist and the Phantom of the Sonata. In 1965, the *Buffalo Evening News* described Cornelia as a "pretty, vibrant woman who still has something of the look of a school girl." She seemed in the prime of her career as an artist and she touted the 1960s as "a good time to be a painter — so many ideas are popping." Her work had roots in the long tradition of the Renaissance, but her treatment of still life had a contemporary look: a woman eating spaghetti, bars of soap over a faucet in a kitchen sink and a table filled with breakfast treats of bacon, eggs, toast and a coffee pot. More somber works included a depiction of the death of Alexander the Great. But something was about to happen that would put her career as an artist on hold for years.

All along the Cornelia trail, workaholic Gould continued to press ahead with his career, or what would become of it. He had been talking for so long about quitting the concert tour that nobody believed him. But he wasn't the boy who cried wolf: he had started reducing his public performances as early as 1961 when Homburger's secretary Verna Sandercock took no advance bookings past 1964. By 1962, he was telling the Fosses, Bernstein and others that he was through and was planning for the end, that he was sick of being a vaudevillian, performing before audiences who were distracting, coughing and waiting for him to make a slipup. "He told me he was tired of being showcased onstage, in front of a crowd," Cornelia said. As well, Gould wanted to create a purer form of music in the recording studio, which he felt would help a listener get closer to the composer and the message of the music. His retirement as a concert performer finally happened without a farewell tour or even an announcement; on Friday night, April 10, 1964, Gould performed his final concert at the Wilshire Ebell Theater in Los Angeles, which was actually a rescheduled concert for one he had earlier canceled. Perhaps that was fitting, in light of the number of concerts he had canceled during his controversial stage career, which had begun in 1951. Gould played four fugues from *The Art of Fugue*, Bach's Partita no. 4 in D Major, Beethoven's op. 109 and Hindemith's Third Sonata. Nothing was wrong with his form, and the nearly sold-out audience, which did not include the Fosses, gave him a warm ovation. After the performance, Homburger suggested Gould may take a sabbatical and return to the stage after a few years. There was one more concert scheduled on Gould's tour, a Mozart Concerto in Minneapolis on April 17, 1964, but Gould canceled it. At the time, no one realized they were seeing the end of Gould's career as a performer.

Meanwhile, Lukas Foss's public career kept moving forward and by the mid-1960s he was firmly entrenched in music circles nationally and internationally. And, although he lacked the charisma of his friend Bernstein, Foss was a fun guy, even dashing at times, and could relate to the audience. The Mozart Christmas concert in New York on December 24, 1964, performed by Foss's Buffalo Philharmonic, was joyful, if at times unsophisticated. According to a *New York Times* review, the "timpanist will produce huge thumps and his tube player great blasts in a manner unheard of from more sophisticated major orchestras . . . and Mr. Foss is willing to crack the Great Maestro façade on the podium. He rushes tempos when he feels like it, he dwells on certain specifics of sonority as only a composer would, he enthusiastically shakes hands with everyone when a piece is over, he prances onto the stage as though wearing sneakers on the way to tennis." When Foss played the piano, he hurries "as the delightful effort of a quirky individual, rather than the unsophisticated gaffs of a non–Madison Avenue type."

When Glenn was separated from Cornelia, he carried with

him sexy photographs of her taken on the sun-basked Hamptons' shore. And then on a ship, someone, presumably a family member or friend, snapped a photo of them sitting together on deck chairs. Both are in sunglasses, wearing warm clothes and smiling (well, as much as G.G. ever gave himself away). Cornelia has her head tilted in a youthful way, as though she is very happy to be there.

Despite attempts to be secretive about their relationship, Glenn and Cornelia began being seen in public, or talking about each other, and soon others began noticing something more than a platonic relationship blooming between the two. Gould's producer, Andrew Kazdin, was one of them. "I knew they were close because Glenn would talk about her like she was his partner and he would refer to her in conversations . . . well, Cornelia thinks this, or that, about someone. I heard that they would talk for hours on the phone when he was in Toronto and she was somewhere in New York," he said. "They would fall asleep with the phones in their ears. There was always talk of the length of [Gould's] phone bill."

Cornelia fit many criteria that Gould was looking for in a woman — she was intelligent, had a broad view of the world, liked stimulating conversation, could speak German, as well as Italian, and could think for herself. Like Franny Batchen, she had an inner strength and a smile that lit up her eyes and put you at ease. She and Gould grew increasingly closer and by 1967, he asked Cornelia to marry him. She says considered it for some time because they were in love. "I didn't really say no in the beginning," she said. Glenn Gould a husband? A stepfather to two children? A domestic animal? Maybe it would work a second time, after the failed, off-and-on romance with Batchen, who was now long gone in the United Kingdom, set to marry another pianist.

Glenn Gould and Cornelia Foss made a rare appearance together in 1967 at a private screening in New York for one of his television programs. "It was a different Glenn Gould that I saw during that day," Kazdin wrote in his book *Glenn Gould at Work*. "Instead of the self-absorbed center of attention, I witnessed an attentive escort to Cornelia. Was she comfortable? Could he get her anything? There was no doubt that Cornelia Foss held a special place in his life." (And yet Kazdin never suspected that they were a couple, never mind had sex; twenty-five years later, Kazdin still maintained Gould never had a girlfriend and that "the piano was his mistress.")

One wonders what Lukas Foss felt about his wife entering into a serious relationship with a man he had admired so much for a decade. In 1967, several years after his wife had begun her affair with Gould, *Saturday Review* said of Lukas Foss: "He is well liked by young people and regularly blasted by the critics. He has accomplished remarkable things, made terrible blunders, and still moves ever onward and upward . . . he is no doubt a Golden Boy, one of the few to make enemies and mistakes and survive both — unsaddened, almost unscathed, and sometimes a little wiser." Foss had become famous enough that a resident in Gould's Toronto apartment building, piano teacher William Vaisey, had a clippings file on him in his filing cabinet.

Also in 1967 in Toronto, producer Judith Pearlman met Gould at Columbia's regional office to discuss the possibility of her producing a film version of Gould's successful radio show *The Idea of North*. New Yorker Pearlman later moved to Toronto for two short periods (a total of nine months) in the fall of 1969 and spring of 1970 to produce the television show. "I met Cornelia in Toronto. I saw [Gould] a lot and talked to him on the phone a lot," she said. Pearlman described Cornelia Foss as having a *fey* personality, "a little quirky . . . she had her blond hair up in a loose, not-very-tight bun with little strands of hair escaping from it. She did not overdress, with not much makeup, and she did not appear as high society." Gould seemed happy around Cornelia, Pearlman added. "It seemed like it was a happy time for Glenn. I never saw him discouraged. He always seemed very cheerful. It was a very good time in his life. And when we were working, he was very productive."

Pearlman believes Gould felt more comfortable with women than men. "You could call Glenn an eighteenth-century man; he was extremely polite and gallant toward women. He liked working with women and was very gracious and very courtly. He called me 'Madame.'" Gould was not as gracious with men, Pearlman said. "He could charm the birds out of the trees when he wanted something, but with men, he could be temperamental, even angry." She said their relationship was professionally intense "but I wasn't attracted to him. It wasn't sexual. Cornelia had the unique perspective of knowing him that way. He'd call me up on the phone and we'd have endless conversations, a lot of musical talk." Gould was reluctant to share his feelings about Cornelia with her, although he would sometimes talk about "his strong likes and dislikes. He was very private but not cold. He was not truly reclusive, just selective. He always had a group of people around; he liked a little family type of group."

But if Glenn was going to have a family of his own, he would have to rupture another family — the Fosses.

But my boss told me, "You're in your early
twenties – you can't just go off and do that!"
– Carol (Hodgdon) Goodfriend

Crushed
by CAROL

Chapter TWELVE

While falling in love with Cornelia Foss, Glenn Gould remained attracted to other women. To the folks at Columbia Records in New York, the pianist had a crush on Carol Hodgdon, the secretary of one of Gould's producers, Paul Myers. "I knew Glenn adored her — many times when he came to my office, he came to see her, not me," Myers said.

"It was thought that Glenn was sweet on her," said his other Columbia producer, Andrew Kazdin, who worked just down the hall from Myers. "He always went out of his way to find her."

Hodgdon was young, bubbly, charming and well educated — "a nice girl from a good Connecticut family, everyone's kid sister," Myers said. Gould met her in 1963 when he was about to make the switch from stage performer to studio musician/ documentary filmmaker.

"He used to call me every day for long, long chats," said Hodgdon, now Carol Goodfriend. "He was obviously very philosophical and was studying the work of [George] Santayana ["Those who cannot remember the past are condemned to repeat it."]. And he was prophetic in technology. Music technology really hadn't been invented but he told me how he was learning to maneuver music with an enhanced sound that became really quite astonishing. He was blending video and music together. Obviously in his brain, he could see what we are now doing on the Internet and in films and theater." Gould seemed attracted to Hodgdon's love of the outdoors. She had majored in music at Smith College, playing the piano and doing some singing, while taking part in competitive skiing, swimming and tennis. "I was an austere athlete," Goodfriend said. She was attracted to Gould, as well — "but I wasn't in awe of him; I grew up as a practical New England girl." Still, the two occasionally flirted. "I was a flirt who liked to have fun, but we never mentioned sex," she said. "I already had a boyfriend and it never occurred to me he might have had a crush on me, but I was naive in those days. I thought of him as a brain guy, a sweet guy, an amazing guy."

In 1965, Hodgdon said, Gould asked her to go to the end of the world with him — Hudson's Bay — for what would become one of the signature works of Gould's new career as a radio broadcaster, his *Solitude Trilogy*. It was supposed to be a solitary, soul-searching journey for Gould in his first full year away from the chaos of an international concert career, but he wanted Hodgdon to share with him the train trip of thousands of miles from Winnipeg to Churchill on the shore on the famous frigid bay. "I was interested in geology and geography and I really wanted to go with him, and it would have been a great adventure," Hodgdon said. "But my boss told me, 'You're in your early twenties — you can't just go off and do that!'" Gould, who was thirty-two, eventually did make the trip aboard the *Muskeg Express* in 1965, presumably on his own, in what became a conceptual and cerebral journey, despite his aversion to the cold in normal circumstances. He interviewed many passengers on the train for his CBC Radio documentary *The Idea of North*, which was followed in his trilogy in 1968 by *The Latecomers*, focusing on the isolation of Newfoundland and in 1977 by *The Quiet in the Land*, about Mennonites confronting modern society. For this series, Gould invented a new art form, which he dubbed "contrapuntal radio," featuring a montage of voices, often speaking over one another, and emotional effects.

In August 1967, Hodgdon quit Columbia while she was dating James Goodfriend, who was Gould's Masterworks literary editor for liner notes that accompanied twenty-five of his record albums. One day not long after, she returned to the New York office to announce she was marrying Goodfriend. Instead of going directly to Myers' office, where Gould was chatting with Paul, Hodgdon went into the nearby office of Gould's other producer, Andrew Kazdin, to talk to her former colleagues. "From my office, [Gould] heard Carol's voice in the other room and he crashed out of the room to see her," Myers said. Upon arriving in Kazdin's office, Gould stretched his arms wide, hugged the woman he had once asked to go to Hudson's Bay with him and gave her *a kiss* in front of numerous witnesses. Myers found it funny that Gould went to such lengths of public affection, despite his supposed "aversion for being touched." Had Cornelia softened him up by this point?

Hodgdon was also taken aback. "I was surprised, and it was the only time he kissed me. It made me feel special," she said. But then the mood suddenly changed when she made an announcement. "I told everybody I was going to get married to James in a couple of weeks and we were going to Europe. Glenn kind of plopped down on the couch and didn't say much."

When the Goodfriends returned from their honeymoon, Gould suddenly did not want James to edit his liner notes anymore, Carol said. Then the scenario took a stranger twist — after James left Columbia Records to become classical music editor of *Stereo Review* magazine, Gould began to grumble that the magazine was starting to give him bad reviews. He told Kazdin that the reason for this was that James was secretly jealous of him because of his friendship with Carol. "I think [Gould] had a type of arrested development with emotions and with women," Kazdin said. "He could be naive."

To this day, James Goodfriend denies that *Stereo Review* gave Gould bad press for any reason. Myers doubted that Goodfriend had shown bias toward Gould. "When he was in the U.S. Army, James had one of the highest IQs and he was honest as the day is long," Myers said. Carol Goodfriend now believes that Gould's bitterness stemmed not from any bad review, but the fact that she married James and he was jealous. Myers believed that the Carol-Glenn relationship was platonic. "Glenn was just enthusiastic about her. She was interested in the outdoors aspect of his life. I'd stake my life on the fact they never had sex."

In the 1960s, Gould did start to lose some of his sexual prudishness, although his naivety took some time to thaw. One night in a restaurant, a man approached him with pornographic photos for sale. Gould was so stunned, he later told Joseph Stephens, "I had no idea there were such things. I was absolutely shocked." Yet a few years later, Gould became a huge fan of the erotic and surreal Japanese novel and subsequent movie *Woman in the Dunes*, in which an insect collector is held captive in a huge sandpit in a vast expanse of seaside desert and becomes a widow's lover there, calming his anxiety by drinking sake. Over the years, Gould reportedly watched the black-and-white film (released in 1964) one hundred times, studying it frame by frame. More than likely he related to the protagonist, Niki, or perhaps the quirky woman, who was part-lover, part-caregiver. Gould might have also related to the plot, which holds that if life is absurd and meaningless, one might as well resign oneself and make the most of it. Gould once said, "To be incarcerated would be the perfect test of one's inner mobility and of the strength which would enable one to opt creatively out of the human situation." In one scene, after binding and gagging the beautiful woman, then releasing her, Niki rolls half-naked with her in the hot and sticky sand as they groan and make love to music that resembles sirens far off in the night, then they curl up in one another's arms. In the end, following years of living with the woman, Niki turns down his chance for escape from the dunes after she becomes pregnant with his child. Gould called it "quite possibly the greatest film ever made."

And so, it is possible that the mid to late 1960s was a type of sexual awakening for Gould, who had previously jammed so many of his energies, perhaps even some of his sexual energies, into his concert career. In his twenties and thirties, Gould seemed to develop a liking for such risqué movies and was enthralled by the sex scenes, according to Paul Myers. "He would suggest we go to the movies and he always picked the ones which were red-hot in those days — Italian movies, *Woman in the Dunes* and *Seven and a Half*," Myers said. "They were always movies with more than the usual sexual interest, although they would be considered innocent by today's standards." Gould rarely talked to Myers about sex or women and "seemed almost slightly prudish." Myers added that Gould loved women's company and to entertain them — "even with a cleaning lady in a hotel, he would stop to chat."

In the mid-1960s, Gould sometimes discussed sex with New York writer and friend Richard Kostelanetz, or rather "theories of the female orgasm." In 1967, Kostelanetz wrote in *Esquire* that Gould's Protestant ideas "haunt his consciousness to this day."

But during this period, of course, Gould had a real-life girl from the sand dunes, Cornelia Foss, and he was about to take a huge step in his relationship with her.

Bach would have been horrified.
— Cornelia Foss

To TORONTO

Finally, in late 1967 or early 1968, Cornelia decided to leave Lukas. Gould biographer Otto Friedrich (a friend of Cornelia's) said that was because serious problems had developed in their marriage, but in an interview with me in 2007, Cornelia would not go that far. "There were a few problems in our marriage, but that's not why I left — I fell in love with someone else," she said. One day, Cornelia put her two children, Christopher (ten), and Eliza (six), into their station wagon and left Buffalo. "I'll never forget Lukas standing by the station wagon and smiling," she recalled. "I said, 'Why are you smiling? I'm leaving you for Glenn.' He said, 'Don't be ridiculous, you'll be back.'"

Word spread around the Hamptons' community of musicians, writers and artists. "When I heard about it all, I was quite taken by Cornelia's guts in doing such a thing — I thought it was brave and daring and, actually, quite romantic," said John Jonas Gruen, who knew the Fosses and published several photographs of them in his book *The Sixties: Young in the Hamptons*. "I mean, taking the children as well as her *cat!*"

Gould's financial records show that he began helping Cornelia with expenses for herself and her two children as early as January 1968 — about $400 a month, even though he was in a brief earnings' slump (Gould showed a loss of about $8,000 in 1968, although he bounced back the following year to show

147

a profit). Cornelia bought a house in Toronto's Rosedale district, not far from Gould's apartment on St. Clair Avenue West, but then she rented it out to a University of Toronto professor and moved with her two children into another house at 55 Summerhill Avenue, just an eight-minute walk from St. Clair. "Glenn and I weren't married, so we decided we shouldn't have the same place," Foss said.

She and Gould saw one another often, sometimes at the homes of friends and colleagues like producer John Roberts, who had met Gould professionally in 1956 and also became his buddy. (In fact, when Roberts moved to Toronto in 1957, Gould was the only person whom Roberts knew in that city and Gould invited Roberts into his family.) "They came to our house for supper and it was quite clear he just adored her with great affection and he talked of her with great enthusiasm," Roberts said of Gould and Foss. Gould never referred to her as his girlfriend, Roberts added, "but they were very, very friendly toward one another. Glenn Gould was, how can I put this? In a sense, he was not a physical person and he didn't like being touched. In all the years I knew him, I never really shook his hand. You had to be careful. I think Glenn forgot he had a body; he was all mind and it never stopped ticking and we always teased him about it. What interested him was the intellectual; he had an amazing concept of music, almost an X-ray grasp of music, a photographic memory. He had a very physical relationship with his instruments." But Roberts added that he did not doubt Gould could have had a sexual affair with Foss. "She was absolutely delightful . . . she was a woman who had a lovely way of speaking and thinking and a very good sense of humor. She was extremely bright and a good match for him."

"She was a very, very lovely, a nice lady, and I liked her a lot," said Lorne Tulk, a CBC engineer who worked on Gould's radio shows. "In some respects, she was something like him . . . lively. Her mind was going all the time and his mind was going all the time, so the two of them got on very well." Gould was fond of Tulk's family and played games with his children.

Foss's children, Eliza and Chris, had some difficulty adjusting to their new home. "It was certainly traumatic at first, but Glenn was very warm and very caring and my experiences with him were great," Eliza says today.

Initially, Chris had "this dynamic of resenting Glenn. I realized he was the stand-in for my father and not really appreciating that. . . . I remember resisting calling him Uncle Glenn. But he was actually extremely respectful and sweet about my father and the fact is that Glenn became someone I ended up loving, adoring."

Judith Pearlman saw Glenn Gould and Cornelia Foss socially for dinner or movies. "They weren't lovey-dovey, but circumspect because her kids were around. But they were intimate in personality and had little verbal jokes between them. It was clear they were a couple, comfortable with each another. The question of sex has always been the big question mark in this case." At one point, Pearlman went to Gould's penthouse at St. Clair and found it, unlike his mind, to be disorderly. "There was no room for anyone else to live in but one person. There were two Steinways, tons of music and papers and records everywhere."

At Cornelia's house, the couple would sometimes invite friends and colleagues for dinner, such as Pearlman and John Roberts and his wife. They would talk about music and Shakespeare and sometimes play corny games such as Twenty Questions. For Gould, it may have been an experiment in fatherhood, in domestic affairs. Foss relished being a host, according to Pearlman. "She was a good host and cooked for us, but Glenn was not." Friends said that Gould could be a cordial guest, but if you went over to his place, you'd be lucky to be offered a glass of water because, most often, he would want to feast off his own menu, which was talking about his music, or his philosophy. (Ironically, in 1971, CBC producer Susan Edwards wrote to Gould, asking him to be a food critic for a television show. He declined.)

In some ways, Gould and Foss made an odd couple — a socialite sometimes in pearls and he in a battleship gray expression and a British driving cap and winter gloves, yet they were both intense intellectuals who liked mind games. She fell for his quirky sense of humor. "He wrote his own review on the back of one of his record covers!" she said. "One day he rolled on the floor laughing because the University of Toronto had started a course called 'The Mind of Glenn Gould.' 'Imagine how ridiculous!' he said. He wanted to go to a class, disguised in a wig, but he never did."

They had some grand times together. Paul Myers socialized with Gould and Foss a number of times in Toronto and New York. In Toronto, Myers said, Gould hated to be spotted by fans, so they would go to the upscale Benvenuto restaurant on a hill with a window overlooking the growing city, where the staff protected him. In Manhattan, Gould's pet eateries were the Stockholm Restaurant on Fiftieth Street and the Egg Basket. At the Stockholm, they kept a necktie available for Gould, who would show up in casual dress. "I don't think he owned a tie," Myers said. "I always told him to please bring a tie and a clean shirt to our recording sessions. Once, he brought a new shirt with the pins still in it. I can see my ties on many of his portraits and record covers. It's quite charming." The Egg Basket was one of Gould's favorites because the chef, Dione Lucas, was world-famous for her egg dishes and would make his scrambled eggs just as he adored them. "He lived on his scrambles," Myers said.

Myers liked Cornelia. "She was pleasant and polite, but a little hazy, slightly vague. I remember she liked poetry." He recalled that Gould was enraptured by Foss. At restaurants "he would sit with his back to the door, but spend a lot of time turning around to see if she was coming in." However, Gould kept Cornelia away from everyone except a close group of friends, Myers said. "He never talked a lot about her and it was a great secret." Other close friends protected Gould and his secret, like John Roberts. "I would bug John for details about Cornelia, but he wouldn't say much," Myers said.

Gould was tight-lipped with the media about his personal life; he agreed to give Kostelanetz an interview for a story in *Esquire*, but Gould told him, "Okay, I'd like to help you. But I have two stipulations. You shan't interview any of my family or friends. They won't honor your request. Second, that we do as much of this as possible over the phone."

And yet stories of Gould and Foss made the rounds in entertainment circles and among friends and family; Gould's cousin Jessie Greig told a friend that Glenn had a girlfriend, but she didn't name her. According to Pearlman, a number of people in the industry knew about the affair and there was a lot of curiosity: "At a party, a psychiatrist took me aside and wanted to know about Glenn and Cornelia, all the gossip. Where did Glenn meet Cornelia, how close were they? He wanted to know more, but I never talked about it."

"There were rumors that Gould was involved with the wife of a musician," said Linda Litwack, Gould's public relations person at the CBC in the 1970s, who also knew Lukas Foss, "but at first I didn't make the connection in my mind, and I don't think a lot of people did. Then at one point, it occurred to me they were having an affair. It was so bizarre." Another rumor, according to producer Andrew Kazdin, was that the pianist had moved out of his apartment and into a hotel and he suspected it had something to do with Cornelia. But that rumor was probably unfounded. This was an affair that seemed heavily weighted toward domesticity. Gould and Foss, who both loved nature, took her kids on trips to hotels in Ontario's vast Muskoka region, where they reportedly slept in different rooms. Her son Chris recalls traveling the back roads: "It was a really uninteresting motor-home environment. I think any-thing pretentious made him ill, frankly." Gould's ledger for July 1968 shows that he used $400 cash for himself, $287 for "Mrs. Cornelia Foss," $21 for flowers and $218 for three motels. In 1969, Gould gave Foss about $6,000 in monthly increments. Gould was also using massage therapist Cornelius Dees on a regular basis and in October he paid Dees $500.

In Toronto, the couple spent a lot of time at Cornelia's house, close to the wooded ravine, an escape in the middle of the city where the couple could go for long strolls along bab-bling creeks, backed by an orchestra of robins and black squirrels. They did not spend as much time at Gould's apart-ment. Marilyn Kecskes, who worked at Gould's apartment building from 1969 and was its superintendent from 1973 until his death in 1982, said that, over the years, he brought few women to the building, which at the time was his studio for practicing and writing. "I don't know any woman who could have lived in that apartment with Mr. Gould — he was so ter-ribly messy," Kecskes said, referring to empty milk containers, newspapers and music scores littering the penthouse.

Not only was Gould reluctant to clean up, but when it came to fixing things, he was no handyman. Gould's assistant Ray Roberts recalls getting a phone call from Cornelia, who was a little panicky over a blown fuse in her house, but Gould had no idea what to do about such matters. Fortunately, Roberts, who was Gould's jack-of-all-trades, was with the pianist at that moment. "Glenn handed me the phone," Roberts said. "She had plugged a kettle, or something, into a wall socket and it had blown and blackened the wall. I told her not to touch it, to get an electrician, which I think she did."

Just as it would be difficult to believe that Marilyn Monroe did not take interest in her husband Joe DiMaggio's baseball playing with the New York Yankees, it's hard to fathom that Cornelia Foss did not like the other love of Glenn Gould's life

— composer Johann Sebastian Bach — or at least his liberal interpretation of Bach's music. "Bach has a religious theme," Foss explained. "You see, my grandfather Rudolph was the dean of St. Lorenz Cathedral in Nuremberg. You can't treat Bach like a clock, take it apart and put it back together. But Glenn liked to play around with it, rather than to stay with the intention of the composer. Bach would have been horrified." Yet Foss, who was not a musician, loved Gould's interpretation of Beethoven's work — "He got that right. He was a great pianist."

Glenn Gould and Cornelia Foss did not talk much about music and yet when they did, the usually thin-skinned pianist was able to swallow her criticism. "In the beginning, she was a bit critical of his piano playing and he loved that," John Roberts said. "It was very good for him; she knew how to handle him. If you knew him well, he could take criticism, but you had to be careful. He would go into the voices of his fictitious characters so it really wasn't him you were criticizing . . . you could never have a confrontation with Glenn; it would be a disaster. But he accepted it from her, he so admired her." With previous girlfriends, Gould had phoned them in the night to get their feedback on his music, but he did not do that so much with Cornelia. In a way, it was a more well balanced relationship than he had with other women — when she was with him, his music was never an elephant in the room. In fact, Foss likely did not influence Gould's music directly, Roberts said, "but he would've had great solace in talking with her. She was a soul mate. He was not normal and had practically no friends. I was one of the few people he didn't cut off." (We now know that Gould had more friends than some people realized.)

As well, Foss was not enamored with the few compositions that Gould had fashioned, including his String Quartet of the 1950s. "They weren't very good," she said.

However, she was impressed with Gould the philosopher. "He had tremendous ideas and thought patterns with a very original mind," she said. "He was interested in so many things passionately." Foss helped to motivate Gould at times, friends said. In fact, it's possible that Cornelia's intelligence, philosophy and theories influenced Gould at the point in his career where he was making the transition from concert pianist to maker of documentary radio, film documentaries and television shows. Foss herself did some apprentice work with filmmaker Anna Sandor and with Gould — she was one of the voices in his radio series *Solitude Trilogy*. But when Foss had sessions away from him, Gould would sometimes get jealous and possessive, sitting in his car, anxiously waiting to pick her up.

During the years of his affair with Cornelia, from 1963 to 1973, Gould was quite productive and made several key decisions about his career, beginning with the decision to quit the concert stage in 1964. In 1971, he also switched his main recording venue from New York to the Eaton Auditorium in Toronto and changed his manager from Walter Homburger of Toronto to Ronald Wilford of Columbia Artists Management in New York. During his time with Cornelia, Gould made an impressive thirty-four record albums, supervised the soundtrack for the movie *Slaughterhouse-Five*, appeared on seventeen television programs, mostly on the CBC, and on dozens of radio shows while inventing the new art form of contrapuntal radio, which included six documentaries and his *Solitude Trilogy* series. As well, he wrote for magazines, conducted lectures and developed his offbeat sense of humor with writings, fictitious characters, a madrigal for a Columbia testimonial dinner and radio spoofs on music critics and competitive sports. After his Cornelia affair ended, he feared that his humorous writing would suffer, along with the safety, security and "quiet charm" his relationship with her spawned.

In the late 1960s and early 1970s, Gould learned to love the technical sides of making documentaries and also recording his music where he could edit for nights on end to get the perfect scene or sound. Immersing himself in technology also meant that he didn't have to get his hands mucky or his feet wet with real life. What he didn't like, he just left on the cutting room floor.

Paul Myers, who knew Gould from 1962 to 1982, wondered if he remained asexual through the years; along with other friends of Gould's, he just could not picture Gould in bed with a woman. "I don't know how far Glenn went with Cornelia," Myers said. "She lived with her children, separate from him. To this day, I wonder. In that era, it was hard to imagine Glenn Gould getting involved with a woman. I couldn't picture Glenn in a [sexual] relationship."

However, Cornelia stressed that her affair was indeed sexual. Although she held back personal details of their affair, and said she did not necessarily want people to see photographs they had taken together, Foss said that Gould was very romantic — "the most heterosexual man I knew. Once, a writer actually told me my relationship with Glenn was not sexual. Of course it was sexual! He was a good lover. He was as far from being a homosexual as one can get — not that I have anything against homosexuals." Foss had heard that, prior to her, Gould had had previous relationships with women and at least one girl-friend. With her, he never talked about having children. "I was in my thirties by then and in those days it was considered too old to have children," Foss said. "Anyway, he had Christopher and Eliza and he was wonderful with them, playing puzzles and helping them with their homework and Chris with his math."

But Cornelia saw disturbing signs in Gould as early as 1968, just two weeks after she had left her husband Lukas, when he had a serious paranoid episode. "It lasted several hours and then I knew he was not just neurotic — there was more to it. I thought to myself, 'Good grief, am I going to bring up my children in this environment?' But I stayed four and a half years! It was so terribly sad, but we were in love. Love is so stupid. I just couldn't leave."

Foss did not discuss details, but others close to Gould said he was convinced someone was trying to poison him. A friend said that Cornelia drove him to a hospital, but he had her drive around in circles and did not go into the hospital, saying the poison was wearing off (Gould was always terrified of getting germs in a hospital). It seemed similar to an episode that Gould had had in 1959, just after moving out of his parents' home into an apartment on Avenue Road in Toronto, when he told Dr. Peter Ostwald that people from an adjacent apartment were spying on him, shining lights through his window and sending him coded messages. Ostwald speculated that Gould had suffered a paranoid delusional episode. It may be no coincidence that Gould had these two incidents at times of upheaval in his life — and he was a man who did not like change. In the 1968 incident, there was no evidence that anyone was trying to poison Gould, despite some obsessive fans getting too close to him. "He had reasonable cause to be paranoid because there were some people after him," his assistant Ray Roberts said. "We had a couple of incidents [in the 1970s] where women came to the studio and had to be escorted away."

Although Gould reportedly never had a psychiatric diagnosis, he may have suffered from one or more mental disorders, including Asperger's Syndrome (see page 220). Cornelia believes that taking too many prescription drugs, or the wrong combination of them, sometimes made Gould delusional. Most of the time, he would seem fine, but then he would become delusional again, she said. Another troubling habit Gould had was occasionally talking to friends about death — particularly his own — and he prophetically told Cornelia he would die at age fifty.

Yet Cornelia seemed to be relatively happy, living in Toronto near Gould; about 1969, she told composer Ned Rorem, a family friend, that Gould was "loving, considerate and yes, tactile." Over the long term, however, Ostwald believed that

Gould's personality, lifestyle and narcissism made it "unendurable" for any woman to live with him. According to the psychiatrist, he could be a control freak, inflexible and manipulative (although Gould could also at times be giving and sympathetic, friends said). Cornelia seemed one of Gould's obsessions. "He'd tell me she did this, and she said that. He couldn't seem to get her out of his mind," said Dr. Joseph Stephens, professor of psychiatry of Johns Hopkins University in Baltimore, Maryland, and an acquaintance of Gould's from 1957 to 1977. Indeed, Gould appeared to have a lot of addictions and obsessions — he often worked seven days a week, worried constantly about his body and his health, and he ate just one meal a day (scrambled eggs at Fran's Restaurant), but he continued to play piano in recording and television studios and was a successful producer. Away from the keyboard, the paradoxical Gould continued to be into an eccentric, donning winter clothes in summer and hankies over his face to shield himself from germs, as his overprotective mother had advised.

During his years with Cornelia, Gould was estranged from both his parents, Cornelia said. Sometime, presumably in the 1960s, Gould had a serious disagreement with one or both of his parents, but Foss could not or would not say why. It is possible that one of the issues was that Gould had entered into an affair with Foss, a married woman with two children, which assuredly would have been against the rules in the household in which Glenn was raised. Even at the best of times in the 1960s, Gould saw his family infrequently, according to writer and Gould friend Richard Kostelanetz. "He would sooner telephone [them] — extend himself literally into their ears — than visit them or even have them visit him." In 1967, Kostelanetz wrote that Gould received his parents' calls often, "but he sees them only a few times a year, mostly for short vacations."

Gould's violinist friend Morry Kernerman also knew of the estrangement. "His mother and father were the nicest, gentlest people, very modest, and I don't think he was smothered by them like some people said," Kernerman said. "I'm Jewish and was raised in a very warm family where the parents were demonstrative with the children. Glenn's parents were not, but their Christian values seemed good and honest and whole-some. But at some point, Glenn disowned them, and it was so hard to believe."

Cornelia said she encouraged Gould to phone his mother and try for reconciliation, but he would not because "he had a tendency to cut off people if they upset him. He was extremely passionate in his views; if someone offered a different opinion, he couldn't bear it . . . and he didn't talk to his parents while I was with him."

Toronto relationship expert Rebecca Rosenblat said the rift may have been brooding between Gould and his mother for years. "It's possible that he had a love-hate relationship with his mother," Rosenblat said. "In the end, his neurosis won out. He may have identified with his mother and saw himself in her. Like a teenager, it could have been a way of finding his own identity at an advanced age, since he seemed to be a late bloomer in some areas."

We do not know how Florence Gould reacted to this estrangement from her son, once the center of her universe, because she gave no media interviews in the 1960s or beyond, left no notes and was as closed-mouth about her personal life as her son was. But it must have been painful for her when Glenn finally left home at age twenty-seven in 1959, then when he quit the concert stage five years later. The estrangement in the 1960s may have been the most painful for her because, besides music, she and Glenn had also shared religion and almost rigid moral standards. Yet life went on for Flora, who remained active in the church, tended to her rose garden at the cottage and worked for a charitable organization that helped unwed mothers and their babies. And, of course, Gould's recording career went on just fine without his parents, as he still played piano on his father's homemade stool.

The prescription drug habit may have been one way that Gould dealt with, among other things, the stress of his estrangement from his parents. In this regard, Cornelia got so involved with treating him, providing nurture to calm his anxious nature, her name was found on his pharmacy bills. That proved to Gould's accountant Patrick Sullivan that their relationship was serious — "I know because I saw his expenses."

Cornelia thought it was her duty, saying, "when people are in love, they help each other." Her care seemed to have a positive effect because at about that time, Gould told an interviewer that, as far as his health was concerned, those years were "the best of my life." During the years with Cornelia, Gould seemed to fall into a nice (for him) routine of working on music and documentaries far into the night, eating around 2:30 a.m. at Fran's, sleeping in until early afternoon, socializing with Cornelia and her kids after supper and keeping this life private.

And Gould was appreciative of those who helped him keep his bubble intact. One of those people was his superintendent, Marilyn Kecskes. "I have never met anyone like Mr. Gould," she said. "He was unique and caring and proper and always very thoughtful to me. He was always inquiring about how me and my children were doing and he was always trying to make a connection, such as asking me what type of cleaner I used for the floors." Gould was concerned when he saw Kecskes's three-year-old son, John, playing with a plastic bow and arrow. Gould said to her, "Mrs. Kecskes, I don't want to say this, but you shouldn't encourage your son to be violent." Kecskes understood. "I thought it was a sweet thing for him to say."

Gould was private and did not like opening his door to anyone. "He used to get parcels from Columbia Records, but I had to deliver them." Kecskes recalls that Gould used to protect his face from people's germs, including hers, in the elevator.

Gould's address in Toronto was kept secret, although some determined groupies and media people found it. "He would never open his door to them — he'd phone me and ask me to please deal with them," she said. "He would say, 'Mrs. Kecskes, somebody keeps ringing my bell!'" Some fans bordered on stalking and to this day there are screwdriver marks on the mailbox for his Apartment 902 in the lower lobby — a testament that someone was trying to force it open to steal the mail of a famous musician.

Of course, women were attracted to Gould. "He had to keep people at a certain distance," John Roberts said. "Too many people tried to get close and it was necessary to have a barrier." One time in Stratford, while playing at the festival, Gould stayed at a secret address to keep women away. "[At the Festival Hall], we found out which stage door to get out. I felt protective of him," Roberts said. In Toronto, Gould struggled to hang on to his privacy. "One night we went to the Windsor Arms for a meal and suddenly, someone was standing behind him, asking for an autograph," Roberts said. "Before you knew it, there was a queue behind him. The situation got so impossible [Gould] got a look of panic. I just stood up and said, 'We're going!' and we left. That's why he used to eat at the Voyageur Restaurant on the [Highway] 401, so not to be recognized."

Kecskes was always on the lookout for Gould's needs; one day when he was out of his apartment, a fierce storm hit the area, shattering windows. The rain swept into his apartment, threatening to damage his piano, but the superintendent got inside and wiped it down. "When he came home, he was very thankful — it was as if I had saved his life." Kecskes developed her own type of crush on the prince of classical music late at night while listening to his music on the rooftop, just above his French doors, but he never knew she was there. "I had the moon and the stars and his music and there was nothing more beautiful."

Gould was a bad driver, Kecskes said, and he scraped the narrow entrance and the wall of the basement parking garage many times with his big cars. If someone was in the garage when he entered, Gould would often circle the block so that he didn't have to meet them, Kecskes said. Cornelia also worried about Gould's erratic driving habits, which resulted in many traffic tickets, license suspensions and numerous accidents. One night in the early 1970s, Cornelia telephoned Ray Roberts to report she had just had a nightmare that Gould had been injured while driving a red car; at the time, he was driving a rented red Pontiac, which was unusual because Gould always said he hated the color red. The nightmare never came true.

Cornelia had her own issues and distractions. A talented sculptress and painter, she had to put her career on hold and she never painted Gould's portrait while they were together. "In those days, I didn't have the peace of mind to be able to paint. Painting is not something you do for fun, like paint by numbers; it's more like someone solving problems in physics. It takes enormous concentration," she said. "I was taking care of Glenn and Lukas and my two children. I went back to Buffalo for Lukas every weekend. I wanted the children to be with their father as much as possible."

Even while she was officially separated from Lukas, Cornelia would entertain friends and musicians at his Buffalo home on weekends. Toronto music critic and Gould neighbor William Littler recalls being at a reception for the media at the Foss home at 26 Richmond Avenue in Buffalo, following a music festival, in the late 1960s or early 1970s. "I remember [Cornelia] was a gracious hostess; it was an old Victorian house." And yet, Gould did not inform his close friend John Roberts and other Toronto friends that Foss was going back to her husband each weekend. And he kept mum on the arguments he was beginning to have with Cornelia, which he would later refer to as "a long, long history of quarrels and relationship disruptions."

Lukas was having his troubles during the time that Cornelia was mostly living in Toronto. In 1968, he was getting bad press for his music and, away from the performance hall, he was ordered to attend driver improvement school after he was nabbed speeding sixty-one miles per hour in a thirty miles per hour zone in Buffalo. His old friend Leonard Bernstein must have suspected that something was wrong with Lukas because his musical interpretations seemed to be falling apart. In the same year Cornelia left one Bach master for another, Bernstein wrote, "[Lukas] is going through a period now of what seems to be publicly destroying the music he's always loved most — Bach. In some of his compositions he takes a piece by Bach and breaks Coca-Cola bottles over it and makes it fragmented and distorted. It's like watching him publicly clawing the stuff out of his brains to make room for something new. There is something so destructive about it." (In another display that surprised some, Lukas invited the rock band the Grateful Dead to perform at Kleinhans Music Hall in Buffalo.)

In Toronto, Gould and Foss looked at many houses and planned to buy one if they married, Cornelia said, and this was confirmed by Ray Roberts. But their plans fell through because Gould refused to get treatment for his emotional problems, Cornelia said, "or even admit that he had them." His drug habit never got any better — in the early 1970s, he was taking about ten Valiums a day, according to Foss — and he was becoming more jealous of her, keeping close tabs on her whereabouts. "I wanted him to get treatment, but he wouldn't," she said.

Gould probably was not seriously interested in marriage, Roberts said, but he believed Gould loved Cornelia. "Oh, yes, I was sure of it; he said he loved her."

He seemed to have fallen hard for her.
He had other relationships with women
that were intimate, but she was
special in his life.
— Ray Roberts on Gould's relationship with Cornelia Foss

The BREAKUP

Chapter FOURTEEN

In January 1972, perhaps influenced by the German Foss, Gould did something he rarely tried — speaking in German. He read a text in German for a promotional recording for CBS Schallplatten in Germany for "Glenn Gould über Johann Sebastian Bach." If it was to impress Cornelia, it did not work. After nearly five years in Toronto, Cornelia felt she could not expose her two children to Gould's phobias and paranoia any longer and she decided to bring an end to their affair in 1973. "The last year became increasingly difficult for me," she said. "My life became more and more restricted as his paranoia became more evident. It really became impossible for me to do anything without being supervised. His personality began to change radically. There was less and less of the Glenn that I had fallen in love with."

Her teenage son, Chris, saw it, as well. "The relationship with him, I think, must have been a little suffocating for my mother," he said as an adult. "On one hand, it was very intense and engaged . . . but [Cornelia] ended up relinquishing a part of herself, and what she wanted to be in life, for his sake. And I think it couldn't be any other way. That's what Glenn needed."

"It was sad for me," Cornelia said. "I realized it was terribly wrong to be with Glenn; he was just too ill. It was nice to go back to Lukas, but I was torn." Foss dismissed the theory that

163

Gould could not have continued a successful relationship with a woman because he was too devoted to his work: "That's non-sense. Everybody has several sides to them."

John Roberts was one of the first to find out about the breakup. He recalls, "Glenn said to me, very sadly, that Lukas had come and taken the children to the airport and back to New York and so Cornelia eventually had to go back, too." When Gould discovered that the children he loved were gone, he knew it was only a matter of time before Cornelia left him, as well, and he was very upset. She did leave, rejoining Lukas in New York, where he had been appointed conductor of the Brooklyn Philharmonic Orchestra in 1972.

"Yes, I regret having stayed so long [in Toronto]," she said in 2007. "I don't regret having been with [Gould], but I regret not going back to my life sooner."

Ray Roberts never met Lukas, but admired him "for stick-ing by his wife. He was telling people he knew that he thought she would always return to him."

Gould stubbornly refused to give up on Cornelia. In 1973 and 1974, he phoned her often in her summer home in Bridge-hampton, New York, and the other home she shared with Lukas in New York City, staying on the phone sometimes for more than two hours, according to phone records, hoping to convince her to come back and marry him. Gould was devastated that she had fallen from the ranks of one of his few close friends to one of his telephone acquaintances, yet Cornelia was torn between the two worlds because while she still loved him, she knew that she could not live with him. Gould hid his emotions from those close to him in Toronto, but he must have been depressed.

Gould did not waste much time getting back to his own music, the sounds of the world he could control. Through the long breakup with Cornelia and her two children, which began in 1973 and continued through 1974, Gould had been a busy boy. To be sure, he had always been a career workaholic, but now the recordings and the radio shows and filmmaking seemed to be taking on an additional role — as a form of escape from the failure in his domestic life. At the end of 1973, Columbia had just released its fiftieth Gould album, he had completed a CBC Radio special on cellist-conductor Pablo Casals, he was preparing for a CBC-TV special *Music in Our Times* and he was filming material for French national television on music and technology. The hectic schedule may also have filled a sexual void, according to sex and relationship authority Rebecca Rosenblat. "When people are passionate about their work and working hard, they might not need sex as much," she said.

Along the way, Gould's influence in music, television and radio remained strong. "Glenn Herbert Gould is not your ordinary society-fleeing recluse," wrote William Littler in the *Toronto Star.* "While it's true that he gravitates toward darkness rather than daylight and individuals rather than crowds, the caves he dwells in come equipped with microphones and tape decks. They facilitate communication rather than severing it. For the paradoxical thing about Canada's most important musician is that retirement from the concert stage has resulted in increasing rather than decreasing his influence."

In 1973, Gould purchased his favorite concert grand piano, the Steinway CD 318. You could always rely on a piano: you hit the keys, it responded, you tapped the pedals, it heeded you, and it had the clearness of tone. People were much more unpredictable — yet Gould liked certain people and he showed his giving side in August 1973, by putting in a rare appearance as a producer for the recording of music by Erich Wolfgang Korngold by another pianist, Antonin Kubalik. He did it as a favor for Kubalik, who recalled that Gould's nightlife apparently caught up with him on the second day of shooting. "He came late and apologized that his alarm clock had gone off at

6 a.m., but he turned it off and went back to sleep!" Kubalik chuckled. Gould seemed to have a soft spot for Kubalik — in 1969, Gould heard of the plight of the struggling pianist who had just emigrated from Czechoslovakia with his wife and two small daughters, sent him a check for $1,000, wrote a letter of reference to the Royal Conservatory for him and advised Kubalik on concert management. All of this was done privately, with no publicity.

In the winter of 1974, Gould was back at filming one of his favorite subjects — himself — in an uncritical series of four French documentaries featuring Gould, his music and his musical analysis, produced by Bruno Monsaingeon. When it was finished, Gould did not show up at a farewell party in his honor. That could have meant that he simply was shy and detested parties, as he usually did, but he might also have become more anxious, and even depressed, about the ever-dwindling hope he had of resuming his affair with Cornelia. Then, in the early summer of 1974, he drove 600 miles to the Hamptons to try to convince Foss to return to Toronto, which was quite out of character for Gould. "He seemed to have fallen hard for her," Ray Roberts said. "He had other relationships with women that were intimate, but she was special in his life."

Some of Cornelia Foss's friends in the Hamptons say they had never seen Gould before, which is not surprising because he preferred nature alone or at least with selected company, apparently not with the Fosses' Bohemian artists. In any event, Gould checked into a motel room in the Hamptons and went to plead with Cornelia. She was renting a bungalow on the beach with a writer's wife, while Lukas was living in another Hamptons' house at the time. "We talked in the bungalow and it was very painful for both of us," she recalled. Foss and Gould also went for a walk along the beach, which made a tragicomic sight with the eccentric pianist in his heavy coat and gloves in the summer heat. "Some of the bathers were staring at him," she said sadly. Cornelia told Gould for the last time she could not return to Canada with him and he finally left with his tail between his legs. "We still had strong feelings for one another and it was sad to see him in so much pain, and that I was part of that pain," she said, but she promised to call Gould when he got back to Toronto.

He may have wept on that long ride home across Long Island, up through Pennsylvania and down the stretch of the New York Thruway, but Cornelia never saw him weep in all the years she was close to him. In fact, it has been said that Gould rarely cried in front of others, except during his relationship problems with Batchen. When asked if she had ever seen Gould cry, Cornelia said in 2007: "Nobody has ever seen *me* cry. Most people have never let others see them cry. Has anybody seen *you* cry?" In any event, June 1974 was a lost month in Gould's professional life — his financial records showed he earned no money in that month — a rarity for him.

Gould apparently told very few people — if anyone — about his failed trip to the Hamptons. John Roberts and Ray Roberts deny knowing anything about it. Meanwhile, Cornelia's promise to Gould fell through when she forgot to call him when he returned to Toronto, and he took this as a sign that she did not love or want him anymore.

At about the time Foss broke up with Gould, a small group of Toronto musicians spotted the pianist brooding in a coffee shop off Highway 400 near Barrie, Ontario, north of Toronto. "We'd just played a gig in Carling in the Muskokas," accordionist Al Adler recalled. "We were on our way home and it was about three in the morning. There he was, sitting by himself at a small table in the corner. It was a hot, sticky night but he had on a coat and white gloves. It was Glenn Gould — we were in awe of him." Adler and his two companions, a singer and a pianist, whispered to one another about trying to get Gould's autograph. "But we didn't go up to him. He was all hunched over, looking sad and in his own world. I think he had a tea, or something, in front of him."

But Gould had not given hope and was not finished with Cornelia Foss just yet.

The VOICE
on the RADIO

Chapter FIFTEEN

It took Gould some time to get his bearings back after the failed Hamptons' trip. Shaken, or at least disrupted, were his confidence and his sense of security, but there remained one place where he was king — his work. In the summer and fall of 1974, he released two Bach albums for CBS Masterworks and a ten-part CBC Radio series on Schoenberg. And then, in 1975, while driving around in the middle of the night, he discovered Roxolana Roslak. The Midnight Man picked up some of his best stuff in the wee hours — his crystal clear thinking about fugues and Brahms, his two scrambled eggs smothered with ketchup at Fran's Restaurant and, on an evening in 1975, Miss Roslak, a woman who would eventually become his accompanist and more.

While cruising the dark streets of Toronto in Longfellow, his chunky black Lincoln Town Car, with Cornelia Foss's bittersweet melody still playing in his soul, Gould listened half-heartedly to CBC Radio. He passed a phone booth on a corner and thought briefly about calling Cornelia, as he had been doing almost nightly since she had said her final goodbye on the cruel Hamptons' shore. The patient Cornelia would still listen to him on the phone as they opined about Nixon and the Watergate tapes or *Brady Bunch* getting canceled. But after such phone calls, the realization that she unbelievably did not want

Glenn Gould any longer would stay with him like a migraine. Suddenly on this night, his longings and negative thought patterns were interrupted by the voice of an intriguing soprano piercing the crackling reception on the radio. Unbeknownst to Gould, it was Roslak, a Ukrainian/Canadian soloist. Years later, Roslak would struggle to recall what she had been singing on the radio that night, but she suspected it might have been *Time Cycle*, which was written, coincidentally, by Cornelia's husband Lukas, with whom Roxolana had once worked. Foss had told colleagues that Roslak's interpretation was the most accurate by all the singers who had performed his song.

Gould was not only captured but enraptured, nearly skidding into a street sweeper, which would have resulted in yet another suspension of his Ontario driver's license. Something in Roslak's voice was worth a broken bone or two; it was a naturally beautiful, creamy voice with warmth, perhaps even sentiment. Gould was not one to embrace openly emotional music, but he sat there, happily slumped, for some time after his car had been turned off and long after the final strains of *Time Cycle* had died up Yonge Street. The next morning, he uncharacteristically rose early and shouted at a CBC executive: "Get me that girl!"

Gould's impulsive attraction to Roslak's voice and his insistence the next day on working with her suggested to some people that there was more to it than musical admiration. "Glenn always had separation anxiety, going back to his mother, and to deal with it, he developed a fetish for the female voice," said Toronto psychiatrist and Gould author Dr. Helen Mesaros. She said that this unusual fetish alleviated Gould's anxiety and produced temporary pleasure, perhaps even sexual arousal and orgasm. "In the absence of a full-scale, mature love relationship, this was the best that he could hope for, a partial experience of love from a distance. Most of his libido as a drive was diverted to higher asexual aims, notably his musical and literary achievements." But as we are discovering, Gould was even more of an enigma than that — he certainly could have worn out the cushions on several couches had he ever submitted to psychoanalysis. According to those close to him, Gould was drawn to sound as a moth to a flame; if not the piano, then an instrument just as sensitive — the human voice. And oftentimes he mixed the two, singing merrily to himself as he played. Women's voices were most appealing to him, particularly when they were spiced with an accent, such as Franny's Scottish brogue, Cornelia's mixture of Italian/German or Roxolana's hint of Ukrainian.

And so it was that Miss Roslak found herself — for better or for worse — in the tipsy but exciting world of an unorthodox pianist and, shortly after, she would be alone on desolate Manitoulin Island with him, singing a Mahler duet to the Hereford cows with a fake German accent.

"I want to hear why you think we had an affair," Roslak said to me in the living room of her quaint old Toronto house one night in the autumn of 2007, twenty-five years after Gould's premature death. She had aged well from the elegant woman into whose arms Gould had fallen three decades earlier.

Slowly but with sufficient drama, I reached into my satchel and pulled out a faded album cover. On its front was a 1977 photograph of thirty-seven-year-old Roslak and forty-five-year-old Gould — a heads-and-shoulders' shot with Roslak standing submissively in the forefront and Gould nestled behind her left shoulder in a bold stance. It seemed as though a brilliant producer had positioned them for maximum impact on the record buyer; indeed, some of the buyers and critics had commented that the picture had a haunting quality about it. Another possibility was that the pose they slipped into for the Columbia Records photographer was a wholly natural one. Whatever the case, history will show that Roslak succeeded in pulling off what no other woman was able to do — capture the reclusive Glenn Gould in a public photograph attached to a girlfriend. And what a striking couple they were: Roslak with her give-away-little Mona Lisa pout and dark flowing hair, which would have been very '70s if this did not smack of an image from the Middle Ages, and Gould with slicked back hair and menacing eyes, like he'd just come down from the castle. I held the record album high for Roxolana to see across her living room, like a prosecutor would flash at a defendant. She did not blink or acknowledge my gesture, not even with the old pout, but instead jumped up to offer me tea and cookies. Without missing a beat, I whipped out a second album cover of her and the famous pianist — a similar Camelot pose, except that this time Gould was standing over her right shoulder with his hand reflectively upon his chin while the soprano was standing in a silk-embossed dress, holding her hands together like they had been bound. Roslak looked more intensely at this record album and raised her eyebrow to me without speaking. "It's the body language of the both of you," I explained.

Next in my interrogation, I produced a third photograph from a magazine, snapped the day of one of the shoots for the album covers, showing singer and pianist smiling widely. "That was shot between takes, I remember," Roslak acknowledged. "Somebody said something and there was a light moment between us."

I would not back down. "Roxolana, I have been researching Glenn Gould intensely for quite some time now and I have never seen this look on his face in the hundreds of photographs published throughout his career. You look like a couple."

The retired soprano sat in a chair and sighed. "You know, I remember that one recording; they sent photographer Don Hunstein down from New York to do the shoot. The idea was to have us photographed outside in nature, and we both liked the idea. It started out as a beautiful day, but then it started pouring, so we had to go back to the studio for the pictures."

"You know, I don't want to do this," I said. "I may not even *need* to do this. But I know that people are going to want to hear the answer."

"It always comes down to sex," she said, shaking her head. "Why does it always come down to sex?"

Most certainly, when he met Roslak in the mid-1970s, Gould needed someone. It was not enough that he was a household name in Canada and in music circles in Europe and Japan, that he would acquire a cult which would motivate a woman from England to tattoo his composition String Quartet onto her back — right now he needed one person. Not only was he coming off the long Coney Island coaster with Cornelia Foss, but his beloved mother Florence was quite ill and he was reluctant to visit her in hospital, partly because he had been estranged from her for a number of years, perhaps partly due to a disagreement over his affair with the married Foss. For the first time in his career, Gould's work was starting to suffer from his personal life and his prescription drug habit had become an addiction. The control he had established in his career as the greatest classical pianist alive had less sway in his everyday affairs, proving that gods can be clumsy down on earth.

During the 1960s and '70s, Roxolana Roslak was one of the prominent operatic sopranos in Canada. Born in war-torn Ukraine on February 11, 1940, she and her family escaped to Innsbruck, Austria, while she was a young child, then to tiny Thorsby, Alberta, when she was nine. Through the stresses of relocation, she found a way to cope through her voice. "I was always singing as a child — I would sing for anyone who would listen," she said. When her family moved to Edmonton, Roslak developed her talent with local opera companies and music-theater productions, then she followed her dreams to Toronto, where she completed an artist's diploma at the University of

Toronto in 1964. The following year, she won a Canada Council grant and worked briefly in small roles at Covent Garden in London, England, but she was back in Canada by 1966. "I was very homesick," she said. "It would have taken a few years to get things going in London. Who knows? Perhaps I would have had an international career, but I was offered a couple of bigger parts in Canada — Fiordiligi in *Così fan tutte* at Stratford and a part that turned out to be seminal in my life, Marguerite in *Louis Riel*." The latter was an opera based on the life of the Métis leader who led rebellions against the Canadian government in the late nineteenth century — it was a big hit in Canada's centennial celebrations of 1967 and put Roslak on the national stage with her rendition of a Cree lullaby. "I was young and would have sung the phone book if anyone had asked me, so it was lucky that *Louis Riel* turned out to be a masterpiece." Roslak described herself in those days as a "very busy singer and reasonably high-profile. Being in Canada, I did a lot of major orchestras and CBC Radio a lot and I got a lot of good reviews and response."

Gould discovered Roslak on his car radio, but their eyes first met in 1975 in the old CBC studio on Carlton Street in Toronto. "He was there in the lobby in July in a heavy coat and scarf. It sounds bizarre, but once you got to know him, his unusual clothes and behavior only seemed strange in the telling," she recalled. "I'd heard his playing. I'd also heard about his eccentricities and mainly that he was a genius, a wonderful pianist and very fascinating person."

In the mid-1970s, friends were encouraging Gould to produce a comedy album with his knack for mimicry and sharp wit, but he dropped that possibility to work with Roslak. Probably one of the reasons he nixed the idea was because he was depressed over Cornelia and worried that the breakup would affect his work, particularly his witty prose and possibly his filmmaking. In a secret note found after his death, he said he wanted to keep the romance with Foss alive "because I fear that the dispiritedness would have a detrimental effect on my writing — specifically on its lighter, humorous aspects which incorporate reflection and for which this relationship served as a yard-stick and a sounding board."

Although he continued to fret about Cornelia while he was beginning his relationship with Roslak, popping anti-depressants like candy, Gould started to work intensely with Roslak, which brought him back to his comfort zone — playing elite piano. Their first project was to perform three songs from the *Lieder der Ophelia* by Richard Strauss in the fall of 1975 on the CBC Television series *Musicamera*. "I was very thrilled to be asked and once I realized I was going to work with Glenn Gould, I was quite overwhelmed," Roslak said. "At the first rehearsal, I was quite nervous. We went through three songs before he stopped and said to me, 'Oh, I see you want to take more time with the tempo. It makes sense, good musical sense.' With that, he freed me, and the pressure was off, then I felt like part of a team, a collaboration. That was freeing, that kind of give and take. People asked me if he was inflexible, and certainly I was full of attention to his advice, but I never felt pressured. He had a tremendous generosity of spirit. That was one of his qualities, and he had an incredible generosity with his talent." Could this be the same, self-worshipping maestro, the Cliché Gould, we've heard about in the more than forty books and at least twenty documentaries dedicated to the subject of the man and his music?

He wasn't always so silky smooth with collaborators, however, especially early in his career when the *Globe and Mail* reviewed his accompaniment with contralto Maureen Forrester and violinist Morry Kernerman: "Superb though Mr. Gould was as soloist, he was less than satisfactory as accompanist. The piano set the pace in the two fast movements of the Sonata for Violin and Piano in C Minor, and it was a pace that gave little opportunity for violinist Morry Kernerman, who, indeed, seemed ill at ease through the entire performance. And if Mr. Gould was inconsiderate of the violinist, he was quite unkind to Miss Forrester. The piano accompaniment to her songs was generally too loud and too demanding."

It would not always be so.

There's a human
behind this [music].
– Gould cultist Natalie Flood

CATHARSIS
through MUSIC

Chapter SIXTEEN

Early in Roslak's professional relationship with Gould, on July 21, 1975, a giant in his life was felled — his eighty-three-year-old mother Florence suffered a stroke and was rushed to East General Hospital in Toronto. Gould was despondent over Flora's sudden illness. She had raised him and had been his first piano teacher, innocently slept with him off and on until he was at least twelve, introduced him to his wonderful world of classical music and pulled him out of full-time school to allow him the opportunity to perform on a world stage. But in recent years, there had been bitterness, regret and even anger between mother and son, so much so that they had drifted apart. Gould's parents even went against his wishes and sold the family's cottage on Lake Simcoe, which had been their country haven for forty years. As Flora lay gravely ill in hospital over four days, Glenn rallied in an effort to see her, but he got no further than the parking lot; he was afraid to leave the safety of his car Longfellow and go into the hospital to visit her, perhaps in part from his fear of catching germs but also likely due to the fact he felt guilty and/or bitter about their long spat. He also harbored some anger and frustration toward his mother for her disappointment over his inability to produce a grandchild for her.

But it all ended there in the parking lot of East General as he slumped in his sunglasses and winter coat, flipping the sun visor up and down, to and fro, while pretending to listen to stock market reports on the radio. Cornelia had bugged him for years to contact his mother and to make up with her, but he had not listened; he could not do it. Even now he could not do it, and it was only partly due to the fact he was worried about getting germs from other patients. The best Gould could muster while his mother was in hospital was to talk to her briefly over the telephone; even at age forty-two, he had not honed his personal communications skills beyond the phone or, in some areas, had not matured past the stage of rebellious teenager. Back at home, waiting to hear updates, one of the first people he called for comfort was Cornelia in the Hamptons. Then he phoned his psychiatrist friend in Baltimore, Dr. Joseph Stephens, for medical advice about strokes and their treatment, but to no avail. Gould never saw his mother again before she plunged into a coma and died on July 26, 1975.

Thanks to his stoic nature and thick Nordic defenses, it was difficult for anyone around him to gauge the impact the death of his mother had on Gould. Through it all, he dealt with his grief by using his mother's own Victorian playbook: chin up and square to the ears, dead face, dignity and control, don't let them see you cry — the same strategy he employed when his dog Banquo was killed by a car in 1960 (he never got another pet). "He went to [his mother's] funeral and conducted himself with dignity," his assistant Ray Roberts said. "I was careful not to poke into his personal feelings. You just didn't do that."

For the funeral, Gould crafted a eulogy for his mother in handwriting which was actually legible for a change — like he was back in the last row at Williamson Road Public School. He penned it on stationary from the Four Seasons Hotel in suburban Toronto, where he had a bed and a mini-recording studio:

Florence Greig Gould came from a Christian home.
From the time she was a teenager, she devoted her

life to classical music − and, in particular, to music for the sacred service − being active in church and young people's groups . . . many of her former students are scattered throughout Canada and carrying on their musical careers today. In later years, no longer able to participate in choral work as she would have wished, several Sunday telecasts were a great source of blessing to her. They never failed to strengthen her faith in our Master. Florence Gould was a woman of tremendous faith and, wherever she went, she strove to instill that faith in others. For the last few years, she devoted her talents to a group of underprivileged mothers in a large downtown church where, weekly, she tried, through music and inspiration, to make their lives a little more meaningful.

And so it went, like a bio from a minister who saw the family only on the Sabbath. The eulogy was void of emotion because revealing oneself was practically a sin. The product of a boyhood in which reason was hammered home over passion, Gould usually hustled himself from situations that could spark social interactions and feelings, even happy ones like birthdays, Juno Awards and December twenty-fifth. Gould did not react to these situations like most people, but rather more intensely while displaying it less. The pain or joy did not surface, and so it hurt his stomach and chest and, in some cases, his pride. If a death descended upon the family, it was best to downplay it, control it, with a eulogy out of the United Church of Canada; if a romance was on the outs, it was easier to write a letter you might never have to post; if there was a confrontation of ideas, best to change your voice to your fictitious, yuk-yuk German composer Dr. Karlheinz Klopweisser and if tears threatened the dam of defenses, it was simpler to rush over to the eighty-eight keys of a piano — like he had done when Gladys Shenner came

to him in tears about her mother — and saturate his senses by
playing something, anything, even Mozart. Here was a guy who,
as a boy, would hum like mad instead of cry when he toppled
on the playground and skinned his knee. If you absolutely
needed to cry or to love deeply, it was more practical to listen
alone in your car to Roxolana Roslak's angelic voice on CBC
Radio. Yes, emotions hurt Gould to the core and he fought
them off and dulled them with drugs signed for by Dr. Percival,
even though they wreaked havoc internally, and soon he would
suffer from hypertension, which had helped send his mother to
the grave. In the 1970s, people did not fully realize the influence that worry and withholding one's feelings can have on the
physical being, that the average person has an average of sixty-
six thousand thoughts per day, two-thirds of them worries
(Gould, an admitted professional thinker, probably topped one
hundred thousand). Stress was a word for architects.

Following his mother's death, Gould took only a brief hiatus
from his work, but we can assume that the event had a deeper
impact on his psyche, his work and his relationships. He could
not just go off in the woods and hum this one away. At the time,
Gould did not know Roslak well enough to confide in her, but
he did continue to telephone Cornelia and also to renew his kin-
ship with his cousin Jessie Greig. "Glenn missed his mother
terribly . . . he was devastated by her death and he became more
introspective," Greig said. Gould told Jessie that, until then,
without siblings and suffering from a distant relationship with
his father, he had not realized what support from family members could do. In the months following his mother's death, he
made numerous visits to nearby Oshawa to visit. "He would
curl up on the chesterfield in his stocking feet and, while I served
five or so pots of tea, he would relate numerous anecdotes, playing guessing games, catch up on family news and through his
word pictures draw me into a world of minds far beyond my
comprehension," Greig said. "During these times, he accepted

me as an equal, never demeaning or holier than thou."

Roslak never met Flora. "He didn't talk much to me about his mother, only about when he was a kid, describing family scenes," Roslak said. "It sounded like it was a happy childhood. He spoke to his father regularly on the telephone. I did meet his father — a very nice, charming gentleman, warm. Glenn had no great animosity toward him, but there was the problem of his father being a furrier and Glenn liking animals so much. Sometimes he talked about his father with affection, though, especially his hydroponic gardens in the house. 'My father has grown these great vegetables!' he used to say with pride." (In his thirties, before he met Roslak, Gould became a vegetarian for a time.)

Roslak was beginning to realize how much of a disaster the pianist was and, within a year, not only was he diagnosed with hypertension, but he became so obsessed with his health, checking his blood pressure so regularly on the hour, his pulse started to chime like Big Ben. Throughout his life, of course, Gould suffered from bouts of eccentricity and hypochondria. Such crises tended to affect his soul, as well. Following the death of his mother, Gould took a renewed interest in the Bible, particularly the ominous Book of Revelations: "The Revelation of Jesus Christ, which God gave unto Him, to show unto His servants things which must shortly come to pass; and He sent and signified it by His angel unto His servant John: who bare record of the word of God, and of the testimony of Jesus Christ, and of all things that he saw. Blessed is he that readeth, and they that hear the words of this prophecy, and keep those things which are written therein: for the time is at hand."

Gould had nightmares about his mother's death, coming to believe that she was in heaven, waiting for him. Whenever he was duly distressed or depressed, he retreated into the state of wonder. "Music protects me from the world," he said. Gould's favorite places to be in the universe were, in order: absorbed in his music, absorbed in his filmmaking, walking alone in nature, working with selected others, and, least favored, being with others in social settings. The latter, of course often turned out to be a "state of worry."

As with Batchen before her, Gould enjoyed working with Roslak. That had been a missing component in his relationship with Foss, although there were redeeming factors with her — notably her two marvelous children, her wide-ranging, succinct philosophy and the domestic security she offered.

And so Roslak came along at a crucial time during a fusion of two of Gould's worlds. It does not seem much of a stretch to suggest that Gould's mourning over his mother was a major contributor in his decision to record the spiritually charged *Das Marienleben* in 1976 with Roxolana. He had performed it live at the Stratford Festival in the early 1960s with soprano Lois Marshall and considered it the greatest song cycle ever written, perhaps partly because of his devout religious upbringing.

To his parents' chagrin, the rebellious Gould had stopped attending church at age eighteen and yet he remained fascinated with the Bible, ESP, coincidences, mysticism and the afterlife. "I believe in God — Bach's God," he said. "And yet I have had all my life a tremendously strong sense that indeed there is a hereafter and the transformation of the spirit is a phenomenon with which one must reckon." Indeed, Gould kept in his possession several Christian books presented to him by his mother, including *The Wonderful Story of Jesus* and *An Argument for Evangelism through Your Vocation*. He believed that artists should seek transcendent experiences and communicate their music spiritually.

In *Das Marienleben*, adapted by composer Paul Hindemith from the poem *The Life of the Virgin Mary* by famous German poet Rainer Maria Rilke, it is quite possible that Gould saw a spiritual and even a physical connection between himself and his dead mother. He admired Rilke and owned his book of poetry, and so he could have identified with the story of the virgin mother (Flora) spawning a diety (himself).

The poem says:

> *Had you a greater vision in your mind of Him before?*
> *How can one fathom greatness?*
> *But look! Behold! For there upon your lap,*
> *Wrapped lovingly in swaddling clothes, lies He . . .*

In the last part of Rilke's poem, "The Death of Mary," the mother and son are reunited in heaven, just as Gould may have hoped he would be with Flora: "Yet the heavens high above are trembling: / Man, fall on your knees, watch my departure, and sing."

Perhaps with this in mind, Gould tried to ease the depression of his mother's death by launching into *Das Marienleben* with Roslak, whose pure, uncontaminated voice had seduced him on the radio, who reminded him that songs about life and death, good and evil, heroes and villains (who also dominated the world of classical music) simplified his life and allowed him to focus. Two years earlier, Roslak had sung as the voice of God, leading an audience through creation in Aaron Copland's *In the Beginning*. "It is a cycle about a mystery," Gould said of *Das Marienleben*. "It is a work of infectious spontaneity, of divine intuition, in which connections are felt to exist long before an exegesis can conform their presence . . . it is the perfect musical counterpart for the concept of Resurrection."

The timing for this project with Roslak seemed just right. "He'd been wanting to do the recording for many years," Roslak said. "I think he wanted Lois Marshall, but I guess somehow it didn't work out." Gould was always on the lookout for a female soloist who could complement him, not only technically but philosophically, but sometimes his alter ego — or, rather, his ego — stood in the way.

Gould was in love with the voice of Austrian/British opera singer Elisabeth Schwarzkopf, whom he considered the premier soprano in the world. He had attempted to make a recording of Strauss songs with her in New York in 1966. "Schwarzkopf thought she would have an accompanist," said the producer of the project, Paul Myers. "Glenn thought he was going to have a very distinguished collaborator, and, of course, that's different. It was very funny." Four songs were recorded without incident but when it came to the song "Morgen!" Gould started improvising too much for the soprano's liking — without consulting with her — and she stopped working with him. The album was canceled.

Perhaps Gould was in awe of Schwarzkopf and couldn't communicate properly with her, or perhaps it was a clash of global egos. Mused Schwarzkopf, "Let's just say it was an unhappy love affair." With the humble, lesser-known Roslak, however, communication and ego were not deal breakers.

But there were other potential duets. At the time, Gould also asked his close friend, mezzo-soprano Joan Maxwell of Toronto, to record *Das Marienleben* with him; he dropped off the score and left it with her for a week, but she was so busy with her husband, businessman Harvey Rempel, and their young family, Maxwell did not have time to read the music. When Gould returned, she fibbed to him that the piece "didn't quite fit my range" even though, in reality, it might have been perfect for her voice. Rempel, who was also close friends with Gould for about thirty years, suspected that Gould had a crush on his wife, saying, "and who wouldn't have had — Joan was blond and stunningly beautiful."

In late 1976 and early 1977, Gould and Roslak recorded the complete Hindemith cycle for Columbia Records at Eaton Auditorium in Toronto. They also taped a CBC *Musicamera* broadcast of *Das Marienleben* in 1976. In the show, available in CBC archives, the chemistry between pianist and soloist is evident, even though Gould is eight feet behind her on the stage, sitting on his father's decrepit homemade chair, flailing away in slow-motion at the piano, but allowing the vulnerable Roslak center stage in her feminine blue dress, lyrics sung like an operatic sparrow. While he provided a tender background for her voice, Roslak provided a beautiful frame for Gould's playing and it was difficult at times to identify the featured performer. *Globe and Mail* critic John Kraglund said Gould and Roslak were an equal couple in the Hindemith recording: "Gould obviously had a strong influence, but he cannot be accused of dominating the performance. The recording is superbly balanced, the piano line always present and never obtrusive . . . Miss Roslak employs a wide emotional range that builds inexorably to the dramatic section." When Gould raised his left hand at the rainbow's end of the long, arching, melodic vocal lines and held it high, he seemed to be touching something that only Roslak could feel. Some hailed this classical music at its best: soulful, reflective, every note and feeling thought out to its natural conclusion. Kraglund called it "a stunning work, stunningly performed." But to others, it sounded mournful, too solitary, as though Roslak's notes and Gould's piano had been strained through a tortured heart. Perhaps all were correct.

This had to be more than music for Gould, who often sought salvation through art, and perhaps it soon became a deep grieving process that provided him more comfort and closure than the eulogy on stationary of the Four Seasons Hotel. It may have also given him an injection of comfort to ease his heartache over Cornelia Foss. Certainly, Gould committed his own soul to the collaboration; in the end, it sounded not like his brighter and breezier *Goldberg Variations*, but rather something old and prayer-bound, as though Flora Gould was playing the organ like mad in the background, and if you closed your eyes, you could almost hear the United Church choir on the chorus behind Roxolana's voice. Gould's work took an hour or so to listen to, but a day's work to comprehend. His piano had a voice — as sensitive as any human's — you simply had to hear through: it sighed; it sung; it moped; it laughed and wept; it was joyous and warm and sometimes it was downright sad. All it lacked was inhibition. It had been here, at the keyboard where he and his mother had fused with the music when he was just old enough to sit on her lap and reach the magic keys with his little hands; after that, said his psychiatrist friend Dr. Peter Ostwald, Gould could always recall "the warm feelings and earlier proximity of both mother and instrument." The only downside to this performance of *Das Marienleben* was that dearly departed Flora would never hear it, and she probably would have liked this one.

Gould orchestrated the mood, Roslak said. "He was in the driver's seat. When he trusted you, he would relax that feeling of control; he didn't trust too many people and rightly so. People could betray him. With somebody that prominent, people want a piece of you. He was just cautious, but he was able to relax with me." However, Roslak knew she was not the choice of Columbia Records for the albums. "They wanted their own singer, a more established name," she recalled. "But he wanted me, and he dug his heels in. He had a lot of power."

Gould won out and later wrote in one of his notepads that Roslak was "among the most gifted vocal artists of this generation."

Roslak may have tapped Gould's fossilized emotions, as well, according to William Littler, the classical music critic of the *Toronto Daily Star*: "He was kind of a romantic; he said he didn't like sentimental romanticism, music which showed its heart on its sleeve, but he did make exceptions, like with [Richard] Strauss." Or perhaps Gould's attraction to Roslak was now beyond the voice.

Meanwhile, the people at Columbia were tickled pink with the albums, one of which won a Juno Award for the best classical album in Canada. "They were very professional together," said Gould's record producer Andrew Kazdin, but he saw nothing in the studio that would lead him to believe Gould and Roslak were starting an affair. "I recorded with them, and I never observed any kind of social relationship, but I can't say it didn't happen. All I did was work with the man for fifteen years. I know where he drew the line and did not want to pry or to make him prudish. I had to withstand the late-night phone calls, the care and the feeding, but he never mentioned anything personal about [Roslak]."

Kazdin's feeling was that Gould never had girlfriends. "That's absolutely the impression I got. He would run like crazy from women and he got letters from many women." Fan letters ended up in New York at Kazdin's Columbia office, including one from a woman in the United States who wanted a meeting with the pianist. Suddenly without warning, the woman showed up one day in the CBS building and requested to see Gould, who happened to be in Kazdin's office. Gould was terrified and barricaded himself in the office. "I found him in a crouched position, cowering behind the door," Kazdin recalled. "I thought to myself that this was nuts." The woman simply wanted to talk to Gould, but CBS officials kicked her out of the building. After that, the producer started what he affectionately called the "Kazdin Detective Agency" to screen fans from his famous client.

Still, Gould was often patient with female fans, even those who tried to visit him against his wishes, such as a persistent American woman, who wrote Gould numerous letters, then traveled to Orillia, Ontario, to meet him briefly in 1966. Gould later wrote to her, "I do not believe that any of us have the right to demand of another person action or actions uncharacteristic of them. I do believe that we may all reasonably expect a life free of intrusions from outside, and, I am, therefore, going to ask you to reconsider very calmly the nature of your actions these last several years and to refrain all together from your attempts to visit or contact me."

Then there was the case of a middle-aged woman under psychiatric care from Austin, Texas, who sent Gould (via Columbia) 174 letters from 1974 to 1978 — averaging twenty pages a letter. "Some of them were love letters, others the story of her life in a kind of diary. She thought eventually Glenn would marry her," Kazdin said. Gould eventually received some of the letters and felt sorry for the woman, who he felt was emotionally disturbed, but he was also intimidated a little and had most of the letters handled by Kazdin. Many women were attracted to Gould, Kazdin said, "partly because he didn't seem attainable to them. He was a very good-looking man, maybe perfect, talented and famous. What more do you need? But I couldn't conceive him having an affair with anyone." This was the impression that stayed with Kazdin long after Gould's death. And yet Kazdin admitted there was a secretive side to Gould. "Glenn Gould's second talent, besides playing the piano, was keeping secrets. He enjoyed the intrigue."

*Come to my heart, that I may
hold you again, as once in May.*
— Roxolana Roslak, remembering Glenn Gould

TRANSITION

Chapter SEVENTEEN

Certainly, as his professional relationship with Roslak blossomed into a social friendship and beyond, Gould kept it private and was loyal — and these were other qualities that attracted Roslak to Gould.

"People close to him thought of him as 'my Glenn Gould,'" Ray Roberts said. "They might talk to a point about him, but when it came to personal things, it would be like they took their coat and closed it, not allowing you in. It was their way of keeping Glenn close to them."

As he got older, Gould went from discreet to very discreet with his romances. In the 1950s, while dating Franny Batchen, he allowed people to see him cry over her, to catch him in a sex act with her and to walk in on them while Franny stroked his hair. During his long affair with Cornelia Foss through the 1960s, Gould was more private. By the 1970s, the relationship was positively stealthy.

Away from the studio and prying eyes, Gould and Roslak developed a bond. "We became quite good friends. I felt comfortable enough with him that I asked for my picture on the album covers!" she said. "I guess it was more of a joke than anything, but I did end up on the covers."

Mutual friends adored Roslak. "Roxie was a friend, such a lovely woman. Loyal. And a fantastic singer," John Roberts said.

"She was almost shy and quiet, and never boasted about herself," said pianist Antonin Kubalek.

In their first year or two, it seems as though Gould and Roslak demanded little of one another, apart from what they brought to the stage and recording studio, but when they began rehearsing in the dining room of Gould's penthouse, their relationship began to lapse into other areas. Roslak became physically attracted to the strange but charismatic Gould. "He was not what you would call a smart dresser or cared much about what he looked like, or anything like that," she said, "but I found him one of the most glamorous people I'd ever known; glamorous in the sense that . . . it was the glamour of his intellect, the glamour of his talent, and even the glamour of his personality. He was a superstar, and he had a superstar personality."

Nevertheless, if there was a particularly unstable time to befriend Gould, this was it; on the other hand, it was a good time for someone to offer their friendship and comfort to Gould. Through this period with Roslak, Gould reported mysterious ailments: between 1975 and 1977, he complained about problems with his hands and his long, strong, flexible, graceful fingers that he had shielded from injury all his life. Forsaking handshakes and sports, those lifelines to his netherworld nonetheless were at risk. In his notepads, he told of pain and stiffness in both hands, numbness in his fingers, pain in finger joints and bumps on his knuckles. In taping television specials with Roslak and others, he said he could not play with his usual precise rhythm and technique and that his hands were out of sync with his mind. And then there was the elevated blood pressure and hypertension. Gould was always trying to come up with remedies for his physical or perceived ailments. "In his St. Clair apartment, he had his own sort of ultrasound machine and a wax bath. It was bizarre," Ray Roberts said. "He would put his arm in this box, filled with paraffin wax and it would coat his arm with intense heat for fifteen or twenty minutes.

He seemed to think it helped." The "injuries" distracted his piano playing, Roberts said. "He didn't tolerate pain like other people because it was such a distraction to him."

Doctors could find little proof that any of this was genuine, although it might have been related to Gould's favorite game — power struggle. He liked two other games, Twenty Questions and Name that Tune, but they were silly little tension breakers — for a supposedly non-competitive guy, he certainly liked to win. But the power struggle game was beginning to get hazardous. Gould, who referred to himself as the "virtuoso" of games, had often flourished in this contest — for example, in a concert at Carnegie Hall in 1962, he had butted heads with none other than world-famous conductor Leonard Bernstein until the latter had no choice but to publicly distance himself from the snail's pace which the pianist chose to play the Brahms D-Minor Concerto while Bernstein's New York Philharmonic squirmed in the orchestra pit (it wasn't personal; Gould often changed the tempo of Bach pieces for better or for worse while snubbing his noses at the critics). But the power struggle game was starting to take its toll on Gould's personal life; not only had he just come off a long estrangement with his mother before she suddenly perished, he was now trying to keep his relationship with Cornelia Foss alive and would not give up the hope that he could convince her she was wrong to leave him, that with her, he could reach even greater heights.

However, Gould kept a stiff upper lip about all of this to most of those around him. At this time of his life, he was seeking less counsel from others than he had as a young man. "People are as important to me as food," he grumbled. "As I grow older, I find I can do more and more without them . . . monastic seclusion works for me."

Yet Roslak seemed an exception in more ways than one. For instance, Gould once said that he preferred not to socialize with artists, but rather with people who had a broader and less competitive view of the world. He even allowed Roslak into his inner sanctum — his quiet penthouse apartment. "We rehearsed there," she smiled. "He had a huge living room and dining room. There were two pianos, and a sofa, and a little table and a room with a TV. It was not pristine or house beautiful."

One of Gould's neighbors at St. Clair, Wolf Leuthner — who lived directly below him from 1972 to 1982 and often chatted with the pianist — took a more shallow, cynical view of Gould's relationships: "His love was his work and I think women were a relief for him to a point; it's like when you go to the Caribbean, where it's hot and your libido gets loose." Leuthner said he saw some things between Gould and women that he would not repeat, out of respect to Gould.

Yet Roslak seemed so much more to Gould than relief. Gould, who had fired a housekeeper for gossiping about his personal life and accused someone else of poisoning him, allowed Roslak to do some tinkering on the large terrace outside the apartment, which had a neglected and overgrown garden. "I thought that, with a little bit of work and some plants and flowers, this could be quite a lovely place," she said. "I managed to persuade him to let me have a go at it, so on one beautiful day in May he commandeered Ray Roberts and his young son, Wayne, to help me realize that magic garden." According to Roslak, Gould sat quietly in his cap, overcoat, scarf and gloves "being terribly entertained, watching the three of us work up quite a sweat as we pruned trees, weeded and planted flowers and a white peony bush." The memory of that day still brings a warm feeling to Roslak and puts her in mind of a work by Richard Strauss, *Allerseelen*, a song about remembrance and loss in its exquisitely poignant final phrase: "Come to my heart, that I may hold you again, as once in May."

We can assume that the easily frightened Gould treaded gingerly with Roslak at first, particularly after being rebuffed for marriage by Foss and Batchen and reportedly refused sex by

Verna Sandercock, yet slowly but surely their relationship started to blossom like the white peony on his balcony and they developed a strong spiritual connection with their music, and with one another. Their spiritualism always began with their work; the musical nirvana was easier to see in Gould, who went into a type of trance at the keyboard, even in the studio. He hummed and sang to himself in a secret language, which drove technicians nuts until it had to be extracted from the records. "He became completely and totally immersed in the music," Roslak said. "He was not in this world anymore and I don't think it was in his consciousness . . . his talent was more than that of a pianist; he was somebody who was able to speak through music. He was original, but most of the time he was very important, and this is what he left us with. With art, you can be just a vehicle that does somebody else's voice or you can be a co-creator and make music that has been done a thousand times before but not exactly in the same way." Roslak said Gould's music had a spiritual quality: "Music is a world of its own to discover and with the magnitude of his talent, his discoveries were limitless. He wanted the listener to see or feel or experience all the things he experienced." When they were recording together, Roslak did not go into a trance like her partner. "I was more aware of my surroundings; I felt anxious and nervous prior to each performance, but once I was doing it, I somehow felt very connected to the spirit of the music — whether it was joyful, sad or tragic, it flowed through you. But I think we were aware of each other, became sort of fused with the music. It takes two entities to bring it alive. I think the chemistry developed, that's why we did a lot of projects together. We shared the same attitudes and the chemistry built over time."

"Creating music together creates a special bond between two people," William Littler said. "Some people say things to one another musically that they cannot do otherwise."

Gould had always maintained a statuesque image of a loner,

who allowed no room in the spotlight for others, but Roslak said he bent over backwards to bring out the best in their teamwork. "He was always eager to explore all the possibilities of the music and, more important, all the possibilities of the particular collaboration at hand," she said. "He would create a very special world deep within the music, and then invite you to join him there. His endless support and encouragement gave me the strength and the courage to delve deeply into that world and become part of that all-encompassing musical experience.... He knew what he wanted, but I never felt pressured — the operative word was collaboration. His musical influence was, of course, enormous, but curiously it did not stifle my own expression; quite the contrary, he had the ability to create such an atmosphere of enthusiasm and discovery, that one felt that anything was possible, and more important — attainable."

This was a different relationship than he had had with Foss, who had collaborated a little with Gould in filmmaking and radio documentaries, but not with his music and, in fact, she shuddered at his liberal interpretations of Bach. However, through his first year with Roxolana, Gould could not or would not let go of Cornelia. In the fall of 1976, a full two years after Foss had dumped him in the Hamptons, he was still telephoning her from Toronto to New York with hopes of reconciliation, sometimes from the Four Seasons Hotel. The following were handwritten notes that Gould made for himself, detailing a number of telephone calls to and from Cornelia in late September 1976. They show Gould's growing desperation with the relationship while he was in and out of hospital for a nose ailment. The television debates mentioned were the United States presidential debates between Gerald Ford and Jimmy Carter on September 23, 1976. When a blank space is left, it likely refers to Cornelia and/or her family. The letter L. appears to stand for Lukas. Quee Wing likely refers to the Fosses' Chinese maid.

(1) Thurs Nose problem at 5; ___ agreed to call later so I could finish chapter.

(2) Thurs ___ called at app 9:00 (My line busy)

(3) "I " " " " 9:15; L. made up "out to watch debates"

(4) "___ called at 9:20; said you did want to watch debates and that I should call after

(5) I did, imm. after; ___became semi-hysterical and said "have to hang up, I'll call tomorrow"! "When? 3 o'clock ("I might be at the hospital") "Then I'll keep trying till I get you?

Fri.

(6b) No call came. I was in the hospital the afternoon

(6) I called at app. 6:00 and was told by Quee Wing that "___were asleep; either ___ or Eliza picked up extension, listened as I left more, then hung up

Sat.

(7) Called at app. 4:00 Today. Eliza said ___ were out and would be back in about 15".

(7a) Called at app. 5:30. L. said you were out and would be back in about 1 hour.

(7b) Called at 7:30. L. said you "were asleep and would be in app. 1-half hrs. – i.e. 9 o'clock.

(7c) Called at 10:15. L. asked whether could call back in half-hour.

(7d) Called at 11:35 – L. said he would "try to get you to call".

The blank spaces left for Cornelia's name are quintessential Gould; nowhere in the thousands of letters found in his apartment was Cornelia Foss ever mentioned, although a number of all-business letters between Gould and her husband Lukas were discovered. A few days after this series of phone calls, Gould placed a call to his old friend Dr. Stephens for a forty-two-minute conversation; it was not unusual for Gould to call the psychiatrist, whom he affectionately called "Herr Doktor" in his exaggerated attempt at a German accent, immediately before or just after he had talked with Cornelia. It was indeed rare for Gould to break down emotionally to anyone, as he had done with Angela Addison during his romance with Franny Batchen in the 1950s, and yet he seemed to confide in Stephens.

Nevertheless, the Gould/Foss Debates and the phone calls continued as Gould apparently fussed and fretted over Cornelia for the next few months, considering and re-considering the affair and what it meant to him and what it still might hold in store while saying little or nothing about it to Roslak. He was having a difficult time closing the chapter, which was no great surprise, considering Gould's penchant for becoming obsessed with things — his music, filmmaking, writing, finding the perfect Steinway piano or watching erotic films. Whenever he turned that incredible focus and one hundred thousand thoughts per day on a subject, watch out below! Or perchance Glenn Gould was simply in love . . . that too profound, too entrapping, too "feeling" emotion. The pianist's reaction seemed to fit the theory of Dr. Anthony Storr, a psychiatrist, who opined in his book *The Dynamics of Creation*: "Those who have had little opportunity of expressing or sharing sexual feelings tend to alternate between suppressing or repressing sexuality and overvaluing it to the point of idiocy . . . it is those who have had little practice in handling their own sexuality who are likely to 'fall in love' in a devastating manner, and who treat the whole matter of love in an all-or-nothing fashion."

In a way, Cornelia had not helped; as their romance had began to crumble, she had reminded Gould how "stupid" love could be, and he was quick to agree. In love with music was just as much of an ecstasy, but easier to manage and less likely to spark other emotions and defenses.

And then, in November 1976, came a lengthy note unparalleled in Gould history, found in his apartment after he died. In the two-page, 391-word document, Gould reviews the status of an unidentified relationship that has obviously deteriorated. Though the woman he is writing about is never named, it is almost certainly about Mrs. Foss and could be dubbed The Cornelia Manifesto.

Gould broke the manifesto into three segments:

> *"Why do I want to retain it"*
> *"Why would I like to be without it"*
> *"What I would advise in the role of 3rd-party observer"*

In the first section, Gould wrote that he was reluctant to admit that he had misjudged the character of the woman and had failed to transform it. He also pined that "I feel at this moment that the daily or stand-by contact with one individual is essential . . . because I felt, until 2 yrs ago, that it would be a life-long contact and cannot conceive of that life without it." He worried that, if he could not be with Cornelia, it would affect his motivation and have a harmful effect on his writing — "specifically on its lighter, humorous aspects which incorporate reflection and for which this relationship served as a yard-stick and a sounding-board." Gould wrote that he did not want to give up the relationship because, as he put it, "I cannot easily surrender the tokens of permanence — safety, security, shelter — from my overview of life."

Under the section "Why I would like to be without it," Gould noted that the relationship had suffered a serious breakdown in communication and had led to frustration. He said he was unhappy to see the woman take a negative stance against him, that she was not concerned about the future of the affair and because "I feel that I have lost all power to influence the other's life-style and outlook."

Gould feared his emotional and physical health would deteriorate if their constant disagreements continued.

Then Gould stepped aside and acted as his own therapist, under the section "What I would advise in the role of 3rd-party observer," and advised an immediate end to the affair, which he termed an "addicting habit." He stated coldly that the relationship was likely "unsalvageable and, in any case, not worth salvaging," and that he would recover. He wrote that time would eventually heal his wounds, but the effects of his humiliations would linger and that the "quiet charm [?] of the past which made it so worthwhile is not likely, even at great emotional expense, to be recaptured."

And so the power struggle continued, at least in Gould's mind. Interestingly, in dissecting the state of the relationship, he never once used the word love, even though Cornelia said that they did indeed love one another. This seems a revealing document on several counts — not the least because the image of Gould berating someone else for "self-pre-occupation" can only, as Gould biographer and historian Kevin Bazzana says, "be described as rich. Once again it gives the lie to the legend that he did not want or could not achieve real contact with another person: the idea of 'daily' contact with another person being 'essential' is not the sort of talk one expects from hermits. But Gould demanded that contact on his own terms — that is the message of this document. His self-regard is entirely on the surface, his inability to accept any world-view but his own, his rejection of a personality that he cannot agree with or change to suit him, the necessity of being able to influence or transform the other. It is easy to see why an intense relationship with Gould came to seem overwhelming to many people." (An intense relationship that ended in such a way may have been overwhelming to Gould, as well. Within six years of his final good-bye to Cornelia, he was dead at age fifty.)

And yet in this manifesto, Gould displayed some sharp rationale, according to psychotherapist Rebecca Rosenblat, an expert on relationships. "It shows that he was able to step out of himself and play therapist — and a damn good one at that! But just because a weatherman can predict the weather doesn't mean he can control it; just because Gould could analyze the way he was didn't mean he could change it." Indeed, while he wrote coldly to himself in his apartment one night as a neutral third party, recommending the discontinuance of the romance, the next night he could have been trying to think of how to get Cornelia and the children to return to him. Gould mentioned nothing in his Cornelia Manifesto about her two children, whom he adored and had hoped to win in a custody battle with the Fosses, even though he did not seem to have any legal grounds for it.

Gould mentioned nothing to Roslak — and presumably to no one else apart from Stephens — about his lingering thoughts about Cornelia. Even Paul Myers, who had often talked to Gould about her, was surprised to hear years later that it had taken Gould so long to get over her. "After [1973], he never mentioned her again," Myers said. "One time I asked him what their status was and he made it clear that it was a closed book." But that goes to show how compartmentalized Gould could be with his friends and associates, such as Roberts, because he continued to phone Cornelia until 1977.

What if Cornelia had finally said yes to marrying Gould? If he'd had someone to convince him to take care of his physical and emotional needs full-time, would he have lived longer? Could there ever have been a Mrs. Gould beyond Flora? Pianist Malcolm Frager believed so: "If Glenn had managed, in his personal life, to just be a little bit less of a genius, a little bit more normal, I think he'd probably still be with us. I mean, if he'd settled down, gotten married and had children, and had something to think about besides himself, he probably would have. It could only have helped his playing, could have lent it greater warmth, greater humanity. And I think to have a happy family life is much more of a challenge than to have a career."

However, Angela Addison, Gould's friend in the 1950s, doubts that Glenn Gould could have married Cornelia Foss, Frances Batchen or any other woman. "There was no way he could have been married to Cornelia," Addison said. "They had wonderful times and I'm thankful he had something to break the tension and the pressure of his life."

It's hard to say whether Gould could have made a good husband and father, Ray Roberts said — "but maybe. People can change. He loved kids."

Some biographers claim that Gould never married because his mistress was his music, but today Cornelia Foss calls that nonsense. "Apart from the paranoia, he would have been a good husband and father . . . but his phobias got worse. He was just too ill."

Others are split on whether Gould might have been a good father. When Myers' son was born in 1967, Gould showed his pleasure for his producer and, according to Myers, said, "I would love to have a son of my own." Myers believes Gould would have made a "terrific father . . . he was hospitable and kind." One could imagine Gould reflecting late at night about the possibility of having his own child, of he or she sitting on his lap while he played, of teaching as his mother had taught him. Cornelia would no doubt produce a child of strong will and intellect — he had seen who she had produced with Lukas — but, of course, there were downsides: she didn't like his Bach. How could she like Lukas's Bach more than his own?

Gould wrote poems for the children of his secretary Jill

Cobb in 1975 and was godfather to children of Joan Maxwell and John Roberts, but the latter was not completely sold on Gould as a dad. "I know Glenn loved Cornelia's children," Roberts said. "They were spellbindingly lovely and there was a lot of her in them. Glenn loved them." But Roberts, who has written a book on Gould and edited another, doubts Gould would have been a solid father. "He was a unique person, so concerned with himself and his work, I doubt he would've had time for a family. He loved our kids and he would play with them. He was Noel's godfather." But Gould did not respect the family's parenting schedule. "When he came to our door it was always late. He'd go straight up the stairs, put the light on and wake them up and invent bedtime stories. The problem was getting him to stop — I had to insist it had to end with Dad as spoilsport. Glenn was an incredibly demanding person; it was a full-time career being his friend."

*Yes, he was different from us, but he was alike,
as well. He enjoyed everyday things – watching TV,
listening to radio, driving around in his car – normal
and natural things. Don't we all have hang-ups?*
– Roxolana Roslak of Gould

RHAPSODY
in MOO

Chapter EIGHTEEN

Some friends said that after Foss dumped him Gould had reduced contact with women. "The [Foss] relationship may have been a watershed, proof that he was not going to achieve a lasting domestic union," said biographer Kevin Bazzana. "He continued to have at least a few romantic relationships in the last decade of his life, including at least three that overlapped for a time in the later 1970s, two of which seem to have ended poorly around 1980." Gould, who never married, became more private into his forties, but it is believed he had at least three intimate relationships in the mid to late 1970s, two in which he told women he loved them, including Swedish music teacher Birgit Johansson, whom he reportedly wanted to marry. Perhaps he was just more secretive or careful about his affairs, even to his close friends; perhaps, after being turned down as a potential husband by Frances Batchen and Cornelia Foss, he lowered his expectations with women. One thing is certain — after Foss, Gould started going downhill physically, and Roslak was witness to that.

Gould did not share details with Roslak about his affair with Foss, and knowing his allergy toward openness, she did not push him, but rather she tried to build a relationship on what she knew about Gould: he had been a child prodigy smothered by his mother, he was a brilliant pianist who had quit the stage in 1964, he was eccentric, he was a good collaborator in music and wanted to try his hand in areas other than piano. For his part, Gould was warming up to Roslak, but what did he really know about her off camera or away from the soundstage, and what was he looking for? We have some idea; in an unpublished want ad he wrote for himself in November or December of 1977, Gould seemed to be getting his wit and desire back in full form as he tried to narrow his criteria for landing a woman:

> *WANTED – Friendly, companionably reclusive, alcoholically abstinent, tirelessly talkative, zealously unjealous, spiritually intense, minimally turquoise, maximally ecstatic, loon seeks moth or moths with similar qualities for purposes of telephonic seduction, Tristanesque trip-taking and permanent flame-fluttering. No photos required, financial status immaterial, all-ages and non-competitive vocations considered. Applicants should furnish cassette of sample conversation, notarized certification of marital disinclination, references re. low-decibel vocal consistency, itineraries and sample receipts from previous, successfully complete out-of-town (moth) flights. All submissions treated confidentially. No paws need apply. Auditions for all promising candidates will be conducted with an on.*
> *Avalon Peninsula*
> *Nfld.*

Even with today's Internet dating, with thousands of potential candidates at the touch of a keyboard, such a partner might be maddening to locate. Gould's want ad, crafted in Newfoundland where he was researching for his radio documentary *The Latecomers*, second in his Solitude Trilogy, seems to be trying to avoid the pitfalls he had found with other women. The intense thought that he put into this want ad suggests he really was looking for someone, at the very least a soul mate. This came one year after his Cornelia Manifesto, in which he revealed to himself that "daily or stand-by contact with one individual is essential" and that he was interested in maintaining "the tokens of permanence — safety, security, shelter." Roslak seemed to fit many of the criteria of the "want ad," particularly "companionably reclusive" and "spiritually intense."

Gould was no chauvinist and allowed himself to be attracted to strong women — as long as they had earned their place — and he especially adored those who harbored fears and yet talked to him about them and tried to work through them. If Gould had genuinely abandoned the thought of getting married after the frustration with Foss, Roslak seemed like a good choice for a partner because, in her late thirties, she had never been married and seemed content to stay single. With her there was no husband in the wings that would create another complicated triangle. But, of course, Gould brought his own demons to a relationship; socially, he lacked confidence and Roslak helped him with that. Away from the recording studio and the CBC cameras, he was not nearly as cocksure, Roslak said. "Glenn couldn't function in social gatherings and he got worse with age, but it didn't factor into my relationship with him because we didn't go to a lot of social things together. I was like him that way. I compromised more with people, but those things took a physical toll on me. I wasn't as antisocial as Glenn, but I was somewhat shy, with a lot of insecurity."

Gould found people distracting. Most times when he was in the company of more than one person, he seemed like a man with intense pressure inside him, as though he were going around all day entrusted with a mission from on high and you interrupted him at your peril. It was as if an orchestra was playing in the mini-auditorium in his head and he had to listen to each note and establish how to use it in the future. This mission was wrapped around him tighter than the heavy clothes he wore, which also kept people at a distance. Living in one world was enough pressure all by itself; Gould lived in two.

However, he did not always look as though he was in musical boot camp — other times, he would drop to his knees to play Scrabble with a child or spend thirty minutes laughing at something silly with Roslak. Part of the reason they did not party with others was that Gould wanted to keep his life with her hush-hush; after the Cornelia affair, which had been slightly more public, he did not want the embarrassment of striking out again. For now, Gould and Roslak settled on a retreat where they could share their inner thoughts and appreciation of the wild.

Manitoulin Island is 350 miles north of Toronto, a large Ontario island separating part of Lake Huron with Georgian Bay, a natural haven of meadows, rocks, 108 freshwater lakes, a one-lane swing bridge and windblown solitude. Ever since he was a boy, Gould had dreamed of starting a farm for old and stray animals on the island. He always had affection for animals and pets, which he generally listed on his "nourishment chain" higher than people and just beneath long-dead German composers. Gould's father, whose job as a furrier, as mentioned, caused tension between his son and him, said of Gould that "already as a child, he wanted to have a farm for old cows and horses and everything. [Manitoulin] is a mystical place, full of Indian traditions, where the great God Manitou is said to have dwelt. Some of my wife's distant relatives had lived there."

The north offered its rugged beauty and its acceptance of Glenn Gould the way he was. There had been solitude and spirit along the seashore as well, until his love with Frances Batchen had ended on the rocks in the Bahamas, and years later, he turned his face to the sandy winds on Long Island with Cornelia Foss. After that relationship ended, the sand and the sea were gone from his life; he didn't even watch his favorite erotic film *Woman in the Dunes* anymore, stopping at roughly one hundred viewings. But Manitoulin was different. "It was important to him and he wanted to share [Manitoulin] with Roxie," Ray Roberts said. "He wanted to bring all critters, even wolves, and teach them not to eat meat. I think he was only half joking. He also wanted me to move there with him."

As well, it was crucial for Gould to get away from his heartaches — the lingering death/resurrection/death of his mother, his dying romance with Foss and his deteriorating health. Mrs. Gould — the only Mrs. Gould — had been dead nearly two years, but surely she was still in his head, particularly out here on the island where the only sound besides the whistling wind were the thoughts whistling around in one's cranium. Gould's photographic memory was grand for the keyboard, poison for things that could haunt him. Surely, one person who could help him with his runaway thoughts was the solitary voice from his *Das Marienleben* recordings — Roxolana. Her initials (R.R.) took on a whole different meaning, and a relaxing one.

Solitude had always been a priority for Gould; much of his creating and learning from recordings, books and scores was done alone and away to maintain the individuality of his interpretations and to resist conformity. "I'm fascinated," he said, "about what happens to the creative output when you isolate yourself from the approval and disapproval of people around you." Occasionally, he did not even mind taking another person with him into solitude, as long as it was the right one — and it appears as though Roslak had an effect on his writing about the subject, particularly *The Quiet in the Land*, a 1977 CBC Radio documentary. Cornelia Foss may have been one of the unidentified voices in his *Solitude Trilogy*, but Gould used Roslak as a sounding board for it, as he had done with Foss for his comedic writing before their relationship turned sour. The sensitivity and compassion of the *Solitude Trilogy* seemed to reflect, among other things, that Gould made a connection between his work and his feelings, his experiences. And so Roslak and Gould drove to Manitoulin, where he was overcoming his agoraphobia — the fear of being away from home and his separation anxiety from his mother, his home and his city — although he still did not like leaving Toronto for long. Roslak had to stay close to him, otherwise The Thoughts might take over: *"Embarrassing, Cornelia? You're darned right it was — all those people in their bathing suits stopping and staring on the beach at the middle-aged man in his wool coat, begging on the sand. They even stopped their damn volleyball playing. There, I've used profanity. This could have been Bach by the sea, but that was all finished and done with now. You never liked my Bach; it turns out it could have been as simple as that."*

Roxolana quieted these negative types of thoughts from time to time in a non-judgmental manner. In a way, she seemed nature-pure and he was always on the lookout for that. One of their favorite pastimes at Manitoulin was singing Mahler to a herd of cows. A photograph in Peter Ostwald's biography of Gould, showing the pianist sitting on a boulder being approached by cows, looking perfectly at home in his heavy coat and cap, was snapped by Roslak. (She sheepishly admitted to me she had been the photographer; there is no doubt that she would have loved to have been in the photo with Gould, but dared not ask him.) Waltzing around with his shoelaces undone, Gould would wave his arms like a conductor and start singing, eventually joined in a duet by Roslak as the cows looked puzzled, and didn't know whether to stand up or sit down in the field:

Pom-pom, pom-pum
Pom-pom, pom-pum
Pom-pomp-pum, pom-pomp-pum
Puppa, puppa,
Padda, padda, padda

Gould later repeated this hilarious performance with elephants at the Toronto Zoo for the 1978 filming of the television program *Glenn Gould's Toronto* with director John McGreevy.

The couple loved the openness of Manitoulin, where you could let your musical notes, your thoughts and your dreams drift to the horizon, or just act corny with a Gregorian chant under a sky of stars. For a man who lived in a world of sound, the island was music to the ears — the birds, the pines creaking, the waves planting kisses along the shore and the crickets serenading Gould through the open motel window until he wanted to go outside in his stocking feet and collect them all one by one. "I think we had a lot in common, which drew us together," Roslak said. "Of course, we shared the music. Glenn was able to structure his life the way he wanted because of his need and desire for solitude and I shared that. I loved to be alone and always have, but I also have a social life. I compromised more than he did. People said he must have been so lonely, but he wasn't alone and he loved those types of settings in nature. I could relate to that. We talked about our solitude and the need to be alone." Perhaps the loon had found its partner?

If solitude is the school of genius, Gould needed it as much for creative thinking as to keep people at arm's length. In the 1960s, he had crafted a radio documentary, *The Search for Petula Clark*, about a singer he had a crush on from a distance. He discovered her music while driving highways north of Toronto. (Gould's love of Clark was unique, considering he eschewed most other kinds of popular music. He listened to her constantly and wrote essays about the effects of her music.) Out of this environment, he would also produce some gems of wisdom with Roslak perhaps as the lone witness:

> *"Behind every silver lining is a cloud."*
> *"I am a child of nature."*
> *"I think one really has to live one's life with a*

spiritual direction in mind."
*"I'm very much the antihero in real life, but I
compensate like mad in my dreams."*

At times, Gould wagged an institutionalized tongue and it
took patience for someone to sit quietly and decipher the ter-
minology in some of his writings such as this: "Hindemith's
method, which endowed his later works with idiomatic con-
sistency [few musicians provide such instant giveaways for the
Who's the Composer version of Twenty Questions], was fun-
damentally phenomenological. 'I vibrate, therefore I am,'
might well have been his motto . . . the two versions of his *Das
Marienleben* provide pertinent illustration: Draft I from 1923
is a passionate, if occasionally untidy, masterpiece; Draft 2 from
1948 is a sober, indeed impeccable revision that approaches its
subject with healthy respect in lieu of ecstatic devotion."

Roslak — whom Gould was now calling Roxie when no one
else was around — would not reveal details, but Gould also
used the quiet of Manitoulin to get a lot of other things off his
chest. Undoubtably they discussed a potpourri of topics: politics; religion; Zen Buddhism; the emergence of the recording
studio; the dumping of some of his addictions, including striking boxes of matches until they were all spent; and, in 1976, the
death of billionaire genius Howard Hughes, known for his brilliance, eccentricities, obsessiveness and secrecy (it comes as no
surprise to discover that the germaphobic Hughes was one of
Gould's heroes).

Roslak and Gould also discussed their fears, including stage
fright, which was one of the reasons Gould quit public concerts in 1964. (Another reason Gould stopped performing,
Roslak theorized, was that "he felt he was not able to have the
kind of control he wanted. There were so many variables and
he liked to feel in control.") Like pianist Frances Batchen before
her, Roxolana Roslak was also frightened of audiences, or at

least what they thought of her, such as on one night in the late 1970s at a Toronto recital when, accompanied by pianist Stuart Hamilton, she got out of breath and choked. "I was always a very reluctant performer; I had terrible nerves, but I was completely driven to do it," she said. In fact, both she and Gould had powerful drives to succeed, which kept them in the public eye. And Gould's emotional needs and other needs kept him performing (until '64) and recording until his death. "Music made up an essential and a huge part of his emotional life," she said. Roslak added that another part of Gould's inner drive was a need to express his talent. "The need of that talent is different from you and I — he was different in a genetic sense. I think he was born different. I never met his mother, but I think she was a very powerful influence in his life."

During their pristine moments together, Gould also opened up about his fears of flying and his fear of catching germs. "He didn't like people to touch him, or to touch people, but I think he touched them in many other ways," she said. While Gould had many irrational fears, Roslak noticed that he had some everyday traits about him, as well. "Yes, he was different from us, but he was alike, as well. He enjoyed everyday things — watching TV, listening to radio, driving around in his car — normal and natural things. Don't we all have hang-ups? I know people not as eccentric as Glenn with just as many hang-ups and problems."

In their type of codependency, Roslak says that Gould helped bolster her confidence and perspective about her worries. "After we finished *Marienleben*, we listened to the tapes and I was terribly insecure, terrified. I told him I was glad it came out so well, that I was just happy we did it and I didn't care if it ever comes out because I was worried about the public's reaction. Glenn got annoyed and said, 'You would feel that selfish you would deny some man in Medicine Hat the opportunity to listen to your music and experience it?' Glenn certainly gave me a big boost in my own ability and, in practical terms, helped my profile. It raised me to another level."

Roslak seemed to be, among other things, a surrogate mother for Gould, helping him through a trying period of physical and psychosomatic illnesses — the hypertension, kidney problems, high blood pressure and the difficulties with his hands. Roslak could be stern with Gould, according to Ray Roberts: "She was pretty persuasive with him, and she certainly had an effect on him. She would get him to do things out of character for him, and that's why I started to suspect they were having a serious relationship. She got onto him about his medication, about taking too many pills. It helped temporarily — he would listen to her for a while, but he didn't necessarily do anything about it." In the mid-1970s, Gould was taking a variety of drugs for real or imagined illnesses: Aldomet (for high blood pressure), Inderal (to slow pulse and respiratory rate), Librax (for digestion), Librium (a tranquilizer) and Indocin (anti-inflammatory). And she fussed about his looks, which were deteriorating from youthful handsomeness to haggard middle-age. No longer with the light brown, almost blond hair, he had become darker, brooding, a philosopher king, eyes more sunken. His reputation alone, on the brink of legend, kept Glenn Gould attractive. Who cared if sunlight was less and less kind to him or if he was developing flab? Machismo was never his appeal.

In 1977, Gould taught Roslak how to drive a car — his spanking new Chevrolet Monte Carlo. "I was shocked," Roberts said. (Due to Gould's erratic driving, his friends referred to the passenger side as the suicide seat.) "She never got her license, but came close to it. He was very supportive of her and he saw that it would have made her more independent. Glenn put away his control issues for a moment and allowed her to pilot him around — imagine that!"

On occasion, the fussy-eating Gould even allowed Rosak to

cook for him. As with Batchen, Sandercock and Foss before her, Gould used Roslak as a sounding board for his music and he told her that he was considering re-recording the *Goldberg Variations*, his signature since 1955 — a risky move to try to match the success of that recording — and revising his self-composed String Quartet of 1956, which had left him unsettled because the critics said it sounded too much like a Richard Strauss piece. After working closely with her in the recording studio and before the television cameras, Gould was comfortable discussing his musical options with Roslak — whether a piece should be deliberate or sprightly, suggestive or assertive, melancholy or heart aglow, more or less, spiritual or secular. Gould also told Roslak that he was seriously considering becoming a conductor — perhaps in live concerts with audiences and for recordings, in which he would both play the piano and conduct (on separate tracks). In fact, he was in the early stages of planning a practice session of conducting with the Hamilton Philharmonic, strictly off-limits to the press. Recalling how he conducted the cows on Manitoulin, it made her chuckle. Roslak loved this side of Gould, which was full of teamwork and sacrifice and seemed to rub off on his girlfriends, all five of whom, like Roslak, became teachers and instructors.

One of the many mysteries that died with Gould was an unpublished song, entitled "Rosemary's Child," found among his notes along with references that Gould wrote it for Roslak. According to Gould biographer Kevin Bazzana, Gould's surviving papers "include many, sometimes remarkably involved, specimens of private humor that he worked up for himself and friends — joke memos, stories set in verse, monologues and scripts, little songs." As was his peculiar custom, he sometimes didn't share them with the people they were written about. Roslak says today she has never heard of a song Gould wrote for her. Then there was a dialogue Gould wrote about Roslak and CBC producer James Kent, who barely knew each other. The dialogue ends with this stage direction: "The sound of heavy breathing is heard."

Evidence of a romantic affair between Gould and Roslak is mainly circumstantial, albeit considerable and suggestive. If nothing else, said Bazzana, their close friendship, "shows in the often haunting intensity of their recording." Then there was the body language between them — on record covers, in their duets and in rare social settings. The fact that Gould allowed Roslak to go to one of his fortresses of solitude — Manitoulin Island — to sing to the cows tells us something.

Over the years Roslak has not admitted she had a romantic affair with Gould, but she does not deny it, either. "Oh, uh, I don't think that's . . . I'm not about to tell you that. . . ." she told biographer Otto Friedrich in 1988. "I would prefer not to discuss his sexual life . . . I have a very strong memory of Glenn, but whether or not he was a homosexual or a heterosexual or asexual or any kind of sexual, that is not the kind of thing that figures very prominently in my recollections. So I'm — you know — I mean, I think he was a very romantic figure. Yes, definitely."

In the fall of 2007, during an interview for this book, Roslak said, "I really am not prepared to discuss personal details. It all comes down to sex. Why wouldn't people think you can't express love in different ways? Love has many guises and expressions, including sex. But people want to know details. Private things are private. I think anybody who was close to Glenn wanted to protect him. I don't want to betray that trust." But Roslak went as far as to say, "Yes, I had an emotional relationship with him. That's all I'll say." That's *all?* For Glenn Gould, that might have been more of an admission than about sex, or a poor concert performance — an emotional affair would be most difficult to admit.

Roslak and Gould kept their close friends and associates mum on their friendship. "I was talking to [CBC producer] John Roberts about Glenn one day," William Littler said.

"[Roberts] said that one day, he confronted Glenn about the mess of his apartment. 'This place needs a woman's touch,' Roberts said, to which Gould replied, referring to a cleaning lady, 'I have one, she comes every week to clean,' referring to a maid." Roberts was very protective of Gould's personal life, as well as his professional life; he stood up for him against the musician's union, which frowned upon the long hours Gould spent in the recording studio.

Gould's producers at Columbia Records in New York, Kazdin and Myers, heard rumors of the romantic affair, but saw no direct evidence of it when they recorded together. "He talked about [Roslak] quite often, about how good she was as a singer, but he said nothing else about her," Myers said.

Roslak's singing coach and sometimes accompanist, Stuart Hamilton, who worked with Roslak for twenty-five years, says now that it was definitely a sexual affair kept clandestine. "Yes, they had an affair — one of [Gould's] great affairs was with Roxie; it was a very passionate and close relationship for several years. She was crazy about him. . . . He carried on his affair with Roxie in his apartment or in hotel rooms. They never appeared in public together, unless they were working," Hamilton said. "He was probably very conservative, old Toronto family WASP. It was tiresome for her to be running around secretly. He took her to New York and she stayed in a room at the Drake Hotel. It was an elegant, expensive hotel . . . he didn't want his fans or anyone else around him." Roslak was working with Hamilton on a daily basis while seeing Gould and she confided in him, Hamilton said.

Ray Roberts remembers being at the Drake on another occasion with Gould: "One time we checked into the Drake, but he complained about how hard the beds were and we had to pick up and move over to a Holiday Inn in New Jersey."

Roslak told a few others about the affair, but they said nothing about it for decades. "I knew about it somewhat," said

Gould friend Ezra Schabas, former music manager of the Stratford Festival, "but it was kept very quiet."

"It was a brief, torrid affair," said a friend of Roslak, asking his name not be used. "I think it was his last affair, and I knew of several."

In the late 1970s and indeed throughout his life, Gould kept a tight lid on his personal life and the media stopped asking questions about it. In 1978, the first of many biographies about Gould was published (the only one in his lifetime) by writer Geoffrey Payzant, *Glenn Gould Music & Mind*. Gould authorized the book, which was as much of an intellectual study as a biography, and did not mention Frances Batchen, Verna Sandercock, Cornelia Foss, Roxolana Roslak or any other of the many women that Gould was close to up until that time. Gould not only approved of the book, he wrote a review of it in the *Glenn Gould Reader*, saying his private life was "austere and unremarkable" and that a book on his life and times would be brief and boring. His coyness acted as a smoke screen for his affairs, which had some kick to them and were windows into his shadowy life. When he went back to his piano, he took his personal experiences with him, and presumably they enriched his repertoire.

> *One develops what one thinks of as an intense need to be*
> *with a particular person . . . while that may be a fascinating*
> *exercise in communication, it's also exhausting*
> *and it distracts you from looking inward, to really*
> *meditate upon the shape of your life.*
> — Glenn Gould

The LIST

Chapter NINETEEN

Gould and Roslak last worked together in 1978 and when they won the Juno Award for *Das Marienleben* in 1979, Gould didn't show up at the ceremony in Toronto to accept the prize. Loyal to a fault, Roslak says the collaboration ended amicably and that their friendship continued until his death four years later, but on a reduced scale (a statement that is rebuked by those close to her, who say it became a full-blown affair). "He wasn't primarily into doing vocal repertoire, but we remained friends," Roslak said. "He called me a lot on the telephone and we talked about everything from music to politics, to dogs and animals, to Mary Tyler Moore. He liked her! And he liked Barbra Streisand's singing. He talked about working with her [on a classical album], but I don't think he did . . . and we talked a lot about mutual friends we had."

Gould preferred using the phone, where he didn't have to self-consciously look into Roslak's, or anyone else's, eyes. He talked so often on the telephone to Roslak and others, his average phone bill for that time period in the late 1970s was about $504 per month, although it sometimes went up to four figures, showing that his need to talk was even greater than his need for prescription drugs, which was at that time $503 per month. He was even talking to his father Bert, who had apparently recovered from Flora's death in 1975 and was engaged to the bubbly Vera Dobson. But Glenn became irritated when Bert asked him to be the best man at their wedding and, turning into Ann Landers all of a sudden, wrote a letter to Bert, which he never mailed. Part of it read:

- *Hope I'm not speaking out of turn ... have kept silent until now. Vera is obviously an energetic lady, tremendously so for her age (theatres, parties and what not)*
- *My point is that I'm not sure it's appropriate for a person of your age to change their spots so radically.*
- *All love relationships are addictive – just as much as alcohol or tobacco. One develops what one thinks of as an intense need to be with a particular person, to translate all your activity, everything that you do in the course of a day, and while that may be a fascinating exercise in communication, it's also exhausting and it distracts you from looking inward, to really meditate upon the shape of your life.*

Gould never became the best man at his father's wedding; in fact, their relationship turned sour once again and Glenn stopped talking to Bert. Throughout her time with Gould, Roslak heard stories about his reputation for abruptly ending relationships with family, friends and colleagues. In total, The List becomes quite ominous: mezzo-soprano Joan Maxwell; childhood friend and journalist Robert Fulford; magazine writer and close friend Gladys Shenner; his revered colleague Leonard Bernstein; his Columbia Masterworks producer of fifteen years Alfred Kazdin; his first date, CBC producer Elizabeth Fox; musician and confidante Greta Kraus; his girlfriend Verna Sandercock; his own mother and father for a period in the 1960s and 1970s; composer John Beckwith; musicologist Harvey Olnick; pianist Anton Kuerti; friend Carol [Hodgdon] Goodfriend and her husband James Goodfriend, who was editor for his liner notes; television director Vincent Tovell; CBC Radio producer Keith MacMillan; violinist Morry Kernerman; musician Bobby Mann; and, in 1977, two psychiatrist/musician friends whom Gould had used from time to time as his unofficial psychotherapists, Dr. Peter Ostwald and Dr. Joseph Stephens.

Maxwell simply referred to this as "The List" and wondered if Gould got the idea from Gilbert and Sullivan's operetta *The Mikado* in which we hear, "I've got a little list . . . I've got him on the list." The music belies the fact that the people on the list are being chopped and that "they'll none of 'em be missed — they'll none of 'em be missed."

"Glenn had a list, too, a list of friendships that ended," Maxwell said. "The dreadful thing about The List was that you were never offered any explanation about what it was that had offended him; you were never given a chance to explain. Suddenly — bang — that was it. It really was unbelievable. I think it went back to the fact that he really couldn't engage in any conversation that might upset him, so rather than offer any explanation, or make any accusation, it was simply trial without jury." Maxwell added that she and her husband Harvey and their two sons had a wonderful relationship with Gould but they suddenly made it onto The List in 1979 and were banned — for reasons unknown to them. Maxwell believed that Roslak eventually made it onto The List, as well. "Glenn had several passionate affairs that we knew about, for instance, and these ended with the woman's abrupt relegation to The List," Maxwell said.

In some cases, it seemed as though Gould stopped talking to people who had criticized him, such as Kuerti, Olnick, Beckwith, Tovell and critic B. H. Haggin. "If you did something to offend him, he would often cut off people for good," Ray

Roberts said. "You became a persona non grata. I was one of the few people to get away with it." Roberts does not know how close Gould ever came to marriage. "At that time, I was only his hired gun — there was no way he would talk to me about something so intimate." But Roberts twice came close to becoming a persona non grata — the first time was in 1977 when Gould was looking for a new assistant. "Actually, I thought he needed somebody else, so I helped him to look, but we didn't find anybody and I stayed on until the end." The other time was in the late 1970s when his widowed father started dating Dobson; during a long drive from Toronto to New York at about that time, Roberts told Gould that Dobson might be good for Bert. "He became angry with me and said he was firing me," Roberts said. "But we had to get to New York, so I was still on his payroll."

Why did Gould, who was sensitive to others' needs in many other instances, have such a penchant for dumping people? Ostwald, who founded a health program for musicians and wrote the book *Glenn Gould: The Ecstasy and Tragedy of Genius*, noted that Gould, like Albert Einstein and Bill Gates, appeared to have some of the symptoms of Asperger's Syndrome, a variant of autism in which sufferers have problems in social situations and may sometimes be cruel toward others without conscience or understanding others' feelings. People with Asperger's tend to stereotype as well as show repetitive patterns of behavior and interests. They can be very intense and focused and may preoccupy themselves with parts of objects.

"He may have used Asperger's to his advantage, both in his piano and his personal life — he cut everything out quite cold-bloodedly to keep himself together," said writer and Gould friend Tim Page, who suffers from Asperger's and wrote a book about it, *Parallel Play: Growing Up Undiagnosed with Asperger's*. "He had to — for him, any loss of control was extra painful. He was always putting himself into a position where he didn't have to worry. For example, almost nobody had his phone number. You would call his answering machine and he would call you back, if he wanted to. And it made him subject to tantrums." Perhaps as a result of Asperger's, Gould was likely not promiscuous, Page added, but rather decided which women he wanted and focused on them. "But that meant he didn't get over [those women] quickly." People with Asperger's may also be sensitive to sound, touch, pain and temperature, as Gould was, and they may also be gifted in music and mathematics, both Gould traits.

Ray Roberts also believes that Gould had Asperger's. "It fit Glenn Gould like a glove. That might be an unpopular opinion because I'm a representative of the Glenn Gould Foundation."

Others, such as psychiatrist Dr. Helen Mesaros, are skeptical of the post-mortem diagnosis and believe there were many psychological and emotional explanations for Gould's quirky behavior, such as his puritanical upbringing. Dr. Joseph Stephens said it was possible that Gould was neurotic (Freud said that civilization owed a lot to the contributions of obsessive neurotics) and that he had a type of disorder, but he could not say for sure because Gould reportedly never went under psychoanalysis beyond the long phone conversations with Stephens and Ostwald. "He was able to function in his music, no doubt about it, but personally, he was a screwed-up guy," Stephens said. "I enjoyed our relationship, and he could be an incredible person, but he also could be an egomaniac, who only wanted to talk about himself and his theories [another symptom of Asperger's]. And he was a terrible driver — he nearly killed me twice in his car. When we deal with geniuses, and Gould *was* a genius, we lay down our arms because there's no way to explain everything. I think he became an unhappy guy at the end of his life."

Relationship expert Rebecca Rosenblat, who did not know Gould but has reviewed his history, believes that he might have been very choosy in letting people into his "messy" life, but once they were in, they walked on eggshells, fearful of making a mistake or causing him pain. Many of the members of this exclusive club were frustrated or angry about getting dumped; Kernerman was so upset, he moved his family from Toronto to Montreal to avoid running into Gould again. However, many others, while sad, had no regrets about being Gould's friend in the first place and put their dismissal down to the cost of doing business with such an unusual man.

Perhaps there were different reasons Gould cut people off and perhaps in the end it was about the power struggle, controlling a situation he could not or would not handle. Obviously confrontation made him squirm, unless he was embroiled in a power struggle he could not avoid. After his death, a number of unposted letters were found in the dead letter office of his apartment intended for people he had ended relationships with, including Shenner, a woman named Eliza and an unidentified woman who may have been Roslak or Monica Gaylord. In another letter, which apparently was mailed to an obsessed American fan who would not leave him alone, Gould wrote: "I tend to go out of my way to avoid whatever confrontations seem likely to result in injuring the feelings of some other person."

It would be easy to portray Gould as a villain if it were not for the flip side of his personality, which was humble, giving and considerate to many women and other colleagues, even those he eventually shunned. "He could be pretty heartless to a lot of people to satisfy his own whims," said Ezra Schabas, who quit as music manager of the Stratford Festival in 1961 because he felt that administrator Gould was too rude and dictatorial. "Most of his friends were people he needed . . . but he was a mixture and could be very kind. He gave my kids signed, long-playing records."

Tovell also felt Gould's kindness, as well as his wrath. "My mother died [in the early 1960s] rather suddenly and Glenn was very upset by this, on my behalf," Tovell said. "I will never forget his solicitude. It was in a sense as though he were sharing in an intimate family experience which had been denied him. That exposed to me a part of Glenn I never forgot; how vulnerable he was to the ordinary vicissitudes of life; how anxious he could be; how deeply concerned he was about what went on around him — about people he knew and the world he was living in."

"Glenn spoke very kindly about a lot of people," Roslak said. "We would talk about mutual friends, but I don't remember him ever being hostile or maliciously unkind."

In the 1950s and 1960s, Gould helped budding St. Catharines pianist Anahid Alexanian get her career kick-started and in 1959, he telephoned a depressed Frances Batchen after their breakup, offering her encouragement. When his producer Paul Myers was writing a novel, a satirical look at colonial life, Gould asked Myers to read it to him over the phone, and he did. "He enjoyed it, even though it never got published. It tickled his funny bone," Myers said.

To this day, Roslak is uncomfortable talking about The List. "I really couldn't say why he had the propensity to do that to people, but it would be too simple to say he just discarded them," she said. "There were things in his makeup, his character and personality that brought him to loggerheads with people. I think with his emotional makeup, he couldn't make compromises. He lived in a pretty black-and-white world, in many instances."

Gould never talked in detail with Roslak about how and why cold rain descended upon many of his relationships, but it was common for him to display different sides of his personality to different people, to compartmentalize relationships. In fact, Gould's relationship with Roslak may have been partly responsible in Gould ending his long relationship with Kazdin —

according to Kazdin himself. "I learned [from a colleague] of the strong possibility that there was a social relationship between Glenn and Roxolana Roslak, the soprano who collaborated with us in the recording of Hindemith's *Das Marienleben*. In fact, during our last phone call together, I had the unmistakable impression that there was a woman with him as we spoke. It has occurred to me that the termination of our friendship might have been somehow related to my unwitting intrusion." Kazdin still does not know why Gould fired him — "What was deep in his heart, I don't know."

Gould was apparently in such turmoil about giving Kazdin the axe, CBC executive John Roberts suggested to him that Gould seek professional help: "I think it's maybe good to go and talk to a psychiatrist. It doesn't mean that one is mentally ill."

Although he was close to Roslak for several years, Gould compartmentalized his friendship with her, keeping some of his own space to himself; for example, he never took her to any of his early-morning jaunts to Fran's Restaurant, across the street from his St. Clair Avenue apartment, and he said little to her about his budding relationship with pianist Monica Gaylord. All through this, Gould's recording and documentary filmmaking continued; in the late 1970s, while he was still with Roslak, Gould tinkered with the idea of transforming into a full-time composer, to have others play *his* music, but it never materialized. "He did compose a few things, String Quartet and *So You Want to Write a Fugue*, but I didn't know him as a composer. Perhaps he felt he didn't have the ability to be the kind of composer he wanted to be," Roslak said. "He did say when he was going to stop playing the piano, he wanted to be a writer."

Stuart Hamilton believes the clandestine relationship of soprano and maestro began to falter in the late 1970s, perhaps not as early as Christmas 1978, when Hamilton accompanied Roslak on the piano for her American debut at the Lincoln Center in New York. (Although acclaimed in Canada, Roslak was unknown in New York, so the Canadian Consulate spent $1,700 on advertising in addition to the $9,000 in Canada Council money that funded the recital at Tully Hall. "I must say the Canadian government has been generous, making it all possible with a grant," Roslak said. About 250 people attended the concert, which obviously lost potential customers to the opening night of the Metropolitan Opera production of *Tosca*, held nearby.)

At about that time, or perhaps a little later, Roslak complained to Hamilton and other friends and colleagues that Gould was phoning her too much in the middle of the night. "He was so demanding on her, so difficult," an anonymous friend said. "She was trying to do her singing in the morning and he would be calling her late at night."

It sounded like Frances Batchen of the 1950s — the Midnight Man was striking again. "I think the phone calls were what started them breaking up," said Hamilton, who proclaimed the ideal vocal coach to be a "curious combination of musician, confessor, nanny and shrink." And yet Hamilton believed that Roslak was interested in marriage or at least a permanent relationship with her pianist. Then, suddenly, Gould cut himself off from Roslak and refused to accept her telephone calls and telegrams, Hamilton said. "She tried everything she could to get back together with him; I think she even went around to his apartment. She was very unhappy and it was very hard on her, which was sad because Roxie is a very dignified, honest person. Her nerves were shattered. She didn't want to break up with him."

Their ecstasy was turning to agony; earth had collapsed onto heaven. Roxolana Roslak had made The List. "Roxie demanded too much in the relationship and that's why she was shunned," a close friend said.

"He had a habit of dumping people," said Littler, who knew Roslak at the time and now works with her at the Royal Conservatory of Music in Toronto. "I think he had a problem with emotional commitment; eventually, people got too close and he wanted to keep something private for himself." Perhaps one of the reasons that Gould severed the relationship was through what Littler referred to earlier — that some people can share something with others musically that they cannot do in everyday life. But, up until this point, perhaps the only girl-friend Gould had cut off was Verna Sandercock, and that could have been partly because she would not go to bed with him.

In the end, Hamilton was not surprised that Gould's relationship with Roslak dissolved. "In ways, he could be insensitive toward women, and they ended up feeling like they'd be used, like Roxie did."

That was another contradiction in Gould's life because he could often be very gentlemanly toward women and, indeed, he seemed to revere them . . . up to a point, or a precipice. "He liked women and was very gracious and very courtly [toward them]. He called me 'Madame' in an eighteenth-century way," said Judith Pearlman, producer of Gould's television special *The Idea of North.* But, of course, she was never romantically involved with him.

Roslak also worked with the late harpsichordist and teacher Greta Kraus, who was a close friend of Gould and confidante to some of his female friends (who also eventually made The List). Kraus once said of Gould, "He could not accept love. I had the feeling that any expression of affection would cause him to panic . . . I know of at least one affair in which he was possessed with absolute jealousy. He couldn't make one phone call without mentioning her. He was stirred by her, passionately wanting to see her. Whether it was ever fulfilled? I assume that with the person I'm thinking of, he drove her to distraction." (We do not know the identity of the woman Kraus was referring to, but it could have been Cornelia Foss, Roslak or someone else.) "And then, whoosh, it was over, from one day to the next, finished! Absolutely finished. Never a word of explanation, not another word. Well, that's a sick mind, isn't it?"

Kazdin speculated that Gould may have schemed to end some relationships, including the one between him and his producer. "He sort of plotted things, planned and plotted. Once, we talked about war and he said he could never fight in a war because he was a pacifist, and yet he said he could work from an underground bunker, where he could plan and plot strategies."

But there may have been a number of reasons why the Gould-Roslak duet did not endure; for one thing, studies have shown that there is a high rate of separation and divorce among entertainers and creative people because of possible ego conflicts, emotional and mental issues, lack of privacy from an adoring public and media, plus demanding workloads and schedules of two such professionals. Sony (formerly Columbia Masterworks) thought enough about the alleged affair between Gould and Roslak to mention it in the 1995 liner notes for a release of *Das Marienleben*. Writer Michael Stegemann said, "Whether Gould ever had an affair with Roxolana Roslak, as his producer Andrew Kazdin and others have indicated, is ultimately irrelevant. What matters is the music itself, and in this respect, these recording sessions appear to have been fulfilling in a way that had not been the case with other female singers with whom Gould had worked."

It could have been that Gould had grown weary of the idea of ever getting married and that the long, sad ending with Cornelia had cemented that. Yes, he said he wanted "safety and security" with Foss, but in the big picture, Gould was not a creature who embraced change, and in his late forties, marriage for such a bachelor would have been a change the size of a Steinway grand. In the early 1980s here was a man who had never moved from his hometown Toronto and had kept the same television network for three decades and the same record company for twenty-five. However, the breakup with Roslak apparently did not stop Gould from his search for the perfect female companion. He was becoming close to Gaylord, but in the late 1970s and early 1980s, he also had telephone/correspondence buddies in his new Columbia public relations rep Susan Koscis, Swedish music teacher Birgit Johansson and budding California conductor Sonia Maria De León. In his notepad, he kept doodling and playing with the names of Roslak and Gaylord on a pad, exaggerating the *R* in Roslak's name and toying with the *M* in Monica, presenting them as though he were a teenager carving girls' initials into a tree. In other notes, he practiced his signature, sometimes spelling Glenn with one "n."

Meanwhile, his all-important work went on as Gould was planning to re-record the *Goldberg Variations* and perhaps his String Quartet. But a major problem arose — his perfect piano, the Steinway CD 318, was aging and in disrepair while losing its rich sound and tone. Gould was now leaning toward renting or purchasing a modified Yamaha concert grand in New York. He liked it, but it had its shortcomings. Always the perfectionist in many areas of life, Gould was constantly searching for the ideal piano, one that fitted his special needs as a sensitive performer. He let his needs for such a piano be known in music circles, and they included: a light, responsive keyboard action; pedal optional; rough keys (as if he were stroking a dog); no after-touch, with the sound stopping the moment he lifted his finger off the key; a minimal effort to push down the keys, even if that meant sacrificing power; an importance in how the instrument felt under his hands rather than how it sounded.

If worded the right way, he could have fit his piano requirements into a want ad much the same as the one he had fashioned for the perfect female companion.

She is an artist who combines astonishing
versatility with extraordinary insights.
— Glenn Gould on Monica Gaylord

MONICA – *The* LINK *between*
two SECRET KINGDOMS?

Chapter TWENTY

The black-and-white photograph at the Canadian Museum of Contemporary Photography shows a pianist in a low slung chair, playing intensely while wearing an overcoat and British driving cap. It is catalogued as No. 74-X-1878, a gelatin silver print taken by prominent photojournalist Walter Curtin. It would be a bizarre shot if it did not happen to be Glenn Gould in his natural environment. The only thing missing from the Master Eccentric are his gloves with cutout holes for the athletic fingers. Nearby in Curtin's collection of notable Canadians is Print No. 74-X-1883. Now this one *is* bizarre. It shows another pianist playing in a jacket, long gloves and a white mask, not unlike the Phantom of the Opera. The only way to identify this pianist is from Curtin's records, which show it is Monica Gaylord of Toronto, who attained some success in the 1970s as a concert pianist and recording artist.

With her mask removed, Gaylord was an attractive, smart, innovative woman ahead of her time in a classical music world dominated by men. The story of her relationship with Gould — seventeen years her elder — is as mysterious as her photograph and it involves the crossing of paths of not only the two unusual pianists, but Canadian Prime Minister Pierre Trudeau and singer Barbra Streisand. And, it is one of those mysteries that Gould's other close friend, soprano Roxolana Roslak, would love so much if her path had not crossed with Gould at the same time.

In the late 1970s, it was known with a nod and a wink in Toronto music circles that Gaylord and Gould had a tight friendship, although to this day she refuses to talk about it. When a researcher contacted Gaylord in 2001, asking for an interview, she sent back a brief note, saying she would talk to him "about anything *but* Glenn Gould." Six years later, as I was researching this project, Gaylord did not respond to three letters I sent to her. Fortunately, when he died, Gould left some clues under scores and old books in his cluttered apartment for historians to comb through, including a number of references to Gaylord. A little violin music, please, as we open this opera, or tragicomedy, of the 1960s. . . .

It begins with Trudeau. "What Glenn Gould was to Bach, Trudeau was to Canada," said actor Christopher Plummer. "He interpreted it with a freshness that was bold and utterly original."

Trudeau and Gould had other things in common — they were both political philosophers and stout Canadian nationalists, CBC celebs who were charismatic and complex, boyish pranksters who enjoyed games such as Twenty Questions, visionaries who kept a record of their dreams and were so enamored with cottage country that images of them that come to mind are of each alone in a boat on the open waters.

If Gould was absolutely private about his women, Trudeau was semi-private. As prime minister, cameras followed Trudeau everywhere and to be snapped with gorgeous ladies suited his ego just fine, but he kept his deeper relationships close to his vest and went to considerable lengths to conceal his affairs from the snoopy public and in some cases from his staff. Classical guitarist Liona Boyd recalls having to wear wigs to disguise herself while running in and out of backdoors and elevators for much of her eight-year affair with Trudeau (1976 to 1983). In a common scenario, Boyd would check in to an expensive Ottawa hotel, sneak over to Trudeau's official residence at 24 Sussex for the night, then return to the hotel to fool the chambermaids by ruffling the bed sheets and ripping open the soap packages to make it look like she had stayed the night. One evening, they made love to Gould's recording of the *Goldberg Variations*, which Boyd had brought as a gift for Trudeau.

Those among Trudeau's staff who knew details about his many women — such as their moonlit skinny-dipping at his cottage on Lake Harrington — remained mum. "There was a code of silence," said his secretary Patrick Gossage. "You simply weren't allowed to talk about it." And the ladies who sometimes overlapped in their relationships with Trudeau often knew nothing about one another. "One night, I arranged a dinner for him in Washington and had a table for all the ex-girlfriends," Gossage chuckled. "None of them knew about the others." And over the years there was quite a stable: Boyd, singer-songwriter Diane Juster; actress Kim Cattrall; actor Matthew Perry's mother Suzanne Perry; singer Gale Zoë Garnett ("We'll Sing in the Sunshine"); ballerina Karen Kain; actress Margot Kidder; and his only wife Margaret Sinclair, whom he wedded unannounced in seclusion in 1971.

Two of Trudeau's relationships, or perhaps crushes, coincided with those of Gould, beginning with singer Barbra Streisand in the late 1960s. Having a crush on Streisand was a stretch for the classical pianist who felt that most pop music was beneath him and far too superficial. "I'm a Streisand freak, make no bones about it," Gould told *Rolling Stone* magazine. He even considered Streisand one of his favorite pop singers — "the greatest singing-actress since Maria Callas." And he adored her tender tune "He Touched Me." Gould wanted to record a classical album with Streisand, which never materialized, but in 1965 in New York, the chance to meet her fell into his lap. Unbeknownst to one another, the two entertainment legends happened to be recording in back-to-back studios. An excited Streisand, who loved Gould's work, found out about it and knocked on his door. When Gould answered, he was stunned to see who was there.

"Hi," she said. "I just wanted to say hello because I'm a fan and, since we were here, I thought I'd stop by and tell you that."

"I know," Gould sputtered, and had nothing else to offer. Years later, he would bemoan his missed opportunity.

Gould's regret about not working with Streisand, or at least getting to know her personally, must have reached a new level in 1969 when he learned through the media that she had started dating Trudeau. Gould was not a fan of Trudeau. "He disapproved of [Trudeau's] lifestyle," Roberts said. Gould preferred his politicians without charm, like Robert Stanfield or Joe Clark. And at times, their politics clashed.

"Glenn was a right winger and a monarchist," said pianist Anton Kuerti, who was friends with Gould and taught Gaylord. "We had a lot of discussions about politics. I was a left winger." (However, there was some evidence that Gould was left-leaning on some issues.)

"Trudeau had an eye for the ladies," said William Littler. "Like with Gould, there were rumors Trudeau was gay because he was single for a long time. When you live alone, people say that. I know — I live alone, but I like it, and I'm not gay." (For the record, Littler always thought Gould was asexual and he knew of no affairs he had with women.) "[Trudeau] did squire a lot of women, but that didn't necessarily mean he had affairs with them. Like [Gould], he liked the idea of women around. But when Glenn allowed them to get close, there were borders they couldn't cross."

Meanwhile, Streisand considered becoming Canada's First Lady. "I thought it would be fantastic," she said. "I'd have to learn how to speak French. I would do only movies in Canada. I had it all figured out. I would campaign for him and become totally politically involved in all the causes, abortion and whatever." Streisand was seduced by the way Trudeau glided around the ballroom floor with even the chandelier dimmed by his luster. Gould, according to some of his friends, would probably have been as stiff as they come in the ballroom, not that he would ever be caught there.

Thankfully for Gould, it did not work out between Pierre and the pop diva as Trudeau broke down and married Sinclair, although the latter once shouted at him, "You can always go back to your American actress!" Trudeau, however, wasn't finished with messing with Gould; after becoming separated from his wife, he began dating Monica Gaylord in the late 1970s — at about the same time Gould was developing a relationship with Gaylord. Gaylord seemed the quintessential Trudeau gal — much younger than him, elegant, intellectual and at ease in the flickering of a candlelight dinner. Trudeau courted her on at least two levels — as a musician for his official parties, where she played her soft, sexy piano for heads of state, and as a date to theatrical premiers. According to Boyd, Trudeau was looking for a woman who could present him with a baby girl, which he craved after Sinclair had given him three nice sons.

The national newspapers kept tabs on the Gaylord-Trudeau dates and the *Toronto Star* carried a front-page photograph of the beaming couple entering a concert hall in Toronto. "She is a frequent date of Trudeau," wrote *Star* critic Sid Adilman. Gould, a voracious reader of newspapers and listener of television and radio news, must have soaked up every morsel as rat poison, brooding in his dim apartment.

Monica Gaylord was born in New York in 1948 to Jamaican parents. She graduated from the Juilliard School of Music in New York. She moved to Toronto with her husband in 1970, but they divorced at about the same time, or before, she met Gould. She was a prodigy like Gould: she had played church hymns at age four and by nine was featured on the popular television series

The Lawrence Welk Show. "Monica Gaylord brings out the adjectives in all of us," said one promo in the 1970s after she performed a combination of classical music and Gershwin's *Rhapsody in Blue.*

Gaylord was a budding piano virtuoso who played for presidents, but she had to supplement her income with children's shows and teaching. Reviewers noted that her keyboard style had a blend of power and charm, and that she was original with warmth of character and brightness of spirit. In 1975, Toronto critic Ronald Hambleton wrote that Gaylord "is endowed with both subtlety and strength and shows admirable calm and warmth."

As for potential male suitors, she seemed to have just the right sprinkle of standoffishness. "I'm an Aquarian," she said, "which means I'm outwardly cool, detached, introspective and inwardly dedicated to a cause — classical music." She often played the works of Canadian female composers "because so many are under the impression there are no women composers in Canada." Gaylord said she had been a liberated woman all her life, adding, "I am not involved with the women's lib movement, although I am certainly not opposed to it and can sympathize with the aims and understand the need for it."

Like Gould, she was not crazy about leaving her house, from which she practiced piano four hours a day and conducted personal sessions in yoga and transcendental meditation — before running at least one hundred times the forty-foot length of her living room and kitchen. When she emerged from her house to perform *An Evening with Monica Gaylord* at Toronto concert halls, which included her favorite piece, Chopin's Ballade in G Minor, she was fit and on top of her game. Gaylord had a cheerful face with dazzling enamel teeth the size of piano keys. "Monica was gorgeous — [Gould] had good taste!" said Linda Litwack, publicist for CBC Television, who worked with Gould on numerous projects. "[Monica] had a kind of psychic connection with him."

In pearls, Gaylord resembled a young Lena Horne, but Gaylord was not quite a nightclub performer. "You need a dynamite image, like Streisand to be a nightclub star," she said for an interview in 1977.

And yet, Gould may have been infatuated with her looks, her style and intelligence. "She is an artist who combines astonishing versatility with extraordinary insights," he said in promotional material on her behalf.

As her friend, Gould may have been biased toward her. Littler said she was not quite good enough to make it big in the classical world. "She had the beginnings of a nice career, but it fizzled out," he said. "That's not uncommon for pianists. We keep turning out new generations of pianists and it's hard for them to sustain a career with another crop coming in. The concert field is over-populated and it can be hard on a person's ego." For a concert pianist to make a career, he or she needs three things, according to Littler: ability, personality and physical appearance. "And your performance begins when you start making your way to the stage from the wings. You need to be a performer, and Glenn knew that, but some others didn't." Littler said Gaylord had the three components to become successful, but she wasn't quite good enough.

Anton Kuerti, Gaylord's piano teacher in the mid-1970s, agreed that she had talent, but it was not outstanding. "She was an average student, a little older than the other students; I didn't think she could make it as a top concert pianist," Kuerti said. "I'm not sure what her aspirations were; I think she wanted to play a little lighter music, perhaps jazz. She was always cheerful, very outgoing."

It is believed that Gaylord began seeing Trudeau in the mid to late 1970s when he summoned her to the Parliament in Ottawa. On November 5, 1978, he brought her to Ottawa to play at a dinner for African presidents and the following day, the *Globe and Mail* reported: "Toronto pianist Monica Gaylord isn't exactly a household name, but she has somehow attracted Prime Minister Trudeau's attention . . . she was the surprise hit of the dinner, the PM's personal choice to play the piano. She was the center of attention as Mr. Trudeau introduced her to his sister Suzette Rouleau."

Like Gould, while Trudeau was gregarious in a crowd and in front of the camera (or his opponents in the House of Commons) and playful and creative in social settings, he retained a deep private side, even a solitary side. One of his favorite quotes was from Cyrano de Bergerac: "I'll climb, not high, perhaps, but all alone." And, of course, his romances were hushed. "For the most part, I kept a watertight seal between my private life and my public life," he said in the 1990s.

Trudeau selected women — like Gaylord and Streisand — who did not kiss and tell; to this day, few of Trudeau's "dates" have gone public. One of the few who did was actress Margot Kidder (Lois Lane in the Superman movies) and that only surfaced in a chapter for the book *Pierre*, long after his death. "His love was elusive," Kidder wrote. "I never heard him use the word about anyone except his ex-wife and his beloved sons, and I'm not sure he altogether trusted the emotion very much. It's as if he gave his love in such tiny, tasteful increments that you couldn't know how big his gift was until you added up the pieces after he was gone."

Trudeau's marriage to Sinclair in 1971 came as a surprise to his adoring public. She turned out to be a rebellious, lively, intelligent flower child, who loved poetry and sewed her own wedding dress. Sinclair was twenty-nine years Trudeau's junior. (Gould had also been dating younger women at that time.) Like Gould, Trudeau likely did not compromise enough with his women and he separated from Sinclair in 1977.

Meanwhile, Gould met Gaylord at about the same time that Trudeau did. But as we have seen, Gould's relationships with women had been a never ending roller-coaster ride. Gould's relationships with Roslak and Gaylord may have overlapped in the late 1970s. Certainly, the two women crossed paths professionally; in 1979, Gaylord accompanied soprano Roslak in a concert. We do not know if Gould was in the audience, but a critic noted, "Miss Roslak's voice was at its loveliest and most expressive in the Lord's Prayer."

Gould may have had a defensive mindset going into his relationship with Gaylord, and he may have felt — in his mid-forties — that marriage just was not in the cards for him. And yet Gaylord won Gould over in other ways beyond her piano. She was intelligent, spiritual, possibly even psychic. And her affection for Gould's music must have stroked his ego. In a letter believed to have been sent in late 1980, Gaylord wrote:

Dear Glenn:

Yesterday, I bought twelve of your records (Bach 2 and 4, Beethoven Concert, English Suites, Wagner, 5th Symph.) of which I listened to the Brahms Intermezzi first. The beauty of your playing and sensitivity brought tears to my eyes and I wanted to tell you immediately. Since I can't phone you directly (I kept getting your answering service), I am writing this letter to tell you how very much I am affected by the energy and your "personal" type of musicality in all of your records. The Emperor is particularly powerful and the 4th very lyrical.

I have great difficulty with words in speaking to you to tell you all of this, so I hope you won't mind this letter. You are my favorite pianist in the world, and I'm delighted to know you.

You're also a terrific person and I pray your life will continue to be fulfilling. Take care.

Love,

Monica

Gould was delighted enough with Gaylord that he shared his piano tuner, Verne Edquist, with her, yet he did not want others knowing about her. "She got my name from Glenn and I tuned her Yamaha Grand," Edquist said. "She had all those beautiful teeth and I remember one day she was having trouble with them and went for a root canal. But I never asked Glenn about her. People used to phone me, but they really wanted to know about Glenn. If you asked him about his personal life, he would tell you not to fight city hall, to mind your own business. I had to worry about my job. I purposely stayed away from his personal life because if you asked or talked about him to others, he would get rid of you. I think that's why I stayed as long as I did."

If Gould and Gaylord were indeed a couple at one point, they would have been on the cutting edge of interracial relationships at that time — not that Gould would have been worried about what people thought about that.

Along with their desire for privacy, Gould and Gaylord were somewhat alike in their offbeat humor and desire to add a personal newness to old musical works, and in their fondness for children. Like him, Gaylord even brought her own adjustable piano stool to concerts. Gould was a fancier of games of all sorts, but Gaylord turned the tables on him by making a tape of twenty selections from her record collection and inviting Gould to identify them. She was a little surprised — Gould was probably irked — to find that he knew only three of them. The man who could play Strauss's *Elektra* from memory did not recognize such familiar trifles as Chopin's Nocturne in E Minor or Schubert's Impromptu in G Flat Major.

On June 10, 1981, Gaylord posted a letter to Gould. The Goldberg she refers to was Gould's budding new version of the *Goldberg Variations*, recorded in 1981 and released after his death the following year:

Dear Glenn:
Enclosed is a copy of the music we discussed last
night. Some of the changes are really (?) funny. Your
String Quartet (what I heard of it) is really (yes)
wonderful. I really (truly) thought the composer was
some highly developed European. I look forward to
hearing it through with the score. Also, I can't wait to
see Goldberg.
> *As always, I very much enjoyed being with you.*
> *Take good care of yourself.*
Love,
Monica
P.S. Lots of reallys in this letter. My enthusiasm for
you is showing.

Perhaps inspired by her spunk and her red dresses (a color
he usually loathed), Gould penned a musical composition for
Gaylord. In a folder of his compositions in Library and
Archives Canada, there are ten pages of ink sketches leading up
to *Monica — Her Madrigal*. The four-part lyrics:

> *Monica Anne, we've tried our best to guide you*
> *And though you've gone your own way, we've defied*
> > *you*
> *Through every season, you've called it treason, yet*
> > *we've still sought to reason with you*
> *We've clearly failed, for you have paled,*
> *You have now turned blue. . . .*

No one knows if Gould ever gave this to Gaylord or
played it for her, but some people believe their relationship
ended badly. To add to the puzzle, after Gould's death, a long,
handwritten text was found in one of his notepads from 1980
to an unidentified woman who could have been Monica (see

Chapter Twenty-Three).

How much Gould or Trudeau knew about one another's close involvement with Gaylord is not known because each traveled in different circles, but she may have given a re-boot to both men's careers — Gould was starting to fade physically and was in flux professionally when she met him while Trudeau had separated from Sinclair and, in 1979, lost to underdog Joe Clark of the Progressive Conservatives in the federal election upset. But both men showed some of their old spark while associating with Gaylord — Trudeau recaptured the prime minister's job in 1980 while Gould in 1981 re-recorded the album that had made him famous. Certainly, Gould knew that Gaylord was dating Trudeau in a public fashion; on March 16, 1982, a front-page picture appeared in Gould's hometown paper, the *Toronto Star* of Gaylord and Trudeau attending a special showing of the 1927 movie classic *Napoleon*. That must have hurt the pianist to the quick. Six months later, Gould was dead of a stroke. In his little telephone book Gaylord's number was found.

But apparently she did not want anyone to know about their friendship. Ray Roberts thought it had been a platonic relationship, but he has no proof. "I know she was in constant contact with him — right up, I thought, until he died."

You make me cry, laugh, feel hatred, horror, yes, everything,
but you also have the most personal sound in your
piano . . . you have suffered much, I'm sure of that
since you play with so much feeling and intensity.
— Svante Karstrom, a Gould fan in Sweden

The LAUGH HEARD
around the WORLD

Chapter TWENTY-ONE

When Glenn Gould stumbled into Birgit Johansson in 1978 in Toronto, he was growing more reclusive, supposedly less the marrying type and perhaps even suspect of women. He had just given up the ghost on Cornelia Foss and was embroiled in up-and-down relationships with Roslak and Gaylord. It was one of the most painful times of his life, psychologically and physically, and, if nothing else, he could have used a really good laugh.

Enter Johansson, a character fitting of the opera of Gould's wacky life. Of all Gould's relationships, Johansson is the only woman who was deceased when I was researching this book (Frances Barrault died shortly before publication), so the relationship remains one of conjecture. Still, family and friends insist that their relationship was a close one. Gould and Johansson met at a get- together involving a number of musicians — and a photograph seen by her former student Jorgen Lundmark bears this out. Supplemented by the culture department of the Swedish government, Johansson was in Toronto to attend a music course under Canadian composer R. Murray Schafer, known for his offbeat works. The mother of three boys, Johansson was separated and soon-to-be divorced from her husband, an officer in the Swedish army. "They met at a party and she said Gould was a wonderful dancer," said Birgit's son

Henrik. "She liked him very much; he was witty and intelligent. And they had a common friend — violinist Itzhak Perlman." Glenn Gould a "wonderful" dancer? That might surprise some people about the supposedly un-athletic Gould, and yet he could dip into his bag of tricks and rise above himself when it came to women who turned him on. And Johansson was some catch — a strong woman physically and emotionally with high cheekbones, attractive features and a smile that lit up her blue eyes, especially when she was fully engaged with others. By age fifty-two, her blond hair had already turned shocking white, but you never thought about age when you were with Birgit; her laugh was so contagious, it could spread to another city.

"She was a very charming, an energetic, powerful woman, always smiling and happy," said Mona Gunnarsson, who worked with Johansson in Sweden in the 1980s. "She was beautiful and sexy, always well dressed."

Johansson had a bigger personality than Foss, Roslak or Gaylord; rather, she was more like Gould's first gal, Franny Batchen, with about the same age difference. Yes, Johansson looked much older than fifty-two, but Gould did not seem to mind that she was six years his elder. The day after their meeting in Toronto, Gould and Johansson went to the Toronto Zoo to share their love of animals; and, so, their romance was on — and, according to those who knew her, it would to continue for the remainder of his life. "Everybody wanted to have an affair with Birgit," said Anders Holdar, who studied piano and drum under Johansson in the 1970s and became a composer.

Gould did not require that his female friends talk music, but it did not hurt if they could. And, of course, Johansson could; at a community music school in Sollentuna, Sweden, she taught pedagogy (the art of teaching music), piano, music theory and theater. "In pedagogy, she showed us the deeper side of teaching music," said Lotta Delebrant, a Johansson student who took over her job for several months in 1979 while Johansson was in

North America for a second visit with Gould. Prior to meeting Johansson, Gould already had some connection with Sweden — he had given a concert in Stockholm in 1958 and was always attracted to the northern European sensibility and way of thinking. In some ways, Sweden was like Canada.

She was born Birgit Adolfsson in 1926 in Karlstad, a small town in the Swedish region of Värmland. Her father, Hugo, was a traveling merchant who sold a variety of goods and also drove a small bus. Her mother, Gertrude, was a housewife who often played piano while her husband sang. The family was religious — from Baptist and Methodist roots, although her grandfather was on the board of directors of a Lutheran church. Young Birgit wanted to study opera, but stage careers were frowned upon in those days in Sweden and an entertainment career was not economically practical. The family did not have a radio, but singing in homes was part of Swedish culture. Birgit officially began her music career as Gould had done — playing the organ — at a Lutheran church when she was eleven years old. As a caregiver with an outgoing personality, she eventually went into teaching at the Music Culture School in Sollentuna, a suburb south of Stockholm, where she became famous for grand entrances, sometimes waltzing into school with a black shawl wrapped around her neck and proclaiming, "I'm here!"

According to her son Henrik, Gould and Johansson were attracted to one another during her initial Canadian visit in 1978. "I believe they fell in love during that first visit," Henrik said. Gould did not propose to her right away, but rather kept in touch with Johansson in Sweden by post and telephone, encouraging her to return to Canada. Because she had shown good leadership qualities in her first visit to Toronto, Johansson was subsequently given part-time teaching jobs in universities in Toronto, California, Florida and other parts of the United States.

During her stays in North America, Johansson and Gould

would find various places to meet, perhaps in the eastern United States, where Gould made numerous automobile get-away trips late in his life to Georgia, Virginia and, reportedly, New Orleans, Louisiana, the world capital for jazz and blues. "They went to New Orleans, from bar to bar, and Gould played the piano. She said it was so much fun!" said Anders Hillborg, a renowned composer who was one of Birgit's students in the 1970s in Sweden. Although Gould publicly pooh-poohed pop music, he sometimes played jazz for frivolity, and Johansson sometimes surprised her students back in Sweden by tossing off her classical role and accompanying herself with soft jazz on a piano. (As a young woman, while still hoping to become a famous mezzo-soprano, she had supplemented her teaching income by playing jazz at restaurants and clubs in Sweden and Denmark.)

During Johansson's second trip to Toronto in 1979, Gould asked her to marry him, some of her family and former students say. "She told us he asked her to marry him," said concert pianist Lennart Wallin. "She was excited and happy, like a little girl." Perhaps as a sweetener to the deal to get her to say yes, Gould collected all of his fifty albums and gave them to her as a gift. She contemplated bachelor Gould's marriage proposal for some time, but she eventually turned him down.

"She said no, and I believe there were a number of reasons," Henrik said. "He was rich and famous and younger than her and she felt so many women wanted him. Also, there may have been some cultural differences . . . differences on how men and women in North America and Sweden viewed one another in marriage."

When she said no, they quarreled, according to Henrik. "Gould protested and said he had once proposed to a woman ten years younger than him, but my mother didn't quite believe him," Henrik said. "He might have said it out of anger. But their relationship didn't stop there. I believe she loved him, and he loved her." Perhaps the woman Gould mentioned was Roslak? Other close friends of Gould's said he was difficult to live with, but Johansson never mentioned that to Henrik: "She never told me he gave her those kind of problems."

Hillborg believes that, at the time, she wanted Gould as a friend rather than a husband. Another reason that Johansson turned Gould down, according to her youngest son, Magnus, was that she wanted to stay in Sweden and be with her young grandchildren, born in 1980 and 1982. "She said he was too young for her, but I didn't believe it," Magnus said.

Yet their relationship remained strong, bolstered partly by the fact that both Gould and Johansson shared considerable pain. In the late 1970s, he was suffering a number of real and imagined illnesses, including back pain, while she had cancer, but would not allow doctors to amputate one of her arms. They were both free-thinking, spiritual souls, who believed in God and sought out alternative treatments, such as the anthroposophic movement, a holistic and spiritual approach to medicine, founded by Rudolf Steiner. Apart from Gould, Johansson rarely let people see the pain she was in. "She never made a big deal out of it to people," Delebrant said.

According to Christina Frohm, who taught under Johansson, "Sometimes she worked with a fever in her body, but she didn't let it stop her."

When Johansson suffered a recurrence of cancer in 1979 — in her knee — Gould apparently soothed her during her second trip to Toronto and she returned to Sweden rejuvenated. In the late 1970s and early 1980s, Gould was not well physically, perhaps partly because of his poor diet, lack of exercise and his ever-present prescription drug abuse. In the summer of 1980, CBC producer Margaret Pacsu was stunned by the number and variety of drugs and tranquilizers Gould took, "mostly downers" to try to slow himself down during an intense taping session with her. Who knows what effect a lifetime of drug consumption had on Gould and his performances; in a 1981 film, a slight tremor can be seen in his hands, perhaps from medication. Another way Gould tried to relax, Pacsu said, was to make silly animal noises and sing her a country western song he apparently had written in his teens.

The next part of this story is hard to digest for some Gould followers and biographers, but Johansson's family and students say that Gould visited Sweden more than once, likely in 1980 and 1982, to see Johansson and to get treatment for his back. He kept it private. Another time, Johansson reportedly went to Heathrow Airport in London to meet Gould. The reason this is difficult for many to believe is that Gould was afraid of flying and had stopped traveling by airplane in the early 1960s — and yet as we have seen in this book, he sometimes did impulsive, fearless things when it came to romance. "She contacted a therapist for [Gould] and he came to Sweden to see a doctor," Holdar said. "He had some sort of rheumatism." It is believed the physician was the late Dr. Lennart Silverstolpe, well known for treating musicians, particularly those who had suffered injuries from unusual methods of playing, such as the hunchbacked Gould with his low piano stool.

In early 1982, Johansson enlisted the help of musician and neighbor Torgny Lundmark to prepare for Gould's secret trip from Canada. Knowing how Gould felt about untuned pianos, she had Lundmark tune the piano in her flat at Frejavagen 25 in Sollentuna. "I remember Torgny and me stood below her apartment window where we believed Gould and Birgit were that night," said pianist Lennart Wallin, who was thirty-four at the time and lived in the same building as Johansson. "It was very exciting to know that Glenn Gould was in our town. Birgit told me the next day that he'd been there. I trusted in what she said. She was not a person who would lie."

To a person, Johansson's family and friends believe all of her story about Glenn Gould and they say she was trustworthy.

"Birgit would not make things up," Hillborg said.

If so, Johansson may have been one of the last people in Gould's thoughts before he had a fatal stroke in the fall of 1982. According to her granddaughter, opera singer Erika Tordeus, Gould proposed to Johansson for the final time just a few days before the stroke, but she turned him down because she was dating a retired police officer. It seemed fitting that Gould's last serious relationship was with a piano teacher — the first had been his mother Flora, who taught the young genius the classics. Some say he never found a woman to match Mama, but we might have found out otherwise with Birgit, had he survived.

*I think in searching out unconsciously people who are
ultimately not available, geographically, emotionally and
spiritually, you can almost predict the ending. I bet Glenn
Gould was one of those . . . he felt he couldn't be deeply
loved. But our moments were special.*

— Susan Koscis

SUSAN K.

Chapter TWENTY-TWO

Along with his friendship with Johansson, in the last years of his life Gould may have been on the verge of yet another intense relationship with Susan Koscis. He had known Koscis, his tall, blond, perky, intelligent, green-eyed publicist at Columbia Masterworks in New York, for less than three years when their relationship seemed to take a plunge toward the deeply personal. Like Birgit Johansson, she had a robust personality.

Koscis was born on Long Island, New York, to a housewife mother, who came from Poland, and a father who became secretary-general of a carpenter's union. Koscis attended Hartt College of Music in Hartford, Connecticut, where she studied piano, but then she went into music administration. "That was my first major mistake; I should have been a teacher and led a nice, normal life," she said. "The music business is a crazy life."

Gould and Koscis were tossed together professionally in 1980 when she started working for Columbia. "Just after I got there, they were gearing up for the big push of his second *Goldberg Variations*," she said. "I'd be warned how difficult he could be and I remember I was very nervous on my first telephone call to him. I wanted to convince him I knew what I was doing. I didn't want to do the 'genius is a nut' articles [as part of the PR duties], but to write about his music and to reach out to a younger generation of music critics, who were not jaded writers." Gould's first interview through Koscis was with Tim Page for *SoHo Weekly*. His story "sat very well [with Gould]," Koscis said.

Page quickly became a pet writer of Gould's and also a friend in his last years — and Page edited the *Glenn Gould Reader* after Gould's death. That was flattering to Page because Gould was always wary of journalists; for instance, in June 1982, he turned down a media request from Pointe Claire, Quebec, citing a "preference for controlled interviews." But Gould was always on the lookout for a friend he could connect with, like the astute Page, who went on to win a Pulitzer Prize in critical writing with the *Washington Post*.

Although Glould claimed that he needed people less and less as he got older, his actions sometimes belied his tough words; at times in the last years of his life, he seemed lonely and longed perhaps for more human contact. In 1980, Gould went to Paul Myers' house in New York and played with Myers' kids on the floor with their train set. "He seemed happy doing that," Myers said. A year later, he even *hugged* another man — Bob Silverman, his editor at *Piano Quarterly*. Since the early 1970s, Gould had had an occasional, and yet warm and sometimes intimate telephonic relationship with Silverman, who was such a fan of Gould, he really never edited anything the musician wrote. When they finally met in Toronto in the summer of 1981, Gould and Silverman talked almost non-stop for three days at the Inn on the Park Four Seasons Hotel, where Gould had a room, a mini studio and, more important, all-night room service.

"I have a lot of energy, but he exhausted me," Silverman said. During a second meeting, Gould's obsessiveness and neediness showed once more as the pair talked from suppertime one day until five in the morning.

Gould first met Koscis in person in New York for a PBS production involving the *Goldberg Variations*. She found him to be a "little odd, shy, sweet and personable, most adorable and strange, a little hiding who he was. I was nervous and excited." Like Gould, Koscis had emotional issues and at the time she was having an affair with a Columbia executive. "For at least half the time I knew [Gould], I was emotionally involved elsewhere and did not see him or think of Glenn in a romantic way," she said. "I didn't see him as a man. I'm sure that came across to him. I was simply not available to him. I did not believe that Glenn was all that available emotionally, either." Yet away from the job, Gould and Koscis became friends. "He would call me every night, very late. He would talk about funny things and say, 'Guess what I did today?' or 'Guess who I talked with today?' I loved the everydayness of our conversations. He became somebody I could count on, who I could share things with. I had enormous respect for his integrity, purity and innocence. He was beautifully untainted."

There wasn't much talk about music, but some gossip. "We knew a lot of people in common and he couldn't stand the new people at the record company," Koscis said. "And we talked about our love of children and animals. He liked to talk about starting a farm where sick animals would come." (Gould often talked about taking in stray and sick animals in a sort of Glenn Gould Puppy Farm in northern Ontario, but, like some of his other projects, it never materialized.) Gould never mentioned anything to Koscis about Birgit Johansson, but, of course, he never mentioned *any* of his other women to her, Ray Roberts or anyone else. He never mentioned the pain and the joy women brought him; rather he continued to take prescription drugs and to plug those raw feelings into his music, telling his millions of listeners, if they had the ear. "I wanted to protect him," Koscis said. "He was always very tender and he did have thin skin and was prone to being hurt, very wounded."

At one point, Gould and Koscis had a sort of falling out. "One night when he called, I was really exhausted; I yawned and probably fell asleep," she said. "The conversation ended soon after. Nothing was said about it and weeks went by without any phone calls, then Tim Page called me and said that Glenn feels terrible about your fight, your silent fight. Apparently, Glenn had taken it badly that night when I yawned as he was talking. So I called him and apologized. I told him I hated him to think I was bored with him, and that opened him up. Imagine — a yawn hurt him!"

Then Gould sort of apologized to Koscis and said, "Of course you were tired." And their friendship resumed with Gould showing compassion for Koscis's troubled love affair with the married man. "He knew that I was insecure and all over the place and he tried to help, especially with the bad romantic relationship I was going through. He kept saying, 'I'm gonna keep working on you until you know about you what I know about you.'" Perhaps this was a more sage Gould than in the past, showing that he had learned something from failed relationships?

When Koscis was informed about Gould's love life, long after his death, she said, "It sounds like he'd been spurned and disappointed by love many times. That does something to one's heart and soul — the scars become tougher." When her affair with the Columbia executive ended, she told Gould, who knew the man, all about it. "He recognized it, said it was good it was over. That was the first conversation we had that was so personal. Then it got more personal, and that changes who you are together." Another night in a music session at the Inn on the Park, Gould made an uncharacteristic remark to Koscis, telling her, "You have Barbra Streisand eyes, and look at those beautiful legs — they go on forever." She was flattered, but also got a little irritated and retorted, "I'm not cross-eyed!" After that, Koscis said she became "free to feel," and a subtle shift began to happen.

She was promoted to a close friend, in much the same way

as Gladys Shenner, Cornelia Foss and Roxolana Roslak had been promoted. "By then, friendship and growing trust was the basis of our relationship, and then came a layer of subtle flirting and noticing and caring. It was a gradual thing that was happening, and I knew it and felt it. Who he was for me really changed. Until then, I never saw him as a man, but here was this attractive man in front of me. And we stared into one another's eyes and talked more personal. He felt he couldn't be deeply loved, but our moments were special. I think I had always been searching unconsciously for people who were unavailable geographically, emotionally or spiritually and I guess Glenn Gould was one of those."

Gould and Koscis never kissed or even hugged one another, she said. "We did the handshake thing and I remember our eyes deeply seared into each other's. I don't remember any physical contact, but I remember wondering could there be, would there be? My understanding was that he was asexual."

She did not think he was homosexual, although at about that time, *People* magazine did a feature on Gould in which writer Joseph Roddy wrote that his "monastic . . . solitude is occasionally broken by friends of both sexes, for varying lengths of time."

Gould was upset when Roddy read him the article over the phone, according to Ray Roberts: "He was mad, and it seemed a clear inference that [Gould] was homosexual." Roddy denied the inference and said he was only referring to male friendship.

None of this stopped Koscis from falling in love with Gould. "Oh, God, I fell in love with him. I didn't realize it until it was too late." It was possible, she said, that Gould felt the same. "He cared for me, you bet, and respected me enormously." He even asked her to move to Toronto to work on a new television project with him, *Ideas*, but at the time, she did not want to move to Toronto. His cousin and confidante, Jessie Greig, was hoping Koscis would be the one to marry him, Koscis said. Greig said

Koscis was a "lovely lady" and continued to correspond with her after Gould's death.

"You never know, I might have been the one. I might have had kids and a life with him," Koscis said. "But could you live day and night with someone who lived the lifestyle he did? In the past, I had put myself in very deep love affairs, but they could not have worked out. I was looking to be rescued, looking for someone to make me feel whole. I think in searching out unconsciously people who are ultimately not available, geographically, emotionally and spiritually, you can almost predict the ending. I bet Glenn Gould was one of those."

While he was a friend and a colleague to Koscis in the early 1980s, Gould struck up a "faraway" relationship with Sonia Marie De León, a music student in Los Angeles. In a number of telephone conversations and letters with her, he sometimes referred to himself as a conductor. Although he had no experience at conducting, he tinkered with the idea of trying it professionally. Their friendship began when De León wrote a letter to Gould, telling him how motivated he made her to become a professional musician. De León, who had been turned off by the "rules and elitism" in classical music, saw Gould as a type of rebellious pied piper who "gave me permission to experiment with my music." As was his practice, Gould would call De León from his Toronto home at about 4 a.m. Eastern Time, which was even late in California at 1 a.m. "I had a weird schedule in those days, so I didn't mind it," De León said. "I came from a poor family, but he cheered me on to do my own thing." Gould showcased his sense of humor and would sometimes call her in a fake accent and pretend he was someone else. "We'd talk about a lot of different things — flowers, food, the weather, what people are like. . . ." Gould never mentioned his health, which was deteriorating, to De León. "To me, he always sounded very positive and energetic."

Certainly, De León said, Gould was in a good mood when

he talked of becoming a conductor. "He talked about *The Idea of North* and his documentary films, but he wanted to become a full-time conductor, to spend more and more time on it," she said. This inspired De León, who was studying piano but eventually went into conducting. She never met Gould, but she said she fell in love with him. "Lots of women did." Suddenly, in late 1981, Gould stopped calling De León and she was never given a reason why.

For a man uncomfortable with change and tight relationships, he was certainly jumping into bed — at least emotionally — with a lot of different women, one after the other, even in the last years of his life at a time when some of his colleagues thought he had cooled it during the Cornelia chill. And apparently, he kept a sentimental place in his heart for Franny Batchen, his girlfriend from the 1950s. Scribbled in his diary around 1980 was a list of people to call, including "Franny." That might have been Batchen, who was distressed in 1979–80 about the death of her close friend, Canadian filmmaker George Dunning. Gould had a way of comforting people, and not only through his music; in 1981, he received a letter from New York musician Ray Alonje, thanking him for his music, which was apparently helping him cope with life in New York, and Gould responded with a "you're welcome" letter. As well, Gould's compassion was seen in 1982 when he granted permission for Theresa Ximenes of New York to use one of his Bach recordings in a film involving animal welfare.

If Gould was displaying compassion and maybe a newfound maturity, some critics suggested it showed in his re-recording of the *Goldberg Variations* in 1981 in New York. Just before recording it, Gould listened to his 1956 version, which he described as a "rather spooky experience," and proclaimed that his spirit had changed in the subsequent quarter of a century. "I could not recognize, or identify with, the spirit of the person who made that recording. It really seemed like some other person, some other spirit had been involved," he told Tim Page. Perhaps the ebb and flow of his personal life, the bumps and the bruises of his love life, the wonderful moments and "safety and security" of life with Batchen, Foss and Roslak and subsequent turmoil in those relationships had left him with something, and that something perhaps affected his music. That is not uncommon in the world of classical music. When Beethoven was going deaf, it was said his agony and frustration appeared in his compositions. Mozart died at age thirty-five, ill and reportedly exhausted by his life and his work, while writing what he believed would be his death knell, *Requiem*. *Goldberg II* may have been Gould's *Requiem*. Whatever the reason, the two *Goldbergs* were indeed different — the earlier version was more energetic, even frenetic at times, while the later version was more introspective.

When he recorded the first *Goldberg* in New York in 1955, Gould was a young, twenty-two-year-old lion of the concert circuit, musically confident and even brash. In his personal life, he was somewhat green and nervous, but still in a relationship with Frances Batchen. By Gould's own admission, the '55 version was very fast in tempo, emotional, alive with special effects and chopped up into thirty-two variations, although its contrapuntal voices were clear and distinctive. Oh, the vibrancy of those ten fingers! They would be childlike, skipping along the keys as though through a meadow, if they were not so educated and accomplished. From the outset, the 1981 version was a different animal. At age forty-eight, he played its opening aria twice as slowly as he had at twenty-two.

"It is hard to shake Gould's death while listening to the new version," said Madison, Wisconsin music critic Jacob Stockinger. "So private is the opening aria, the listener feels like an intruder into a very personal act, such as meditation or prayer."

In a video of the 1981 version, Gould's amazing fingers

showed speed on occasion, but they slowed considerably to pause, to reflect, to organize, to produce calculated phrasing and a spiritual pulse throughout the music, to cry one note, one drop at a time. In the video, he looks older than forty-eight — hair thinning, big glasses, hunched on his father's old stool at the piano, teeth chattering — a man withered, perhaps humbled and yet musically enriched by the life experiences he often sought to avoid. In the latter recording, Gould is clearly heard humming and singing (twice as loud as in 1955) and even groaning as though he is in pain. "There was such joy of life in the first [*Goldberg*]," said Gould's friend Peter Yazbeck. "He called me every day to play me the first version over the phone. But there is obviously such pathos in the second one. I think that's because he knew he was going to die."

Far removed from the pressure and influence of the concert crowds of the 1950s, and perhaps more affected by loved ones, in 1981 he was stopping to reflect about life whereas in 1955 he was just beginning to live. The first version of the *Goldbergs* belonged still to Bach — however, just before his death, Gould claimed the story as his own. The 1981 *Goldberg Variations* went on to win two posthumous Grammy Awards in 1983, Best Classical Album and Best Instrumental Soloist Performance without an Orchestra. Clearly, his state of worry had actually benefitted his state of wonder.

Chris phoned us and said, "We just lost him."
— Gould friend and actress Susan Douglas Rubes

DEATH

Chapter TWENTY-THREE

As his fiftieth birthday approached on September 25, 1982, Columbia Masterworks wanted to hold a celebration, as did some of his family, but Gould was bah-humbug over parties or anniversaries to the point he would sometimes work through Christmas. Around the time of his final birthday, Gould seemed in an unusually serious mood and even talked to his cousin Jessie Greig about death and his own funeral, fearing that nobody would show up if he died. A decade before, he had told Cornelia Foss that he would not live past fifty. To friends and colleagues, Gould looked ill and aged, but Koscis put a smile on his face by showing up from New York to present him with a black cashmere scarf. "It was soft and the perfect color for him; he loved it," she said.

Within the following week, Gould seemed back in form, chipper and working. He telephoned his old surrogate mother, Susan Douglas Rubes, whom he had often stayed with in New York, and told her he was working on an opera about Kafka's book *The Metamorphosis*, about a man who turns into a creature and is shunned by his family, which he had been tinkering with since the mid-1950s and had not finished. "I think he was both writing and composing the opera; he talked about it enthusiastically," Rubes said. "He didn't seem sick to me, at least not on the phone."

In his last years, Gould was also working on a screenplay of the Japanese novel *The Three-Cornered World*, which captured Gould's salvation-through-art mantra and in which a painter-poet escapes to a mountain spa to work as a hermit, trying to avoid secular and emotional distractions, but meets a beautiful mistress whose face he cannot quite capture on canvas. Also in Gould's plans were the official release of his second run at the *Goldberg Variations* and a visit from his old New York producer Paul Myers, who would be passing through Toronto in early October.

But on September 27, Gould was sleeping in a room at the Inn on the Park when he awoke with a headache and a numb feeling down his leg. He called Ray Roberts, who phoned his doctor, but the physician did not seem concerned, perhaps because of all the false alarms with Gould in the past, and it was not until several hours later, as Gould's condition worsened, that anything was done. Finally, Roberts could wait no longer and drove Gould in his big Lincoln to the Toronto General Hospital, where an examination revealed he had suffered a stroke caused by a blood clot in the brain. The next day in his hospital bed, Gould was able to talk to Roberts, his father and Greig and even to play one last game of Twenty Questions. There was another family connection of sorts — Rubes' son, Chris, was an emergency room physician at the hospital and he helped to care for the man who had played with him as a boy so many years earlier in Manhattan. "He recognized Chris and felt he was in good hands. It was nice for Glenn," Rubes said.

For his first three days in hospital, Toronto General officials heeded the family's request not to alert the press to the fact that the international star was seriously ill, which might have been front page news in Toronto. But on September 30, Gould slipped into a coma and tests showed he had suffered serious brain damage. The pianist's grave illness was released to the media and the news went around the music world like a shock

DEATH

261

wave. At the offices of Columbia Records in New York, Koscis was summoned to her boss's office, but she was not initially told why. Having a poor relationship with her new boss, she suspected she was going to be fired; instead, to her shock, she was informed that Gould had had a stroke and was in hospital on death's door. She had to prepare a press release and updated biography for his impending death. "I was sitting there with all these executives," she said. "They knew Glenn and I were close. I went into another office and I don't exactly remember my reaction, but I probably screamed." Koscis spent the weekend in a flood of emotions while she pieced together the obituary of the man she loved. The last time Koscis had talked with Gould on the phone was just before he had become ill, to read him an advance copy of an article by Ed Rothstein in the *New York Times*. "He really liked the article; he said 'no one has ever gotten me that well,'" she said.

On October 4, 1982, Gould was taken off life support and died at 11 a.m. He always hated mornings. "We probably found out before most people," Rubes said. "Chris phoned us and said, 'We just lost him.'"

An autopsy showed a blood clot filling the right cavernous sinus, likely caused by an infection ten days earlier. At the time, Gould had complained he had a cold and sinus pressure. Another clot was found in his internal carotid artery; otherwise, there was no other way to check for the damage of a lifetime of emotional suffering and heartache. The autopsy also showed a minor degree of arteriosclerosis, some enlargement of the heart consistent with chronic hypertension and a mildly fatty liver, probably due to dietary insufficiency. According to Dr. Peter Ostwald, who reviewed the autopsy, "No physical abnormalities were found in the kidneys, prostate, bones, joints, muscles or other parts of the body that Gould had so often complained about."

In Sweden, Birgit Johansson was devastated. On the day

Gould died, she was having a meeting with her students. "I remember I was in another building at the time," recalled her son Henrik. "She came in and showed me this note someone had given her, 'Glenn is dead.' She said, 'Oh, why couldn't I have given him the time? Was it because of me he died? Why didn't I do more for him? I was too concerned with myself.'" His mother became very depressed, Henrik said. "I thought she would die; she went into a high fever in the hospital and it grew worse over a period of months. She had to take a year off teaching her students . . . but, finally, after six months there was a concert she had promised to do and she went through with it. It kept her going and she recovered." (After Gould's death, Johansson got letters from him, which he had posted before his stroke, but after she read them she burned them to protect his privacy.)

He was as revered in death as he had been in birth by his parents. Headlines around the world marked the passing of a talented, eccentric musician. Gould had worried with his cousin Jessie that no one would go to his funeral and yet in Toronto some 3,000 people attended a memorial service at St. Paul's Cathedral, mostly colleagues, fans and the acquaintances with whom Gould had carried on years of telephone conversations and letter writing. Some of his close friends were there, as well, such as Susan Koscis, Monica Gaylord, John L. Roberts and Ray Roberts. Birgit Johansson, who had vowed to Gould never to make their relationship public, flew in from Sweden and stood anonymously at the back of the church, listening to a record of Gould's *Goldberg Requiem*. Cornelia Foss did not attend. "I didn't think it would be appropriate to go," she said. Instead, Cornelia, her children and even Lukas quietly reflected in New York on the strange pianist who had impacted their lives for so many years. Franny Batchen was unwell in England, but lit up a few cigarettes, stared through her window into the rain and remembered that night long before when Glenn Gould had been in an audience to applaud her piano playing. Then she went into her den and played their song, the Berg Sonata.

Gould's close friend of twenty-five years, John Roberts, gave a touching eulogy about a genius, an innovator and "in his own way, the purest and most moral person I have encountered." Gould left half of his estate — about $750,000 — to the Salvation Army and the other half to the Toronto Humane Society. Singer Petula Clark checked in from Paris: "I am very sad . . . I admired his work and looked forward to meeting him some day to thank him for the kind compliments that he paid me in the past."

Roslak was also sad. "It was terrible he died so young, but I don't think anything could have been done about it, because of the way he was," she said.

Suddenly, everybody was talking to the media about Glenn Gould, and yet some mysteries still lurked. After the funeral, Gaylord phoned Ray Roberts. "When Glenn died, Monica put her arm on me," he said. "She phoned me and told me to keep my trap shut about her close relationship with Glenn. They had a closeness and she didn't want it to come out. Like he did with some other women, they touched each other emotionally."

Gould was buried at Mount Pleasant Cemetery in Toronto near his mother Flora . . . once again he was reunited with Mama.

It took Koscis a long time to grieve. "I cried for over a year," she said. "On the first anniversary of his death, I organized a Glenn Gould Film Festival [in New York]. I channeled my grief." Koscis tried to put Gould's personal life in perspective: "I don't think anyone could have had a lasting relationship with him, unless she was extraordinarily sensitive about his needs and had extraordinary self-awareness. It would have taken an extra special woman."

Some clues about Glenn Gould's love life may be found in a number of letters and notes in his handwriting, penned perhaps to himself in the middle of the night. Found in his gloomy, twilight penthouse after he died in 1982 were the Cornelia Manifesto of 1976 and the want ad for a woman in 1977, but the most talked about note was written in 1980:

> *Love letters to Dell – You know, I am deeply in love with a certain beautiful girl. I asked her to marry me but she turned me down but I still love her more than anything in the world and every minute I can spend with her is pure heaven; but I don't want to be a bore and if I could only get her to tell me when I could see her, it would help. She has a standing invitation to let me take her anywhere she'd like to go any time but it seems to me she never has time for me. Please if you see her, ask her to let me know when I can see her and when I can –*

Since 1982, there has been much debate about this Dell letter, to whom it refers, and if, indeed, it is about real people. It is written in the third person, supposedly asking a third party to help the writer get the woman to contact him. Dell could refer to the woman or to the third party. If this is not about Cornelia Foss, it certainly parallels the way her affair with Gould ended. After turning down his marriage proposal, she left him in 1973, but allowed him to call her for nearly four years. In 1974, he drove to the Hamptons in an unsuccessful effort to get her to return to Toronto. She promised to phone him, but she says she forgot; then, in September 1976, a desperate Gould placed at least eleven phone calls over three days from Toronto to Foss in New York and Bridgehampton, but only once did she come to the phone and then she said she was too busy to talk. On the other occasions, Gould got Foss's daughter Eliza, her husband Lukas and their maid on the line and asked them to please get her to return his calls. Perhaps another clue in the letter is that

Cornelia's maiden name was Brendel, which could be shortened as a nickname to Dell. To this day, Cornelia seems uneasy with the Dell note and doubts that it is about her. She turned down this author's offer to read the note to her in her summer home in the Hamptons in 2007. "He was so private, he'd roll over in his grave, worrying that someone might find writings with his emotions on them," she said.

Another person who might have been Dell in Gould's mind was Charles [Chuck] Daellenbach, whose name was pronounced Dell-enbach. He was a tuba player, who founded the group Canadian Brass. He made at least one recording with Monica Gaylord and performed onstage with her. If he was Dell, then perhaps Gould in his letter was referring to Gaylord. Both Gould and Daellenbach had relationships with Gaylord in the 1970s and 1980s, although it isn't known for certain how close these relationships were. Gould noted in his diary on May 22, 1980: "There was a call on the [telephone] service from Chas. D.; I can only assume that, whatever the official pretext, he was really calling on behalf of M. and I have no intention of returning the call." Gould often referred to Gaylord in his scribbling as M.

Another possibility is that the Dell letter may have referred to Johansson, although it is believed that she continued to see him after 1980.

Some believe the Dell letter is not about a real person at all, but a fictional character for one of the operas Gould was always talking about writing but never completed. If so, it is possible that the Dell character was based somewhat on Cornelia because Gould often mentioned that his work was "quasi-autobiographical."

Indeed, Cornelia said in 2007 that Gould may have been writing something "indirectly" for her which he never finished. "There were a lot of things he never finished," she said.

Breakups with girlfriends seemed to spark such a reaction in Gould; in 1956 when Batchen dumped him, he went on an unprecedented vacation to the Bahamas, but instead of enjoying the fruits of the warm Caribbean, he holed up for days in a small hotel room, struggling to write an unnamed opera, perhaps *The Metamorphosis*. When life was too painful for Gould, he retreated into art.

Author Kevin Bazzana speculates that the Dell letter is likely unimportant in Gould lore — he believes that Gould did not write the letter, but rather copied it from somewhere because of the corrections he made to it and the form in which it was written. "Or it could have been his stab at fiction," Bazzana said.

Another mysterious document found in Gould's handwriting after his death — written to an anonymous woman in 1980 — continues to baffle researchers. Even in the secluded lair of his dark apartment, writing to himself, he remained so private he rarely identified his women. The text reads:

How good is our friendship?

In my opinion, so good that it has created an almost tensionless atmosphere.

Because; we met and developed it when we were seemingly of one mind: one purpose; we both fell in love talking about tranquility of spirit and we re-enforced each other's determination to find that quality and bring it into our lives.

I talked about hierarchies of friendship i.e. that I didn't believe in them. I said that there are moments of intensity which have nothing to do with longevity, intimacy, proximity, etc. We, in my opinion, reached that plateau very quickly and till now have maintained ourselves there in miraculous fashion.

We've also reached that plateau because, like all good Navajo Café customers, it hasn't made any sense to play games, to employ strategies of any kind; we've behaved, I think, as though we really might never see each other again and have therefore been completely honest.

Which, however, doesn't necessarily mean we've made ourselves as clear to each other as we'd like to think.

Last week, we had the first (and I hope last) mini-fallout from unclearness. I took a little too much for granted; I just assumed that my prevailing interest in a reclusive lifestyle was understood and I didn't realize how ready you were to interpret that as rejection.

But I think now we reach a larger problem, and more urgent need for clarification.

Because our relationship has, no doubt about it, escalated; there's a psychic intensity which is really quite extraordinary — it's also immensely productive and comforting and assuring.

But it can resemble — if one wants to let it — a physical intensity; of, if not that, one can easily convince oneself that its natural course is in the direction of physical intensity.

And that isn't necessarily so, in my opinion.

Some people do try to make it so; some succeed, most fail.

And if there is a confusion of purpose between us and a corresponding need for clarification, that's where it's going to arise. Because nothing that's happened, or could foreseeably happen in our relationship, is going to change or begin to change the way of life that I decided many years ago to lead.

Change would be destructive and produce the kind of resentment that would rather quickly cause our relationship to flounder.

Therefore: no change is contemplated. Can you live with that? Is psychic energy per se hard for you to deal with?

> *I tell you this now only to avoid the kind of*
> *confusion that could add even a moment's uneasiness*
> *to what is a really remarkable relationship.*
>
> *I intend that, if you are willing to continue, we will*
> *bring each other such peace as "passeth under-*
> *standing."*

It is not possible to tell for sure who this note is about — it could be about Gaylord, Johansson, Roslak, Koscis or perhaps an unidentified woman. Some people believe the mystery letter is about Gaylord, not Roslak.

"It sounded to me like [Gaylord] was a psychic or a spiritual person," said a friend of Gould, Roslak and Gaylord, who asked not to be identified, "whereas Roxie was more earthy — she wanted more, especially in the physical end." Gaylord conducted lessons in yoga and transcendental meditation, and yet one might attach Roslak to this letter because of the reference to their meeting as "seemingly one mind, one purpose" due to their music collaboration, and the religious ending of "such peace as passeth understanding." Their recording of *Das Marienleben* was a religious work.

Roslak and Koscis deny knowing anything about the letter. Gaylord is still not talking and Johansson died in 2003 without ever going public about Gould. There was a Navajo Café in Santa Barbara, California, where Johansson taught from time to time, so it is possible that it is about her. Her family says Gould asked her to marry him, but this could have been a flip-flop on the part of the often-contradictory pianist, who had various stages of love and avoidance with some of his women.

Notice that Gould actually used the word *love* — possibly the only time he got caught using it in reference to a real person in all the writings found after his death.

A genius in love.

Whatever HAPPENED TO . . .

Chapter TWENTY-FOUR

FRANNY (BATCHEN) BARRAULT

It is 2008 and Glenn Gould has been dead for more than twenty-five years. Or has he? In a middle-class townhouse in Richmond, England, eighty-two-year-old Frances (Batchen) Barrault sits in her den, flooded with cigarette smoke and memories of her old lover. She is frail, suffering from Parkinson's disease, and slouches in a chair, opening a package of cigarettes with trembling fingers. The room had already been cluttered with stacks of books, music scores and a big white piano, but now cameramen are setting up for a photo shoot for a documentary about Gould.

"How long will this take?" she asks.

The door is closed to her nearby living room, where her husband Graham, a renowned chemical engineer, is watching television. He is an amateur pianist and, years earlier, they walked down the aisle to their favorite music, Bach. But Graham does not like to talk much about Franny's favorite pianist, Glenn Gould.

As interviewer, I ask her about the Berg Sonata, which Gould taught her in 1953 and which she sometimes plays on the anniversary of his death. Suddenly, Barrault gets up, walks over to the piano, sits on the stool and turns into young Franny Batchen once again. Her fatigue dissipates as she starts to play the Berg Sonata. Knowing her history as being nervous under pressure and considering her age and health, it is an inspiring sight to everyone in the room.

In the interview that day — more than fifty years after she left Gould for New York — Barrault said she was enriched by Gould and those she knew in Toronto in the 1950s, and yet throughout her life, she has continued to struggle for peace of mind.

When she first went to New York in 1956, she briefly continued her quest to become a prominent pianist, as well as a piano instructor, but she said her new teacher — Eduard Steuermann — was critical of her playing and she gave up performing and teaching for five years. "My personal pattern after a failure had always been to begin again, apply the rigorous self-discipline, hope for the best and then encounter the inevitable failure, or what I considered failure," she said. Following an eight-year stint in New York, Batchen moved to Edinburgh, Scotland, where she became a professional photographer for a brief period. Batchen said that Gould visited her in Edinburgh and that he wanted her to return to Toronto with him, but she insisted on staying and helping one of her ailing aunts. (In 1964 and 1965, Gould turned down invitations to play in the Seventh Earl of Harewood Edinburgh International Festival in Edinburgh, though he had wound down his concert career by then.) When Gould went back home, Batchen apparently became depressed and, according to one friend, was suicidal. When Gould heard that his former girlfriend was depressed, he phoned her, and his encouragement helped cheer her up.

She sought more spiritual growth, renewed her faith in God and became a semi-abstract painter, going into a trance for some of her work to seek divine guidance. Before she died in November 2009, Frances said that her memories of Gould were sweet. Like many of Gould's former girlfriends and female friends, Barrault also became a music teacher.

CORNELIA FOSS

After moving to Toronto to be near Gould for more than four years, Foss returned to her husband, Lukas, in 1973. They remained married nearly six decades, residing in Manhattan with a summer home in the Hamptons, until Lukas died at age eighty-six in 2009.

Cornelia has fashioned her own career as a landscape and portrait painter and art teacher. According to one critic, her life with Gould may have enriched her work: "It's as if Ms. Foss, who has always been a fine painter, went through an epiphany and arrived at these simple frameworks of landscape. Through them, she describes her own inner scene of enduring grief and love of life." Her work can be viewed on the Internet through the DFN Gallery (www.dfngallery.com). In 2008, she finally painted her first portrait of Gould.

To this day, Foss thinks of Gould as "a wonderful, extraordinary person, passionate about so many things." And yet, she feels uncomfortable looking at photographs of him and seems to be in pain when she talks of the man she had an affair with for nearly a decade.

For many years, she cared for Lukas, who had Parkinson's. Lukas will go down as one of the most innovative American composers of the twentieth century and one of the most versatile musicians as a conductor, teacher and pianist. Their daughter Eliza grew up to be an actress and their son Christopher a corporate strategist. They still talk of their "stepfather" Gould fondly. Lukas did, as well, and never held a grudge, friends said. "[Lukas] had a Zen of understanding of his place in life," said Buffalo musician Charles Haupt. "He was an incredibly forgiving person, too. He never held a grudge. Never."

ROXOLANA ROSLAK

After her breakup with Gould, Roslak got on with her singing career and did well, although she never reached the heights she had with Gould. In 1982, she did some stage directing in Toronto and acted in the movie *Anne of Green Gables* as Madame Selitsky. In 1987 at age forty-eight, Roslak quit singing professionally. "Women with high voices have the shortest careers next to dancers," she explained. "Your body can't do it anymore, and your instrument is your whole body. Your age alters and your voice is part of that process. Luckily, I got into teaching. I found out I could relate to others one-on-one. I was able to get results and I enjoyed it." She remains a teacher at the Glenn Gould School at the Royal Conservatory of Music in Toronto for students seeking a professional career in music.

To this day, despite the painful ending to their affair, Roslak retains a warm feeling about Gould and her part in his legacy, and she has been involved in some posthumous lectures and discussions about his work, but she does not live in the past. And she does not try to analyze his quirky nature, preferring to believe "he was born different."

Meanwhile, Roslak's former coach and accompanist Stuart Hamilton is perplexed why she has been reluctant to talk about her affair with Gould, just as Batchen and Foss remained silent for so many decades. "Why do these women insist on keeping their mouths shut? It must be about loyalty, about their relationship with him," he said.

VERNA (SANDERCOCK) POST

Verna Post moved to Hawaii in 1965, gave birth to two children, became a teacher at Hawaii Community College, then a voice coach at the University of Hawaii. Today, Post has some regrets about not taking Gould up on his offer to romance her. "I was too uptight and worried about getting pregnant. This was the 1950s, not the sexual revolution of the 1960s," she said. "Things just weren't that open. Glenn and I were products of that Protestant, Canadian background, and I didn't want to be the girlfriend of a celebrity. I remember what happened to Ingrid Bergman." (In 1949, actress Bergman became the center of an international scandal when she left her husband and young daughter to be with Italian director Roberto Rossellini.)

In a special place in her home, Verna keeps an embroidered ceremonial scarf with gold threads, which Gould brought back for her from a tour of Israel and she chuckles when she sees old record albums from the 1960s with photographs of the pianist wearing a gray wool vest she knitted for him. Whenever she feels particularly sentimental, Post leaves her footprints in the sand of a long beach in the Pacific and thinks about the man who called her "Puss" and "Angel" and wanted her to travel the world with him at the height of his career.

GLADYS (SHENNER) RISKIND

Gladys's writing career likely never surpassed that story she wrote about her heroic pianist in *Maclean's* so long ago. "I guess I peaked in my twenties," she says today. In December 1963, just three months after Gould refused to talk to her again, Shenner married an American corporate lawyer in Toronto, Jay Riskind. Their marriage — which produced son Jonathan, the Washington bureau chief for the *Columbus Dispatch*, and daughter Jennifer, an actress/fundraiser — lasted fifteen years before they divorced. Gladys now lives in a Chicago suburb.

She has many fond memories of Gould and she rivaled Verna Sandercock as Gould's soul mate of the late 1950s and early 1960s. "I wonder if there was another woman in Glenn Gould's life who had as close a relationship as I did? It would be interesting to find out, but I doubt it . . . But nobody knows about me," Riskind said. "He was dependent on my warmth."

MONICA GAYLORD

She has kept her word not to speak publicly about her close relationship with Gould. Gaylord did not become famous, but she had a fine career as a classical pianist and harpsichordist. She did some touring and recorded an album featuring black musicians.

After Gould's death, Gaylord continued to see Pierre Trudeau off and on into the mid-1980s. In 1991, Trudeau got the daughter (Sarah) he was looking for from lawyer Deborah Coyne, although he never married Coyne.

Gaylord has had a long career as a music teacher. Since 1986, she has taught — like Roslak — at the Glenn Gould School of the Royal Conservatory of Music in Toronto. One wonders how she discusses Gould with her students.

BIRGIT JOHANSSON

After Gould died, Birgit Johansson burned the letters he wrote to her and refused to talk publicly about their affair. "I think she wanted his letters to remain private," her son Henrik said. "She wanted to keep their world, their reality, away from the public. And I think [the way it ended] was too painful."

"If she made Gould a promise she would not make their affair public, she would keep that promise," said her former student Anders Hillborg, now a composer. "She was a highly moral person."

Gould's death sent Johansson into a tailspin of depression and illness and she had to take a year off teaching, but she recovered and went on to open a small restaurant in Stockholm. She married a police officer, known in Sweden as Super Cop, and cared for him after he suffered a stroke. She died in 2003.

ANAHID ALEXANIAN

The promising pianist coached by Gould never made it big in

classical music. In the mid-1970s, she moved from Canada back to her parents' homeland of Armenia where she continued to play piano at concerts and to do some teaching and composing, but her dreams of becoming famous were gone. She never married and began to live a type of reclusive life. "She went off the deep end," her sister Armine said. Like Gould was at times, Anahid became paranoid, Armine said. "She lived under Communist rule in Armenia and she thought they were trying to kill her. Even now she has the feeling like she is in danger."

In several telephone conversations with me in 2008, Alexanian said she was interested in talking about her relationship with Gould, but she never did. She believed her telephone was being bugged and was reluctant to pass on her story. "I don't want any harm to come to you," she told me. Yet, her memories of Gould remain "wonderful."

SUSAN KOSCIS

Her relationship with Gould might have shifted into romance had he lived. Gould changed the way Susan Koscis thought about men: "After that, it was difficult for other men to measure up to him in values and integrity. Yeah, he was weird, but he surrounded himself with people he cared about and who he felt comfortable with. He made his life work around his phobias and, for an artist, had a reasonably happy life. How crazy is that? Having worked with many artists and musicians, others who were considered more normal and mainstream, and yet they had numerous divorces and affairs. It struck me that he created the kind of life that worked for him."

Koscis is now vice president of arts and culture for the Search for Common Ground, an organization based in the United States that helps societies in conflict to find non-adversarial, non-violent solutions to diverse community, national and international problems.

ANGELA ADDISON

Gould encouraged Angela Addison's writing and she became an author of children's books and poetry. Living in Victoria, British Columbia, she is married and has three children. "He was quite angry when I married at age twenty-five. He thought I was giving up my musical and writing career," she said. At one time, she wrote a few chapters of a book about Glenn, "But I got so involved with family, I never finished it."

Addison believes Gould could never have married. "He just couldn't be as totally consumed by the music and have enough left.... He wanted somebody he really loved in his life, day-to-day, and he probably needed that desperately, but he also knew he couldn't hold up his end. In some ways, he would have really benefited from being married, but he made the choices he did and lived by them and he suffered a lot of horrors because of that. When you listened to Glenn, you got the feeling you weren't quite sure if he was chasing the music or if the music was chasing him. He seemed completely driven by the need. That's a recipe for disaster in a marriage. It's better to keep close friends than to be married."

CAROL (HODGDON) GOODFRIEND

Gould asked her to go to Hudson's Bay with him (she declined), then he was disappointed when she married the editor for his liner notes at Columbia Masterworks, James Goodfriend. Gould never spoke to them after she announced her marriage in 1967. The couple has traveled the world as art dealers.

"It was terrible," Carol Goodfriend said of Gould's death. "If he were still alive, he'd be a real force for innovation in music and technology today."

SONIA MARIE DE LEÓN DE VEGA

After being telephone pals with Glenn Gould during the last years of his life, when he tinkered with, among other things, conducting, De León says Gould inspired her. She has become a respected symphony and opera conductor with the Santa Cecilia Orchestra in California. She was the first woman to receive a Vatican invitation to conduct a symphony orchestra at a Papal Mass. She founded the Discovering Music program that introduces classical music to students in low-income neighborhoods, an endeavor Gould would have loved.

MARILYN KECSKES

Marilyn Kecskes remained superintendent of Gould's old apartment building on St. Clair Avenue in Toronto until 2007, where she occasionally went to the rooftop to remember him. "People still come to the building from all over the world to see his apartment," she says. "His music remains very personal to me — when you hear his recordings, you know it can't be anybody else." After his death, she suffered an emotional breakdown and, like Gould, she became afraid for a time to meet people. But then Kecskes helped to found Out of the Cold, a program that gets the homeless off the streets during Toronto's cold winters. Gould, who left half his money to the Salvation Army and the other half to the Toronto Humane Society, would have been proud of his superintendent.

CYNTHIA (MILLMAN) FLOYD

Gould coached her and helped kick-start her career. Cynthia Floyd taught at the University of Ottawa for many years and was the chairman of its music department. Although she gave workshops and concerts on the fortepiano, she never made it big as concert pianist. "I felt I disappointed [Gould]," she says. "I was missing a key ingredient; I didn't have perfect pitch like he did. But I'm glad I didn't. I've enjoyed my career as a teacher."

JESSIE GREIG

Gould's first cousin and soul mate became an elementary school teacher in Oshawa, Ontario. She said of Glenn, "He had a profound effect on people. His courage, stepping out into the unknown all his life with the music and writing, enabled me to be a better teacher. He challenged me. For example, he was always giving me ideas for lessons. When he fell in love with haiku, I would have my students write it and then we'd read it together. Later we wrote it to one another."

Greig died in 1996 at age seventy.

BERT GOULD

After marrying Vera Dobson in 1980, Bert sold the Southwood Drive home where Glenn grew up. He died in 1996 at age ninety-four, outliving his son by fourteen years.

MORRY KERNERMAN

Gould's friend and accompanist had a successful career as a violinist and music teacher. He remains perplexed by why Gould broke off their friendship, but still considers him brilliant. "I've worked with the greatest musicians in the world, but no one measures up to Glenn Gould," said Kernerman, who lives in Toronto.

ANDREW KAZDIN

Gould's New York record producer of fifteen years found himself cut off by the pianist for reasons he still does not understand. He wrote a book on Gould in 1989, *Glenn Gould at Work: Creative Lying*, which some people thought was a trifle cynical. Kazdin says of Gould, "He's still thought of as one of the leading pianists of his generation. Sometimes his interpretation of standard music was so perverse, people would go, 'Ooooh!'"

BARBARA FRANKLIN

In the 1950s, Gould fantasized about traveling the world with her like two white swans. She certainly got around on her own as a soprano and actress, appearing on many television shows and in theater in New York.

ANTONIN KUBALEK

Gould helped this Czech immigrant get started in North America. He has gone on to become a renowned concert pianist, recording artist and teacher.

STUART HAMILTON

A Gould friend in the 1950s and accompanist for Roxolana Roslak, Stuart Hamilton has been one of the most recognizable voices and faces in Canadian opera as a concert organizer, lecturer, broadcaster, teacher and accompanist. He was awarded the Order of Canada in 1985.

JOAN MAXWELL

This mezzo-soprano made a concerted effort to slow Gould's drug use in the 1950s and he became a godfather to one of her children. She was a Canadian opera star until a back injury curtailed her career in 1969 and sent her into teaching in Toronto and at the University of Ottawa, where she was Professor of Music. She died in 2000.

JOHN L. ROBERTS

A friend to Gould for more than two decades, he has given presentations at many Gould festivals and symposiums. He compiled and edited two books on Gould — *The Art of Glenn Gould: Reflections of a Musical Genius* and, with Ghyslaine Guertin, *Glenn Gould: Selected Letters*. Roberts lives in Calgary.

PAUL MYERS

He wrote a biography on Gould's friend and colleague, *Leonard Bernstein*. Myers lives in London.

RAY ROBERTS

Gould's assistant from 1970 to 1982 and his close friend, Ray Roberts is a director of the Glenn Gould Estate. "Cornelia's talking about their affair was in a strange way gratifying to me," Roberts said when my article in the *Toronto Star* revealed Gould's relationship with Foss. "Many people thought he was gay, and I made the statement when he died that he was not homosexual. Some gay groups and other people were surprised."

SUSANNE HAMEL-MICHAUD

Gould's beautiful ballet friend, who turned down his request to go to Russia with him in 1957, became a poet and essayist. In 1995, she wrote the book *Glenn Gould: My Lovely and Tender Love.*

GLENN GOULD

Decades after his death, Gould still casts a long shadow in the entertainment world, as much as any classical musician. His recordings still sell very well and he has inspired filmmakers, novelists, poets and cult followings around the world. "If he were still alive today, he would be treated like Elvis," Ray Roberts said.

In 1998, Canada's national news magazine, *Maclean's*, voted Gould the number one artist, ahead of the Group of Seven painters, and the fifth "most important Canadian" of all time. In a nation that often downplays its talents, he has become a type of hero and an explorer. Sometime in the distant future, far off in space one of the first human-produced sounds that aliens might hear is a prelude and fugue by Bach, recorded by Gould and put aboard two *Voyager* spacecraft launched in 1977. They might note, "Is that humming in the background?"

Since Gould's death, it has taken the secrets a long while to come tumbling out of his closet, but now, with the research from this book, it is clear that Gould's wonderful depth of feeling and style at the piano likely were not shaped only by divine talent or a verbal diviner from his dedicated mother, but also by his emotional experiences. And apparently, he still has sexual charisma. After viewing a video clip of Gould playing Brahms, a viewer remarked, "This is fantastic. It really does seem as though he is having an orgasm. It is also turning me on a bit, given he is quite good-looking. I would quite like to have sex with his youthful ghost, but Gould being the Last Puritan, I'm sure that I am now guaranteed not to be haunted."

Even in death, Gould seems haunted by old ghosts and rivals. In CBC's *The Greatest Canadian* television series in 2004, Prime Minister Pierre Trudeau was named the number three most influential Canadian of all time with Gould lagging, but still in the ballpark, at number fifty-five. Ironically, actor Colm Feore has played both Gould (*Thirty Two Short Films About Glenn Gould*, 1993) and Trudeau (*Trudeau*, 2002).

No, that sound coming from Mount Pleasant Cemetery in midtown Toronto is not Beethoven rolling over.

Acknowledgments

Most of the material in this book is original from interviews I conducted with more than one hundred people, many of whom knew Glenn Gould well. Some of those, especially his close female friends, had never been interviewed.

There are many people and sources to thank, beginning with the women — particularly Frances (Batchen) Barrault, Cornelia Foss, Roxolana Roslak, Verna (Sandercock) Post, Susan Koscis and Gladys (Shenner) Riskind. I applaud their courage in talking openly with me about a subject that was very private for them for decades.

Few of the people in Gould's personal life turned down my request for an interview. The most notable exception was Monica Gaylord, who did not respond to my three letters.

Photographs were graciously made available by Barrault, Post, Koscis, Riskind, Warren Collins, John Jonas Gruen, Carol Goodfriend and Stan Sellen.

For background information and analysis, Kevin Bazzana is an author's dream. He is sharing, sensitive and honest. Bazzana's two books on Gould (see below) were meticulously researched.

Special thanks go to filmmakers Warren Collins in Toronto and William Morris in Richmond, England, who helped so much with background and interviews for my section on Frances Batchen.

Thanks, as well, to the many friends of colleagues of the late Birgit Johansson in Sweden, who helped me put her mysterious relationship with Gould into better focus.

Toronto historian and author Mike Filey was helpful with his call in the *Toronto Sun* for Gould friends to contact me.

For anyone undertaking a project such as this, the Glenn Gould Archive in the Music Division of the National Library of Canada in Ottawa is an invaluable source of materials.

Thank you to producer/director Peter Raymont of White Pine Pictures in Toronto, who optioned my early research to make the 2009 documentary *Genius Within: The Inner Life of Glenn Gould*.

And to my longtime agent, Robert Mackwood, owner of Seventh Avenue Literary Agency in Vancouver, and publisher Jack David and editor Jen Hale at ECW Press. Also to Hollywood screenwriter/director Shane Salerno, who is encouraging me to write a feature film on Glenn Gould.

Thanks also to the Glenn Gould Estate and the Toronto Public Library, especially the Toronto Reference Library, and the University of Toronto Faculty of Music.

Finally, thanks to my family, particularly my wife, Jennifer (Vanderklei) Clarkson, who has apparently, and thankfully, become immune to living with a writer. And to all the people listed below who gave me interviews.

Sources

AUTHOR INTERVIEWS

Addison, Angela. Telephone. November 11, 2007.
——. Telephone. November 14, 2007.
Adler, Al. Telephone. October 3, 2007.
Adler, Herbert. Email. August 15, 2008.
——. Email. August 18, 2008.
Alexanian, Anahid. Telephone. August 5, 2008.
——. Telephone. April 6, 2009.
Alexanian, Armine. Telephone. June 3, 2008.
——. Telephone. May 22, 2008.
Annandale, Robert. Telephone. September 23, 2007.
Aubrey, Dan. Telephone. May 6, 2008.
Audrey (Spector), Nicole. Email. September 10, 2007.
Axworthy, Tom. Telephone. April 28, 2008.
Barna, Yvonne. Telephone. November 15, 2007.
Barrault (Batchen), Frances. Telephone. October 17, 2007.
——. Telephone. October 28, 2007.
——. Telephone. October 21, 2007.
——. Telephone. November 4, 2007.
——. Telephone. November 11, 2007.
——. In Richmond, England. January 20, 2008.
——. In Richmond, England. January 21, 2008.
——. In Richmond, England. January 22, 2008.
——. Telephone. February 3, 2008.

—. Telephone. February 13, 2008.
—. Telephone. June 15, 2008.
—. Telephone. November 28, 2008.
Barry, Elizabeth. Telephone. May 21, 2008.
Bazzana, Kevin. Telephone. September 20, 2007.
    —. Email. December 4, 2007.
    —. Email. December 11, 2007.
    —. Email. July 2, 2008.
    —. Email. July 14, 2008.
    —. Email. June 18, 2009.
    —. Email. September 15, 2009.
Beckwith, John. Telephone. November 7, 2007.
Burns, Bruce. Telephone. February 8, 2008.
Boyd, Liona. Telephone. May 6, 2008.
Carroll, Owen. Telephone. June 3, 2008.
Collins, Warren. In Toronto. October 17, 2007.
    —. Mail. October 18, 2007.
    —. In Toronto. October 22, 2007.
    —. Telephone. October 29, 2007.
    —. Telephone. January 13, 2008.
    —. In Toronto. February 1, 2008.
    —. In Toronto. February 11, 2008.
    —. Telephone. February 13, 2008.
Cooper, Susan. Telephone. March 20, 2008.
Delebrant, Lotta. Telephone. January 24, 2009.
Delebrant, Thomas. Telephone. January 24, 2009.
De León de Vega, Sonia Marie. Telephone. November 15, 2007.
Doolittle, Clarence. Telephone. May 27, 2007.
Dunn, John. Telephone. March 25, 2008.
Edquist, Verne. Telephone. March 12, 2008.
Elliott, Robin. Telephone. 2008.
Engel, Howard. Telephone. May 21, 2008.
Floyd (Millman), Cynthia. Telephone. June 1, 2008.
Foss, Cornelia. Telephone. June 25, 2007.
    —. Telephone. June 26, 2007.
    —. Telephone. July 9, 2007.
    —. In Bridgehampton, New York. July 10, 2007.
    —. Telephone. July 12, 2007.
    —. Telephone. August 20, 2007.
    —. Telephone. August 21, 2007.
    —. Telephone. August 23, 2007.
Franklin, Barbara. Telephone. November 7, 2007.

—. Telephone. November 8, 2007.

Frohm, Christina. Telephone. January 22, 2009.

Gillard, Cheryl. Email. May 2008.

Gesser, Sam. Telephone. February 16, 2008.

Goodfriend (Hodgdon), Carol. Email. December 1, 2007.

—. Telephone. December 10, 2007.

Gossage, Patrick. Telephone. April 28, 2008.

Guilbert, Christine. Telephone. February 27, 2008.

Gruen, John Jonas. Email. August 28, 2007.

—. Email. May 14, 2009.

Guertin, Ghyslaine. Telephone. February 17, 2008.

Gunnarsson, Mona. Telephone. February 8, 2009.

Hahn, Paul. In Toronto. May 28, 2008.

Hamilton, Stuart. Telephone. November 3, 2007.

—. In Toronto. November 6, 2007.

Hillborg, Anders. Telephone. January 15, 2009.

—. Email. February 10, 2009.

Holdar, Anders. Telephone. January 20, 2009.

Homburger, Walter. Telephone. February 8, 2007.

—. In Toronto. January 28, 2008.

Huff, Frances. Telephone. March 25, 2008.

Joachim, Otto. Telephone. December 18, 2007.

Johansson, Anders. Telephone. February 3, 2009.

Johansson, Henrik. Telephone. January 18, 2009.

—. Telephone. January 25, 2009.

Johansson, Mareuka. Telephone. February 3, 2009.

Jonzon, Agneta. Telephone. April 1, 2009.

Hamel-Michaud, Susanne. Telephone. November 2, 2007.

Kallman, Helmut. Telephone. December 20, 2007.

Kazdin, Andrew. Telephone. November 11, 2007.

Kecskes, Marilyn. Telephone. February 10, 2007.

—. In Toronto. August 16, 2007.

—. Telephone. August 23, 2007.

Kernerman, Morry. Telephone. March 17, 2008.

Kombrink, Ilona. Telephone. February 15, 2008.

Koscis, Susan. Telephone. September 27, 2007.

—. Telephone. October 1, 2007.

—. Email. December 3, 2007.

—. Email. December 4, 2007.

Kostelanetz, Richard. Email. September 5, 2007.

—. Email. January 12, 2008.

Kubalek, Antonin. Telephone. January 29, 2008.

Kuerti, Anton. In Toronto. January 15, 2008.
Leuthner, Wolf. Telephone. March 20, 2008.
Lightbourn, Naomi. Telephone. January 28, 2008.
Littler, William. Telephone. December 8, 2007.
—. Telephone. December 15, 2007.
—. Telephone. January 24, 2009.
Litwack, Linda. Telephone. December 10, 2007.
—. Email. December 11, 2007.
Louie, Alexina. Telephone. January 24, 2009.
Lundmark, Jorgen. Telephone. November 4, 2008.
—. Email. November 4, 2008.
Lundmark, Torgny. Email. February 11, 2009.
—. Email. February 12, 2009.
MacDonald, Brian. Telephone. March 30, 2008
MacDonald, Sylvia. Telephone. January 2, 2008.
MacFeeters, Ron. Telephone. February 19, 2008.
McCoppin, Peter. Telephone. April 9, 2007.
Mesaros, Helen. Telephone. May 10, 2008
Milligan, Doris. Telephone. May 27, 2007.
Miller, Donna. Telephone. November 7, 2007.
—. Telephone. November 9, 2007.
Morris, William. Email. October 6, 2007.
—. Mail. October 7, 2007.
—. Email. October 20, 2007.
—. In Richmond, England. January 20, 2008.
—. In Richmond, England. January 21, 2008.
Myers, Paul. Telephone. December 5, 2007.
Nigosian, Peter. Telephone. August 5, 2008.
Page, Tim. Telephone. March 10, 2007.
—. Telephone. February 6, 2009.
Palvetsian, Kohar. Telephone. June 18, 2008.
Palvetsian, Nevi. Telephone. June 19, 2008.
Palvetsian, Syraun. Telephone. June 18, 2008.
Pearlman, Judith. Telephone. September 20, 2007.
—. Telephone. September 26, 2007.
Post (Sandercock),Verna. Telephone. November 20, 2007.
—. Email. November 22, 2007.
—. Telephone. December 4, 2007.
Pringle, Pat. Telephone. May 27, 2007.
Rempel, Harvey. Telephone. November 10, 2007.
—. Telephone. November 12, 2007.
Riskind (Shenner), Gladys. Email. September 23, 2007.

—. Telephone. September 24, 2007.

—. Telephone. September 30, 2007.

—. Telephone. October 2, 2007.

—. Telephone. June 25, 2008.

—. Telephone. July 15, 2008.

Roberts, John. Telephone. January 7, 2008.

—. Telephone. January 11, 2008.

Roberts, Ray. In Toronto. November 18, 2007.

—. Telephone. January 30, 2009.

Rogers, Mary Alice. Telephone. November 15, 2007.

Rosenblat, Rebecca. In Toronto. August 25, 2008.

—. In Toronto. September 8, 2008.

Roslak, Roxolana. In Toronto. October 5, 2007.

Ross, Michael. Email. 2008.

Rubes (Douglas), Susan. Telephone. November 20, 2008.

Rubes, Jan. Telephone. November 20, 2008.

Sandstrom, Jan. Telephone. January 16, 2009.

—. Email. January 18, 2009.

Saville, Graham. In Richmond, England. January 20, 2008.

—. In Richmond, England. January 21, 2008.

Schabas, Ezra. Telephone. March 10, 2008.

Schafer, F. Murray. Telephone. March 10, 2009.

Schwartz, Carmel. Telephone. November 7, 2008.

Sellen, Stan. Telephone. October 29, 2007.

—. Telephone. February 13, 2008.

Simon, Jeff. Email. March 1, 2007.

—. Email. March 2, 2007.

Semerjian, Haig. Telephone. April 28, 2008.

Silverman, Robert. Telephone. May 22, 2008.

—. Email. May 24, 2008.

Snow, Michael. Telephone. November 12, 2007.

Sonnenberg, Ben. Telephone. January 5, 2008.

—. Email. January 6, 2008.

—. Email. January 7, 2008.

Stephens, Joseph. Telephone. June 13, 2007.

BOOKS

Barrault, Fran (Batchen). *Poems of Love and War 1939–1945*. Richmond, England: Lotus, 1990.

Barrault, Fran (Batchen). *The Confidence Quotient*. Richmond, England: Lotus, 1995.

Bazzana, Kevin. *Glenn Gould: The Performer in the Work*. New York:

Oxford University Press, 1997.

Bazzana, Kevin. *Wondrous Strange: The Art and Life of Glenn Gould.* New York: Oxford University Press, 2003.

Beckwith, John. *In Search of Alberto Guerrero.* Waterloo, Canada: Wilfrid Laurier University Press, 2006.

Bergman, Rhona. *The Idea of Gould.* Philadelphia: LevPub, 1999.

Glenn Gould: A Life in Pictures, introduction by Tim Page. New York: Doubleday, 2002.

Carroll, Jock. *Glenn Gould: Some Portraits of the Artist as a Young Man.* Toronto: Stoddart, 1995.

Clarkson, Michael. *Intelligent Fear.* Toronto: Key Porter, 2002. New York: Marlow, 2002.

Cott, Jonathan. *Conversations with Glenn Gould.* Chicago: University of Chicago Press, 1984.

Friedrich, Otto. *Glenn Gould: A Life and Variations.* Toronto: Lester and Orpen Dennys, 1989.

Fulford, Robert. *Best Seat in the House: Memoirs of a Lucky Man.* Toronto: HarperCollins, 1988.

Gruen, John Jonas. *The Sixties: Young in the Hamptons.* New York: Edizioni Charta, 2006.

Hafner, Katie. *A Romance on Three Legs.* New York: Bloomsbury, 2008.

Hamel-Michaud, Susanne. *Glenn Gould: Mon bel et tendre amour.* Quebec: Les Éditions Petit Hublot, 1995.

Kazdin, Andrew. *Glenn Gould at Work: Creative Lying.* New York: E. P. Dutton, 1989.

McGreevy, John, ed. *Glenn Gould: Variations, By Himself and His Friends,* Toronto: Doubleday, 1983.

Mesaros, Helen. *Bravo Fortissimo Glenn Gould: The Mind of a Canadian Virtuoso.* Baltimore: Heritage Special Edition, American Literary Press, 2008.

Page, Tim, ed., *The Glenn Gould Reader.* New York: Alfred A. Knopf, 1984.

Payzant, Geoffrey. *Glenn Gould Music & Mind.* Toronto: Key Porter, 1978.

Ostwald, Peter F. *Glenn Gould: The Ecstasy and Tragedy of Genius.* New York: W. W. Norton, 1997.

Roberts, John P. L. and Guertin, Ghyslaine, eds. *Glenn Gould: Selected Letters.* New York: Oxford University Press, 1992.

Roberts, John P. L., ed. *The Art of Glenn Gould: Reflections of a Musical Genius.* Toronto: Malcolm Lester Books, 1999.

Rorem, Ned. *Facing the Night: A Diary (1999–2005) and Musical Writings.* Emeryville, California: Shoemaker and Hoard, 2006.

Schoenberger, Nancy. *Dangerous Muse*. Cambridge: Massachusetts: Da Capo Press, 2002.

Southam, Nancy, ed. *Pierre*. Toronto: McClelland & Stewart, 2002.

MAGAZINES AND NEWSPAPERS

Addison, Angela. "The Ultimate Soloist: A Portrait of Glenn Gould." *Bulletin of the Glenn Gould Society*. October 1988.

Angel, Amanda. "Celebrating Lukas Foss's 85th Birthday." *East Hampton Star*. June 19, 2007.

Bazzana, Kevin, ed. "Florence Greig Gould." *GlennGould Magazine*. Spring 2007.

Bernstein, Leonard. "The Symphonic Form is Dead." *Time*. August 30, 1968.

Carroll, Jock. "I Don't Think I'm At All Eccentric." *Weekend*. July 7, 1956.

Clarkson, Michael. "The Secret Life of Glenn Gould." *Toronto Star*. August 25, 2007.

Elliott, Robin. "Constructions of Identity in the Life Stories of Emma Albani and Glenn Gould." *Journal of Canadian Studies*. Spring 2005.

Friedlander, Mira, "Jessie and Cousin Glenn." *Toronto Star*. September 20, 1992.

Fulford, Robert. "Growing Up Gould." *Saturday Night*. December 1982.

Greig, Jessie. "Glenn Gould the Man." *Bulletin of the Glenn Gould Society*. October 1986.

Kind, Silvia. "Glenn Gould the Man." *Bulletin of the Glenn Gould Society*. October 1988.

Kostelanetz, Richard. "The Glenn Gould Variations." *Esquire*. November 1967.

Page, Tim. "Glenn Gould: The Last Months." *GlennGould Magazine*. Spring 2001.

Rasky, Frank. "Classical Pianist (Monica Gaylord) Kicks off Series of Lake Concerts." *Toronto Star*. July 4, 1977.

Roddy, Joseph. "Apollonian." *New Yorker*. May 14, 1960.

Roddy, Joseph. "Glenn Gould." *People Weekly*. November 30, 1981.

Shenner, Gladys. "The Genius Who Doesn't Want to Play." *Maclean's*. April 28, 1956.

Swift, Patricia. "Mrs. Lukas Foss Has Many Roles, Wife, Mother, Homemaker and Artist." *Buffalo Evening News*. September 21, 1963.

Townsend, Dorothy. "An Informal Visit with Lukas Foss." *Los Angeles Times*. August 17, 1961.

FILMS AND TELEVISION

Glenn Gould: On the Record. National Film Board of Canada. 1959.
Directors Wolf Koenig and Roman Kroitor.

Glenn Gould: Off the Record. National Film Board of Canada. 1959.
Directors Wolf Koenig and Roman Kroitor.

Music in Our Time. Canadian Broadcasting Corporation. May 6, 1974.

Glenn Gould's Toronto. John McGreevy Productions. Director John
McGreevy for his series *Cities.* September 27, 1979.

Glenn Gould: A Portrait. Canadian Broadcasting Corporation. 1985.

Thirty Two Short Films About Glenn Gould. Rhombus Media. Director
François Girard. 1993.

Glenn Gould: The Shadow Genius. Canadian Broadcasting Corporation,
Life and Times. 1998.

Extasis. Kultur Films Inc. 2003.

Glenn Gould: Hereafter. Ideale Audience and Rhombus Media. Director
Bruno Monsaingeon. 2006.

Genius Within: The Inner Life of Glenn Gould. White Pine Pictures.
Producers Peter Raymont and Michèle Hozer. 2009.

ALSO

Emanuelli, Sharon K. "Oral History Interview with Edith Robinson
Wyle." Archives of American Art. March 9, 1993.

Maxwell, Joan. An address to the National Capital Opera Society.
Ottawa, 1997. Later published in *GlennGould Magazine.*

Ostwald, Peter. "Glenn Gould as a Patient." A paper presented to the
symposium and film festival "Glenn Gould: Variations on Musical
Genius in our Time." San Francisco. November 18, 1995.

Tovell, Vincent. "At Home with Glenn Gould." Canadian Broadcasting
Corporation Radio. 1959. Released on CD by the Glenn Gould
Foundation in 1996.

Website of the DFN Gallery in New York. www.dfngallery.com.